Protecting RAF Airfields & Install~ ~ast Asia 194?

Through the eyes of the squadrons and flights of the R.A.F. Regiment

ROBIN F FINLAYSON

Acknowledgements and Copyright

The Operational Diary sections and the front cover of this book, contain public sector information licensed under the Open Government Licence v3.0.

The Operational Record Books held at The National Archives and used in this book are listed below:

AIR 29/134 - **2941 -2943 Field Squadrons**

AIR 29/136 - **2945 Field Squadron**

AIR 29/138 - **2941 -2945 Field Squadron Appendices only**

AIR 29/884 – **4401 – 4408 Anti -Aircraft Flights**

AIR 29/885 – **4410 – 4436 Anti -Aircraft Flights**

AIR 29/886 – **4437 – 4450 Anti -Aircraft Flights**

Design concept, layout and illustrations by Robin F Finlayson.

Front cover picture: No.4448 A.A. Flight (copy of original colourised)

Published in paperback in September 2018

Visit Robin F Finlayson's Facebook page for further series and other publication updates.

Dedication

This book is dedicated to all who have served and specifically those that paid the ultimate sacrifice in this campaign.

The records used in this book identify those that passed away and as such are listed and remembered below.

1544605	Leading Aircraftsman	Stobbs, R.	2943 Field Squadron
1446658	Leading Aircraftsman	Scrase	4417 A.A. Flight
1450246	Leading Aircraftsman	Partridge, L.C.	4413 A.A. Flight
1234366	Leading Aircraftsman	Chapman	4402 A.A. Flight

Key Abbreviations

Abbreviation	Meaning	Abbreviation	Meaning
Rank		G.H.Q. India	General Headquarters India
A/C – A.C.1	Aircraftsman Class 1	Flt	Flight
A/Cpl	Acting/Corporal	H.Q.	Headquarters
F/Lt - F/L	Flight Lieutenant	M.F.H.	Medical Field Hospital
F/O - FO	Flying Officer	M.U.	Maintenance Unit
G/Cpt	Group Captain	N.A.A.F.I.	Navy, Army, Airforce Families Institute
L.A.C.	Leading Aircraftsman	R.A.F.R.	Royal Air Force Regiment
Maj	Major	S.H.Q.	Squadron Headquarters
P/O	Pilot Officer	Sqn - Sqdn	Squadron
Sgt	Sergeant	**Other**	
S/Ldr – S/L	Squadron Leader	A/C	Aircraft
W/Cmdr.	Wing Commander	A.L.G.	Advanced Landing Ground
Post, appointments or positions		Cwt	Cubic Weight
Adjt	Adjutant	D.F.C.	Distinguishing Flying Cross
A.O.C.	Air Officer Commanding	E/A	Enemy aircraft
A.V.M.	Air Vice Marshall	Hy/A.A.	Heavy Anti-Aircraft
B.O.R.	British Other Ranks	H.M.T.	His Majesty's Troopship
C.D.O.	Command Defence Officer	L.A.A.	Light Anti-Aircraft
C.O.	Commanding Officer	L.A.A.M.G.	Light Anti-Aircraft Machine Gun
DR	Despatch Rider / Driver	L.M.G.	Light Machine Gun
G.D.O.	Group Defence Officer	M.C.	Military Cross
i/c	In Command	MM	Military Medal
O.C. - OC	Officer Commanding	M.T.	Mechanical Transport
M.O.	Medical Orderly	O.P.	Observation post
N.C.O.	Non-Commissioned Officer	O Group	Orders Group
S.M.O.	Senior Medical Officer	Recce	Reconnaissance
Structural, unit or type		R.V.	Rendez Vous
A.H.Q. India	Air Headquarters India	U/S	Unserviceable
A.M.E.S.	Air Ministry Experimental Stations – Radar Installation	W /(R).T.	Wireless (Radio) Transmission

Contents

Acknowledgements and Copyright..1

Key Abbreviations 3

Introduction...8

  Background to the formation of the R.A.F. Regiment 8

  Background to the Operations in South East Asia 8

  Operation overview and the role of the R.A.F. Regiment 10

    Field Squadron – Role and Structure 12

    Anti-Aircraft Flight – Role and Structure..13

Unit Formation - R.A.F. Regiment, Secunderabad 14

  Overview..14

  Operational Diaries 19

    April – July...19

    August to October..28

  War Establishment of an Anti-Aircraft Flight – No. India/664................................35

  Formation Order No.385...37

  Formation Order No.430...40

  Formation Order No.493...42

  Formation Order No.2943 and 2944 Squadron (R)...45

  Amendment to Formation Orders 47

No.221 Group - Supporting British Army IV Corps...48

  Overview..48

  Operational Diaries 53

    May 53

    June 53

    July 54

    August 56

    September..59

    October 64

    November 70

December 77

No.4416 A.A. Flight – Movement Order No.1 90

No.4416 A.A. Flight – Nominal Roll 93

No.4416 A.A. Flight – Xmas Menu December 1943 94

No.4448 A.A. Flight Photograph 1943 95

No.4448 A.A. Flight – Crest 96

Group 222 - General Reconnaissance 97

Overview 97

Operational Diaries 100

July 100

August 101

September 104

October 106

November 108

December 109

No.4413 A.A. Flight -Training Programme 6th – 11th September 1943 110

No.4413 A.A. Flight -Training Programme 13th – 18th September 1943 111

Group 224 – Supporting Indian XV Corps 112

Overview 112

Operational Diaries 124

April 124

May 124

June 127

July 142

August 157

September 169

October 177

November 183

December 197

No.4402 A.A. Flight – Temporary Operational Ground Order 215

No.4402 A.A. Flight – Gun Post Sketch Map 218

No.4407 A.A. Flight – Duties of Officer i/c R.A.F.R. Flight – A.M.E.S. 219

No.4407 A.A. Flight -Storage and Care of Ammunition memo 220

No.4407 A.A. Flight - Group Defence Officer visit memo 222

No.4407 A.A. Flight – Explosives, Supply & Distribution memo 224

No.4407 A.A. Flight – Standing Order No.4 - 'Orders for Gun Post Duties' 226

No.4407 A.A. Flight – Standing Order No.5 – 'Orders for Corporal i/c Watch' 228

No.4407 A.A. Flight – A.A. Pit Sketch Plan 229

No.4407 A.A. Flight – Reconnaissance Report (Parashuram Landing Ground) 230

No.2941 Squadron Warning Order 232

No.2941 Battle Diary No.1 Flight 234

No.2942 Squadron Xmas Menu 236

No.2944 Hill Parties Chakrata 237

No.2944 Daily Syllabus of Training...240

Group 225 - General Reconnaissance 243

Overview 243

Operational Diaries 246

September...246

October 247

November 249

December..251

No.4428 A.A. Flight – Defence Orders 253

No.4428 A.A. Flight – Sketch of Gun Post 256

No.4428 A.A. Flight – Flying Boats Protection 257

No.4428 A.A. Flight – St Thomas Mount Airfield Defence Scheme 259

Group 231 – Heavy Bombers 260

Overview...260

Operational Diaries 264

May 264

June 264

July 266

August 267

September... 268

October 271

November 281

December.. 288

No.4437 A.A. Flight – Movement Order 294

No.4437 A.A. Flight – Part 2 Standing Orders - Defence (614) 300

About the Author 306

Other books by the Author 306

Planned books for this operation and campaign series................................. 306

Bibliography.. 307

Introduction

Background to the formation of the R.A.F. Regiment

Germany's use of airborne troops in Crete, to attack and destroy airfields behind the frontline in May 1941, was a significant change in strategy and Britain had to urgently rethink how it planned the defence of its aerodromes. A Committee was set up in June 1941, chaired by Sir Findlater Stewart, tasked with looking at ways to improve aerodrome defence.

In December 1941, the Cabinet approved a recommendation that the Royal Air Force should form its own aerodrome defence corps. The R.A.F Regiment was formed by Royal Warrant on 6th January 1942 and became operational on 1st February of that year.

Background to the Operations in South East Asia

The pre-war plan, developed to defend Singapore and the South East, was based on the assumption that the Japanese would attack from the sea, travelling 3,000 miles from their islands, allowing sufficient warning for reinforcements to deploy.

When the actual attack came in December 1941, the Japanese surprised the British forces by invading Malaya, over land from China and down through Indo-China. Without air superiority and the need for a revised defensive plan, to counter the attack, it wasn't long until the British forces were outmanoeuvred and by February 1942, Singapore had fell. The momentum of the attack pushed the British and Indian forces into its longest ever withdrawal and by May 1942, most of Burma was taken.

The monsoon (May to September) in 1942, the worst since 1897, stopped the Japanese Army at the India- Burma border. With the Allies locked in battle in Europe and North Africa, and build-up of resources for the invasion of North West Europe, the defence of India was not a high priority. Holding the India-Burma border was the only feasible option for the British and Indian forces.

Two fronts were held along the border:

1. Imphal – British IV Corps and 23rd Indian Division
2. Chittagong – 14th Indian Division

The British-Indian forces in the east of India were placed under the Eastern Army and despite limited resources, political pressure required an offensive against the Japanese, as soon as possible after the monsoon. The first Arakan offensive, aimed simply to reoccupy north Arakan and capture the Akyab Island, lasted from September 1942 until March 1943. The offensive progressed well up until February 1943, when a counter attack by the Japanese, threatened the Eastern Armies supplies lines.

Lieutenant-General 'Bill' Slim was brought in to take over the command of the offensive and sustained it for the next two months, until the monsoon arrived.

Although the Eastern Army was back at the point at which it started the offensive the previous year, the forward airfields at Chittagong, Cox's Bazaar and Ramu were retained. The monsoon period would be used to develop new tactics, structures and jungle warfare capabilities for the next offensive phase.

The command structure for this theatre had a major overhaul and on 15/16th November 1943, the South-East Asia Command (SEAC) was born and charged with directing operations against Japan. Admiral Lord Louis Mountbatten was appointed the Supreme Allied Commander and Lieutenant-General Slim became the commander of the Fourteenth Army (renamed Eastern Army).

Air Chief Marshall Sir Richard Pierse became Air Commander SEAC, his charge to take Burma with the Eastern Air Command. Made up of the 3rd Tactical Air Force (3TAF), a Strategic Air Force, Troop Carrier Command and a Photographic Reconnaissance Force. The groups of 3TAF are tabled below.

Table Showing the main R.A.F. Groups in 3TAF and their Roles

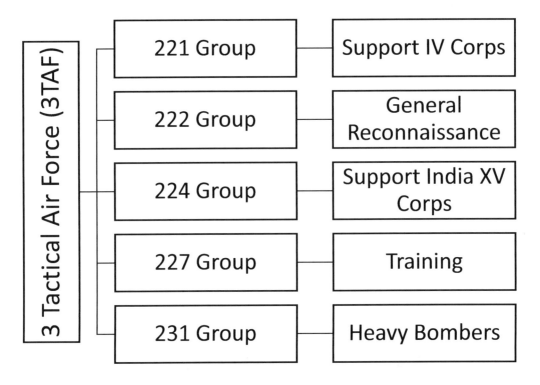

Operation overview and the role of the R.A.F. Regiment

'Units of the R.A.F. Regiment have proved themselves of the greatest value in this campaign, of which the insecurity of airfields and warning establishments in forward areas has been a feature. When Radar Stations were established at St. Martin's Island and later in the Maungdaw area, the unusual situation existed of Radar Stations being actually well in advance of the front line and within range of the enemy's guns and night patrols. It says much for the R.A.F. Regiment personnel that the Radar crews enjoyed undisturbed conditions in which to carry on their work under such trying conditions. It has proved to be quite unsound to rely on the Army maintaining troops for local defence in times of crisis when the land situation deteriorates. This is the time when they are really needed by us, but this is the time when they are inevitably withdrawn to take part in the land battle.' Air Commander, Third Tactical Air Force.

In 1942 there were around 4,500 Ground Gunners organised primarily in Defence flights detached to and integral with flying squadrons and further distributed throughout South East Asia protecting radar and other important installations. In May of that year, A.H.Q. informed the Air Ministry in London that more Ground Gunners and anti-aircraft machine guns were needed, to provide vital direct defence of airfields and installations.

In June, the Director of Ground Defence arrived in India to assess the situation and concluded that AHQ India had done little in response to ground defence, although also acknowledged that the number of personnel needed far exceeded the number available in theatre.

In November 1942, with a training school established at R.A.F. Secunderabad, Ground Gunners from Defence flights would be trained as members of the R.A.F. Regiment and form the backbone of the Corps in SE Asia in new Anti- aircraft flights. Although the Army would still hold primary responsibility for airfield defence, the R.A.F. would provide local ground and anti-aircraft defence, utilising the scarce Regiment resource and "Backers -Up" R.A.F. tradesmen, who would provide support in the protection of the airfields and installations.

The initial resource estimate for the Regiment was just under 5,700 officers and men. Made up of 15 field squadrons and 90 A.A. flights. This was significantly more than those currently employed in defence flight duties and with continual pressure to reduce resources, arguments continued between London and Delhi. The final agreement was that the resource would stay roughly the same for 1943 as those currently employed, but in 1944 the allocation for the Regiment would significantly reduce to just over 2,500 officers and men. The unit allocation for 1943 would be for 6 field squadrons and 50 A.A. flights, accounting for just under 2,800 officers and men. The balance would later be partially consumed through the formation of 12 additional A.A (India) flights in January 1944. These flights would be slightly smaller than the standard A.A. flights, with a total of 35 airmen, and due to officer shortages, most of the new flights were commanded by Sergeants.

The field squadrons and A.A. flights would be allocated to Air Groups, with priority of resource to where the Japanese were at greater risk of attacking, both by air and land. The map below shows the general location of the Air Groups to which R.A.F. Regiment units would be deployed.

Map showing Air Group location and R.A.F.R. allocated areas 1943

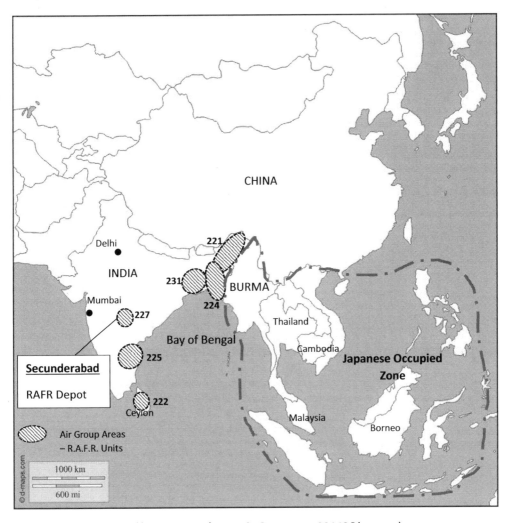

(Author Adapted - http://d-maps.com/carte.php?num_car=32142&lang=en)

Field Squadron – Role and Structure

The primary role of the field squadron was to provide ground defence for aerodromes, which included a counter attack capability and an ability to secure, and take control of enemy held aerodromes.

The field squadron was organised into five flights, three rifle, one support weapons and one headquarters flight. Each Rifle flight had 3 ten men sections, which included local fire support with a L.M.G team and a Grenadier. The Support flight had 3 L.M.G teams and a Grenadier section that would provide suppressive support fire for the rifle sections as well as providing counter attack capability.

Field Squadron establishment

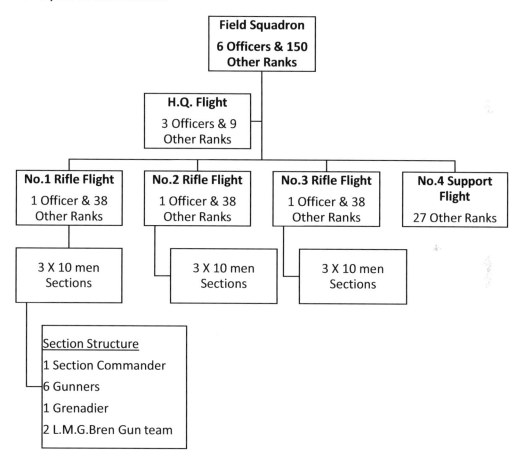

Note that the Squadron Second-in-Command would also be No.4 Flight Commander.

It should also be noted that although designated as field squadrons, their establishment was more akin to a standard rifle squadron, the squadron ORBs normally designated with the letter "R" after their number.

Anti-Aircraft Flight – Role and Structure

The primary role of the Anti-Aircraft (A.A.) flight was to provide light anti-aircraft defence, against low-level attacking and dive bombing aircraft. The unit could also use its weapons, if required, in a ground to ground role, against tanks and personnel.

The anti-aircraft flights were structured into 3 Gun Sections and a Flight headquarters. Each section would man 3 twin 0.303m.m. Browning machine guns, fixed to Motley Stork mountings, with ammunition, belt fed. Although the Browning machine gun was the standard issue anti-aircraft weapon, some units would retain their Lewis machine guns, until upgraded.

Anti-Aircraft Flight

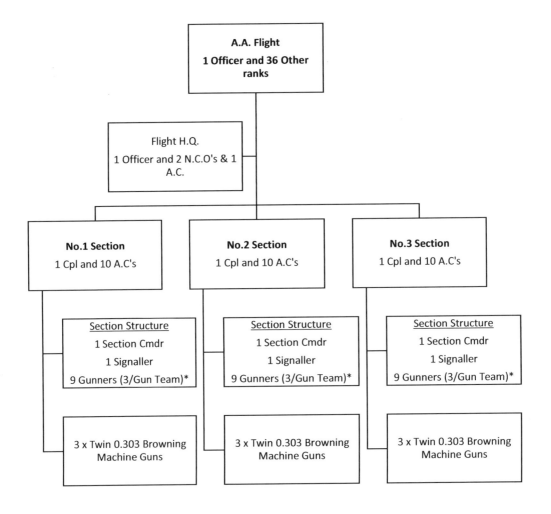

* Each Gun Team includes a Spare Gunner.

Unit Formation - R.A.F. Regiment, Secunderabad

Overview

The re-organisation of the Defence flights into new R.A.F. Regiment field squadrons and A.A. flights started in April 1943. By the end of July, six field squadrons and 16 A.A. flights were formed and a further 34 A.A. flights formed by the end of October of that year.

Formation of R.A.F. Regiment Units at the R.A.F.R. Depot, Secunderabad – 1943

Month	A.A. Flights	Field Squadrons
April	4401, **4402, 4403, 4404**	**2941**
May	**4405, 4406, 4407, 4408**	**2942**
June	4409, **4410**, 4411, 4412	**2943**, 2944
July	**4413**, 4414, 4415, **4416**	**2945**, 2946
August	**4417, 4418**, 4419, 4420, 4421, **4422**, 4423, 4424, 4425, 4426, 4427	
September	**4428**, 4429, 4430, 4431, 4432, 4433, 4434, 4435, **4436, 4437**, 4438	
October	4439, 4440, 4441, 4442, 4443, 4444, 4445, 4446, **4447, 4448, 4449, 4450**	
Establishment Numbers	50 Officers and 1,800 Airmen	36 Officers and 900 Airmen

Note units in bold are included in this book.

Although the training school at Secunderabad had been operational for more than a year, it became clear that the focus would have to move from the training of airmen in ground defence, to properly training and equipping the new field squadrons and A.A. flights. The training school was renamed the R.A.F. Regiment Depot, on the 1st March 1943, its training establishment expanded and a new site located just 1 mile from its current location.

The expansion of the training establishment meant that it now had a Commanding Officer, a Chief Instructor, a Medical Officer, and Adjutant, with nine wings, equally split into formation, squadron and A.A. wings. The standard training programme started with 3 weeks individual training, after which airmen were posted to either field squadrons or A.A. flights, where further training would take place at unit level, before being posted to their respective airfield or A.M.E.S sites.

The first tranche of units in April/May, consisted of 2 field squadrons and 8 A.A. Flights. The first field squadron, No.2941, was formed on the 9th April and was uniquely made up of officers and men of an old "Special" A.A. Squadron, preferring the designation of No.1 Squadron. Although it was able to undertake a small amount of flight training, very little organised training happened during its 4-weeks at Secunderabad, as it lacked sufficient equipment and had to totally reorganise, following the replacement of its all original officers. By mid-April the squadron was instructed to move by flights to the airfield at Agartala.

The second field squadron, No.2942, was formed on the 6th May, following four weeks of training as individual flights. A few days later the squadron was instructed to move to the airfield at Comilla, and although the movement would be by flights, the accommodation proved inadequate and after a quick rearrangement the squadron entrained together. As seemed to be common, the route seemed to be poorly organised by Movement Control, with carriages, food and accommodation provision being inadequate and routes taking weeks longer than they should have, with men who became sick, having to be left at various hospitals on the way.

No.4407 & 4408 A.A. Flights were formed on the 6th May 1943, under Air H.Q. (India) Formation Order No.385 and with an establishment of 1 Officer, 1 Sgt, 4 Cpls and 31 Airmen, in accordance with Est. India/644. Leaving Secunderabad, they entrained and arrived at respective airfields of Chittagong and Imphal, by the end of the month.

The second tranche of units in June/July, consisted of the final 4 field squadrons and 8 A.A. flights. No.2943 Field Squadron was formed on the 18th May as No. 2903, but was subsequently amended on the 5th June, with an establishment of 6 officers and 150 gunners, in accordance with Establishment No. India/633 (E.C.). On leaving the depot for the airfield at Jessore, the squadron had only one appointed officer, the Adjutant.

No.4410 A.A. Flight was formed on the 19th May 1943, a full complement of men, 9 twin Lewis Guns, with mountings, but no couplings. Other weapons included seventeen 0.303 rifles and bayonets and twenty 9m.m. Sten guns, the former would be distributed to airmen not on gun post duty. The standard allocation of ammunition included 37,700 rounds of 0.303, 1,250 rounds of 9m.m. and 72 Grenades. The flight received instructions in June to proceed to the airfield at Cox's Bazaar.

Although No.2945 Field Squadron was formed on the 13th May, it didn't leave Secunderbad, for the airfield ay Chharra until July. The squadron entrained in two groups with the advance party leaving with 3 Officers and 50 airmen and days later the remainder of the squadron marched out of the Depot. The detail of its establishment and weapons allocations are tabled below.

Squadron Headquarters Flight

3 Officers	9 Airmen
1 S/Ldr. x Squadron Commander (Sten Gun)	Staff N.C.O's 1 x F/Sgt. & 1 Cpl. (Sten Guns)
1 F/Lt. x Second-in-Command (also Support Flight Commander (Sten Gun)	3 A.C. x Signallers (Rifle)
	2 A.C. x M.T (Rifle)
1 F/O x Adjutant (Sten Gun)	2 A.C. x Stretcher Bearers (Rifle)

Rifle Flight

1 Officer (per flight)		38 Airmen (per flight)	
Flight Headquarters		1 Sgt x Flight 2 i/c (Sten Gun)	
1 F/O x Flight Commander (Sten Gun)		1 A.C. x Signaller (Rifle)	
		6 A.C. x Spare Gunners (Sten Guns)	
No.1 Section	No.2 Section	No.3 Section	
1 Cpl. x Section Commander (Sten Gun)	1 Cpl. x Section Commander (Sten Gun)	1 Cpl. x Section Commander (Sten Gun)	
6 A.C. x Gunners (Rifle)	6 A.C. x Gunners (Rifle)	6 A.C. x Gunners (Rifle)	
1 A.C. x Grenadier (Rifle Dis.)	1 A.C. x Grenadier (Rifle Dis.)	1 A.C. x Grenadier (Rifle Dis.)	
2 A.C. x L.M.G team (L.M.G. & Sten Guns)	2 A.C. x L.M.G team (L.M.G. & Sten Guns)	2 A.C. x L.M.G team (L.M.G. & Sten Guns)	

Support Flight

1 Officer		34 Airmen	
Flight Headquarters		1 Sgt x Flight 2i/c (Sten Gun)	
1 F/Lt. x Flight Commander, also Squadron Second-in-Command (Sten Gun)		1 A.C. x Signaller (Rifle)	
		1 A.C. x Spare (Sten Guns)	
		6 A.C. x Spare Gunners (Rifle)	
No.1 L.M.G. Section	No.2 L.M.G. Section	No.3 L.M.G. Section	No.4 Grenade Section
1 Cpl. x Section Cmdr. (Sten Gun)	1 Cpl. x Section Cmdr. (Sten Gun)	1 Cpl. x Section Cmdr. (Sten Gun)	1 Cpl. x Section Cmdr. (Sten Gun)
1 A.C. x Signaller (Rifle)	1 A.C. x Signaller (Rifle)	1 A.C. x Signaller (Rifle)	1 A.C. x Signaller (Rifle)
2 A.C. x L.M.G team (L.M.G. & Sten Guns)	2 A.C. x L.M.G team (L.M.G. & Sten Guns)	2 A.C. x L.M.G team (L.M.G. & Sten Guns)	4 A.C. x Grenadier (Rifle Dis.)

No.4413 A.A. Flight formed on the 11th June 1943 was the first R.A.F.R. unit to be posted to Ceylon at an airfield at the southern point of the island, at Koggala in July. No.4416 A.A. Flight formed on the 12th June, continued training at the Depot, without a formerly appointed commanding officer and it wasn't until the 18th July that the flight commander was officially appointed and on the same day instructed to move to the airfield at Kumbhirgram.

The next tranche of units in August, saw 11 A.A. flights formed. Drawn from a "Pool" of gunners at the Depot, No.4417 A.A. Flight was formed on the 7th July and trained as a complete unit on foot and arms drill, infantry section leading & fieldcraft and L.A.A.M.G. instruction. The flight commander gave subsidiary lectures for the unit on security (incl. P.O.W.), Japanese tactics, the Campaign in Malaya, Singapore, the Dutch East Indies and Burma and on the Japanese Army. On the 14th August the flight left the Depot, in high spirits, for the airfield at Khurda Road, lead out by the Depot band, with the salute taken by the Depot Commanding Officer and Chief Instructor.

On the 23rd August No.4418 A.A. Flight left Secunderabad for Imphal, where its first task was to disperse its sections, protecting 3 different A.M.E.S. sites.

The next tranche of units in September, saw another 11 A.A. flights formed. Whilst undergoing A.A. training at the Depot, No.4428 A.A. Flight was formed. It was soon posted to the airfield at St. Thomas Mount, Madras, it's main strength coming from its relatively low average age, excellent morale and already experienced in prolonged spells in forward areas.

Formed on the 14th August No.4436 A.A. Flight had already been trained, before its flight commander arrived at the Depot, where they were immediately posted to the airfield at Khulna. They left with 7 days rations, with 8 other flights by train for Madras.

A similar experience fell to the flight commander of No.4437 A.A. Flight, who on being introduced to his unit was instructed to move to Diamond Harbour, Madras. Although issued with the standard weapons, what stands out is that the nineteen 0.303 Browning Machine Guns are recorded as u/s, with fire and safety attachments omitted and the mounting holding down bolts for the base plates missing.

The final tranche in October totalled 12 A.A. flights, which concluded the 1943 formation of the new R.A.F.R. units totalling 6 field squadrons and 50 A.A. flights. Of the final units formed, No.4448 A.A. Flight spent its last four weeks at the Depot under the training supervision of its flight commander and sergeant. The last two weeks of October was spent kitting out the men, drawing weapons, ammunition and equipment, plus weapon and fieldcraft training. The flight commander led two outings, over the desert and hills around Secunderabad, although gruelling, were claimed to be very successful. A final flight in attack over rough ground, showed the unit could move well, including rock climbing in full battle order. To the probable relief of the men, the unit was soon posted to the airfield at Dum-Dum.

Following a final 3-week training course No.4449 A.A. Flight left for Cholavarum and the last unit No.4450 A.A. Flight, became the second unit posted to Ceylon, to the northern airfield at Sigiriya.

Operational Diaries

April – July
2941 Field Squadron – Entrained to Agartalla (April)

The "Special" A.A. Squadron was reformed at SECUNDERABAD, R.A.F. Regiment Depot, as 2901 Squadron and personnel drafted in to make a total of 6 Officers and 150 B.O.R's. Formation date was 9/4/43. The majority of the old "Special" Squadron of 110 men was retained – the few exceptions being lost on medical grounds and about 50 new men drafted in to make the full establishment of 150 B.O.R's. The 3 Flight Officers of the "Special" Squadron were exchanged for 3 new officers and, in addition, 2 more officers were posted to the formation to make up the establishment of 6 officers, including the Commanding Officer.

Very little training was carried out at SECUNDERABAD during the four weeks the Squadron remained there, as the changes in officers and men, organisation and equipment of the Squadron, made it impossible to carry out much organised training, although a certain amount of Flight training was done as time permitted.

Equipment of the Squadron was not complete when orders were received to move to AGARTALA. The officers of No.1 Squadron, as the Squadron was popularly termed, were:-

S/LDR.H.J.FORBES.M.M.,   F/LT.F.G.MACGREGOR,   F/O.F.W.EVANS, P/OW..LITTLEFAIR,   P/O.J.D.BAXTER   and   P/O.H.G.REDINGTON   (as Adjutant).

Other ranks were:-

1 F/SGT., 4 SGTs., 14 CPLs and 131 A.C's; a complete establishment of :- 6 Officers and 150 Other Ranks. One CPL: Cook attached.

The Commanding Officer was instructed to report to Air Headquarters, INDIA, and from there proceeded to Air Headquarters, BENGAL, where he received instructions to report to AGARTALA on the 18/4/43. The Squadron commenced move from SECUNDERABAD by Flights, the first movement taking place on the 14/4/43 and continuing for the three following days. The Squadron completed the movement by the arrival of No.3 Flight at AGARTALA on 23/4/43.

2942 Field Squadron – Entrained to Comilla (May)

This Unit came into being about the end of the first week of May. It was at Secunderabad and for the previous four weeks had been training as 4 individual Flights. On May 4th we were told that we were to be inspected on May 6th by A.O.C. Training Command, A.V.M. Vincent and from that point forward we could consider ourselves a Squadron. The C.O. was later told that the actual Formation Order was dated 29-4-43. The Officers, all of had been together at Secunderabad were,

S/Ldr. J.E. Hosking.   Age 44 C.O.

F/Lt. G.E. Cattell.   Age 36 2nd i/c

F/O. W.G. Chaffin.   Adjutant

F/O. A. Jordan.   Age 29 No.1 Flight

P/O. W. Budgen   Age 35 No.2 Flight

P/O A. Pelly-Fry   Age 36 No.3 Flight

F/Lt. Cattell acts as No.4 Flight Commander.

The Senior N.C.Os. were,

F/Sgt. Harris.   Admin.

Sgt. Chapman.   No.1 Flight

Sgt. Snaith.   No.2 Flight

Sgt. Quigley.   No.3 Flight

Sgt. Whitworth.   No.4 Flight

The inspection duly took place on May 6th and passed off satisfactory. That morning the Squadron and the Officers were photographed but the former was a bad group and no copies are available. The Squadron was under orders to leave for Comilla, journeying by Flights, on the 10th – 13th inclusive and an advance party of F/O Chaffin, F/Sgt Harris and 6 men went ahead on May 8th, travelling via Bezwarda and Calcutta.

Thereafter following a few days of hectic organisation, obtaining equipment arms, ammunition etc., and on the evening of the 10th No.1 Flight (F/O. Jordan) moved off. At the station it was discovered that the accommodation provided on the train was quite inadequate and a hasty rearrangement of plans ensued. As a result the whole

Squadron entrained together on May 12th in 3 "T" Cars with one "C" Car for arms and baggage. Just prior to moving off on the 12th all ranks were vaccinated owing to a Small Pox scare. The journey was a very uncomfortable one. It seems we had been wrongly routed by Movements Control from Secunderbad and no one knew anything about the convoy at the stations we passed through. So we had to make our own arrangements as we went.

The route we were forced to take was the Central Provinces one and it was very hot. The carriage had no fans, no ice containers, appalling lavatory accommodation (one native type latrine per coach of 50 men) and in all five men succumbed to various forms of sickness en route and had to be left at various hospitals. The convoy reached Calcutta (Howrah) at about 08-30hrs on Sunday May 16th and the men were given a much needed opportunity of cleaning up and stretching their legs. They were allowed to go out into the town till midnight and that night slept on the train which was in the siding. There were no absentees. The following day the baggage was loaded and transferred to Sealdah and the convoy left at about 16-00hrs for Golundo Gat. The rest of the journey was uneventful and the Squadron arrived at Comilla at about 23-00hrs on 17th May were the Adjutant, F/O Chaffin had transport laid on and all arrangements made. From Calcutta to Camilla the Squadron had been in the charge of F/Lt Cattell as the C.O. and F/O Jordan had remained for a further day in Calcutta to attend to various things. They left Sealdah at 22-00hrs on 17th May and arrived at Comilla at 22-30hrs on the 18th, one day behind the rest of the Squadron.

4406 A.A. Flight – Entrained for Amarda Road (May)

4356 A.A. Flight, R.A.F. Regiment, was formed at Secunderabad, (R.A.F. Regt. Depot) on the 9th May 1943. F/O G.B. Chambers was posted to fill the vacancy of Flight Commander & granted the paid acting rank from that date. The "other ranks" personnel shown in Appendix "A" were also posted and the units establishment was completed with 1 Sgt., 4 Cpls., 31 AC's. (India 664). In view of this flight being an independent unit in certain respects (See

Formation Order, Appendix "B") it is necessary to draw on the personnel, all of whom are Gunners, Group V, for such duties as clerks. Four have been detailed at Secunderabad as signallers: and when the M/T establishment of 1 Motor Cycle and 4 vehicles arrives, it will be necessary to find at least four drivers. This unit is employing 1 Cpl and 1 airman in the "Orderly Room". This makes six men at least off strength off the flight for its primary duty. Before leaving Secunderabad on orders from A.H.Q. India, to Amarda Road, the flight was brought up to establishment in personal weapons 20 Sten Guns and 17 rifles, and every man was kitted up to scale so far as supplies permitted. Deficiency "chits" were issued. The Depot were unable to supply any machine guns, either Lewis, Browning of V.G.O., and the reason for this appears to be that as new units such as this are being formed, the personnel for these units are drawn in small batched from R.A.F. Squadrons & other units. It is considered that it would be an improvement if the whole of these gunners were withdrawn from these R.A.F. units & they brought their weapons with them to Secunderabad where they could be pooled and re-issued to new units.

4407 A.A. Flight – Entrained via Calcutta to Chittagong (May)

Unit formed at R.A.F. Regiment Depot under Air H.Q. (India) Formation Order No. 385 dated 6.5.43. The Unit was one of the earliest to be formed under the new policy providing for the organisation of the R.A.F. Regiment om India into self-contained Units. Established strength on formation was 1 F/Lt. commanding and 36 Gunners (Est. India/664). Establishment provided for equipment of 18 L.M.G.s, type not specified.

F/LT. L.R.H. Portlock appointed to command the Unit.

Unit left R.A.F. Regiment Depot for R.A.F. Station, DOHAZARI. Movement Order No.1 issued. Travelled by "M" Coach to Calcutta (Howrah), via Nagpur, arriving 23.5.43.

4408 A.A. Flight – Entrained via Calcutta to Imphal (May)

4358 A.A. Flight formed, formation order no.385 Established and Equipped in accordance with Establishment India/664. Commanded by F/O (A/F/L) 104923 GRIERSON G.J.
Flight entrained for Imphal.

2943 Field Squadron – Entrained to Jessore (June)

The Squadron was formed at the R.A.F. Regiment Depot, SECUNDERABAD under formation Order No.394, dated 18th May, 1943 as 2903 Squadron R.A.F. Regiment. Amendment to formation Order No.96 dated 5th June, 1943 altered the number of the Squadron to 2943. The strength of the Squadron was 6 Officers and 150 Gunners in accordance with Establishment No. India/663 (E.C.) F/O F.N. Hallam was appointed the Adjutant on formation of the Squadron, but no other definite appointments were made up to the time of leaving the Depot.
F/O's A.E.M. LEWSEY, S.J. CLARK and F.N. HALLAM left with 75 B.O.R's leaving F/LT T.F. RYALLS and F/O's H.W. FREEMAN and A.E. COLLADGE to follow on the next day with a similar number of B.O.R's, as per Movement Order.

4410 A.A. Flight – Posted to Cox's Bazaar (June)

'A' FORMATION ORDER. No.397 19 May '43 Formed at SECUNDERABAD. Est. India 664 (E.C) 1. F.L.T., 1. SGT., 4. CPLs, 31 Armen. Equip. 9 Twin Lewis Guns, 9 Mottly Stork Mountings, (no couplings)1008 Mags,17 Rifles and Bayonets, 20 Sten Guns, 100 Mags. Ammo.' .303:- 37,700 Rnds., 9.m.m.1,250 Rnds, 72 Grenades
'B' Posted to Cox's Bazaar as an A.A. Flt.

2945 Field Squadron – Entrained to Chharra (July)

In accordance with A.H.Q. India. Formation Order No.416, No.2945 Squadron R.A.F. Regiment, was formed at Secunderabad, Deccan, on 31st May, 1943.

ESTABLISHMENT.   INDIA/663/E.C.

OFFICERS.	S/LDR.	F/LT.	F/O.orP/O.	TOTAL OFFCIERS.
Squadron H.Q	1.	1.	1.	3.
Total 3 Flights.			3.	3.
Total Squadron	1.	1.	4.	6.

AIRMEN.	F/S.	SGTS.	CPLS.	A.Cs.	TOTAL AIRMEN.
Squadron H.Q.	1.		1.	7.	9.
Total 3 Flights.		3.	9.	102.	114.
Support Flight.		1.	5.	21.	27.
Total Squadron.	1.	4.	15.	130.	150.
TOTAL ALL RANKS.				156.	

ALLOCATION OF WEAPONS.

DETAIL	Rifle No.4.	Rifles No.1 Discharger.	LMG.	STEN.
Squadron H.Q.				
Officers (3).				3.
Staff N.C.O's				2.
3 Signallers.	3.			
2 M.T.	2.			
2 Stretcher Bearers.	2.			
Total Squadron H.Q.	7.			5.

1 RIFLE FLIGHT.				
Officer.				1.
Flight 2nd in Command.				1.
Signaller.	1.			
Section Commanders.				3.
6 L.M.G. Gunners.			3.	6.
6 Spare Gunners.				6.
18 Gunners.	18.			
3 Grenadiers		3.		
TOTAL.	19.	3.	3.	17.

TOTAL - 3 FLIGHTS.	57.	9.	9.	51.

SUPPORT FLIGHT.

Officer. (included in H.Q.)				
Flight 2nd in Command.				1.
Spare.				1.
Signallers.	4.			
Section Commanders.				3.
L.M.G. Gunners.			3.	6.
Spare Gunners.	6.			
Grenade Section Commander.				1.
1 Signaller.	1.			
4 Grenadiers.		4.		
TOTAL SUPPORT FLIGHT.	11.	4.	3.	12.
TOTAL SQUADRON.	75.	13.	12.	66.

During this period training was carried out at the Depot, but no Officers were officially appointed to the Squadron.

It was announced that the following Officers were appointed to No.2945 Squadron:-

Squadron Commander. 66276 F/LT (A/S/L. w.e.f. 31/5/43) GARNER. R.H.A.

Second-in-Command. 114320 F/O (A/F/L. w.e.f. 17/7/43) GARNETT. T.R.

Adjutant. 118315 F/O STUART HART K.

No.1 Flight Commdr. 127657 F/O OTTOY N.A.J.

No.2 Flight Commdr. 104078 F/O WILMOT F.C.P

No.3 Flight Commdr. 123710 F/O ASHTON J.E.E.

No.4 Flight Commdr. Second-in-Command.

An advance party of 3 Officers and 50 airmen marched out of the Depot, and left for R.A.F. Station, CHHARRA by train. This party took the baggage for the whole Squadron, and was accommodated in one 3rd Class T bogey, and one E.V.P. truck. These trucks having missed a connection at NAGPUR were attached to the CALCUTTA Mail. En route at Tumsar Rd. 1033871 LAC BLAND cut off the top of his thumb in a door.

The remainder of the Squadron marched out of the Depot, and also left for CHHARRA in 2 T bogeys. This party was badly delayed, and reached its destination a day late.

4413 A.A. Flight – Entrained to Koggala, Ceylon (July)

No.4413 A.A. Flight, R.A.F. Regiment was formed at SECUNDERABAD on 11.6.43. as per formation Order No.415 A.H.Q. letter reference 3218/44/Org. dated 11.6.43.

The Flight left SECUNDERABAD by train en route KOGGALA.

4416 A.A. Flight – Entrained to Bezwada (July)

A.H.Q. INDIA Formation Order No.415 was received notifying the intention to form No.4416 AA Flight, R.A.F. REGIMENT DEPOT SECUNDERABAD in the first instance.

Events leading up to the receipt of this order were briefly that on the 12th June 1943, 1 Sgt, 4 Cpls, and 31 ACs. Were provisionally allotted to what was known as 16 AA Flight. No officer was appointed until the 17th June when F/LT. F.C. WILSON was provisionally appointed to the unit. On the 4th July F/O WILMOT replaced F/Lt. WILSON, bit on the 8th July F/Lt. WILSON was reinstated. During all this period training was proceeding, some changes being made to personnel. No information was received all this time regarding the official formation of the unit. At the time of receipt of the Formation Order referred to above, the attached is a copy of the Nominal Roll of the Flight. The Officer was not officially appointed until receipt of A.H.Q. (I) Signal received at the R.A.F. REGIMENT DEPOT on the 18th July when A/F/Lt. F.C. WILSON 104081 was appointed Q/C Flight and the order to move the Flight to R.A.F. STATION KUMBHIRGRAM (SILCHAR) was received.

Copy of the Movement Order of the Flight from SECUNDERABAD to KUMBHIRGRAM attached herewith (App. "B"). Departure of Flight from SECUNDERABAD and arrival at BEZWADA.

4417 A.A. Flight – Training at Secunderabad (July)

No.4417 A.A. Flight was formed at the R.A.F. Regiment Depot, in accordance with A.H.Q. India, Formation Order No.430, dated 7.7.43 (See Appendix "A").

PERSONNEL were drawn from the "Pool" at the Depot.

ESTABLISHMENT was in accordance with that laid down for A.A. Flights by A.H.Q. India and comprised of 1 Flight Lieutenant, in Command, 1 Sergeant, 4 Corporals and 31 Gunners.

ARMS consisted of 19 Browning .303 L.M.G's. 21 STEN Machine Carbines and 17 Rifles, complete with bayonets.

AMMUNITION, according to scales.

TRAINING as a complete Unit, commenced under instruction from the Depot staff and consisted of Foot and Arms Drill, Infantry Section Leading and Fieldcraft and L.A.A.M.G. instruction.

101221 F/O H.E. HAROY was posted to fill the F/LT. O.C. vacancy, and supervised all instruction by the Flight N.C.O's. Lectures were given by him Security, including Prisoners of War, Japanese tactics, the Campaign in Malaya, Singapore, the Dutch East Indies and Burma, and on the Japanese Army.

Some changes to personnel occurred, due mainly to hospital admissions of recurrent malarial cases.

4418 A.A. Flight – Formed at Secunderabad (July)

Flight formed at R.A.F.R. DEPOT (India) SECUNDERABAD- 12.7.43

COMMANDING OFFICER: F/LT. R.T. Ferrier-Jones

N.C.O.s: Sgt. Stone, Cpl. Nash, Cpl. Jones, A/Cpl. Cusse, A/CPl. Oates

B.O.Rs.: 31.

EQUIPMENT:

ARMS: .303 Brownings (A.A.)   19

      Rifles S.M.L.E. Mk III 17

      Sten Carbines   21

      Grenades   72

AMMUNITION: .303 37,700 85% Ball, 10% A.P., 5% Tracer

      9m.m. 2,000

MOUNTINGS A.A. Motley Stork   9

STATIONERY: One pack

COOKING UTENSILS: Miscellaneous

TRANSPORT: Nil

FURNITURE: etc. Nil

August to October

4417 A.A. Flight departed for Khurda Road, via Bezwada Waltair (August)

The Flight Commander was informed of the probable move of the Flight to an unnamed destination and that training at the Depot would cease on Saturday 14th August, leaving the whole of the following week clear for removal preparation.
On receipt of the first definite information concerning departure, the Movement Order, together with the week's programme was drawn up by the Flight Commander.
All Section Commanders were called together, and given orders individually, for duties throughout the week, as laid down in Appendix "B".
Nominal Rolls checked. Kit Inspection. Arms drawn from Armoury.
Instruction in assembly and erection of Motley Stalk Mountings.
Inspection Parade. Lectures by Flight Commander and M.O.
Kitting out parade and preparation packing. 1103685 SGT. BARKER replaced SGT. FENWICK as second in command.
Checking of Pay Books, Identity Discs. Final arrangements with R.T.O.
Medical Officer's Inspection. Pay Parade. Ammunition and 14 day Rations drawn. Baggage Party load wagon allocated, in Sidings, Secunderabad.
Final instructions from the Depot Commandant, W/CDR. KENNEDY to F/LT. HARDY.
Flight Commander's Inspection.
Depot Commandant's Inspection.
Embussed in M.T. for SECUNDERABAD Railway Station. The Flight debussed about half a mile from the Station, and marched the

remainder of the way, headed by the Depot Band. All the men were in very high spirits. A salute was taken at the entrance of the Station, by W/CDR. KENNEDY, accompanied by S/LDR. GARDINER - Chief Instructor.

Departed for CALCUTTA, via BEZWADA WALTAIR, and KHURDA RD.

4418 A.A. Flight departed for Imphal, Manipur State (August)

The Flight left the Depot, Secunderabad on 23rd August 1943, for Imphal, Manipur State. The move was carried out smoothly and without difficulty. On arrival the sections were deployed in accordance the following:-

To 583 A.M.E.S. - H.Q. Section
                  No.1 Section
To 857 A.M.E.S. - No.3 Section
To 885 A.M.E.S. - No.2 Section and Sgt. Stone.

All sections were comfortably settled as above on 1st September, 1943.

4428 A.A. Flight departed for St Thomas Mount, Madras (September)

No.4428 A.A. Flight, R.A.F. Regiment was formed at R.A.F. Regiment Depot (India) Secunderabad, by the terms of Formation Order No.460, dated 14th August 1943 at Air Headquarters, India. The Flight was formed on the basis of Establishment No. India/644(E.C.), which provides for one British Officer (F/LT. C.O.) and 36 British Other Ranks (including one Sergeant and four Corporals). At the time of its formation No.4428 Flight was undergoing the current A.A. Training course at R.A.F. Regiment Depot, Secunderabad.

Posting of Commanding Officer to No.4428 Flight was authorised by Command Routine Order, No.90.

No.4428 Flight posted from R.A.F. Regiment Depot to R.A.F. Station, St. Thomas Mount, Madras. By this time it had become apparent that the main strength of the Flight consisted of gunners with a relatively low average age and of excellent initial morale. The majority had been in India some 18 months and had already undergone a prolonged spell of service in a Forward Area.

4436 A.A. Flight departed for Madras (September)

Unit Formation Order No.460 A.H.Q./INDIA 14/8/43. F/Lt. W.G. Chaffin 107944 posted to Unit as C.O. A.H.Q. B. Signal No. P707 dated 5/9/43.
F/Lt. W.G. Chaffin arrived at R.A.F. Regiment Depot Secunderabad to take over unit which had been formed and trained by Depot personnel. Flight posted to R.A.F. Station Khulna.
Collected remainder of equipment etc. and ready to move off.
Flight paraded and left for station at 07.00hrs. 7 days rations taken for journey. Left with 8 other A.A. Flights for Madras at 11.00hrs.

4437 A.A. Flight departed for Diamond Harbour, via Madras (September)

I have been appointed O.C. of No.4437 A.A. Flight w.e.f. 5.9.43. I am to proceed to SECUNDERABAD by CALCUTTA - MADRAS MAIL on the 15.9.43.
No.4437 A.A. Flight R.A.F. Regt. has been formed as per FORMATION ORDER NO.460. A.H.Q. INDIA. I have just been introduced to my Flight before proceeding to its first operational 1 locality i.e. DIAMOND HARBOUR via MADRAS, CHITTAGONG, CALCUTTA. Authy. A.H.Q. 4324/iv/Mov. Dated 9.9.43. A rather roundabout route.

The above planned journey will take us approx. three weeks to reach our destination. A more considerate plan would have been six day rail journey direct to DIAMOND HARBOUR via CALCUTTA.

The present strength of our Unit is a s follows:- Officer Commanding, 1 Senior N.C.O., 4 N.C.O.'s and 31 B.O.R.'s.

Our equipment on departure consisted of 19 u/s .303 BROWNINGS (Fire and Safe attachments were omitted on initial issue) 9 Motley Stalk Mountings - less holding down bolts for base plates, 17 Rifles, 20 Sten Machine Turbines, 30,000 rounds of .303 ball ammunition, 3,600 rounds of tracer, 1,800 rounds of A.P., 72 grenades (Mills 36) and a First Aid Box. |

4447 A.A. Flight departed for Alipore (October)

4447 A/A Flight formed in accordance with Formation Order 493 Ref.3226/18/ORG III dated 7/9/43. Original personnel - see Nominal Roll at App. A. Training, kitting & general organisation proceeded with.
OC F/LT. Cayne admitted to GOUGH Hospital. Sgt. Gibbons i/c Flight.
Flight left SECUNDERABAD for ALIPORE. Authy BPO/D.14109 d/d 6/10/43.

4448 A.A. Flight training at Secunderabad and posted to Dum – Dum (November)

INTRODUCTION. This record covers the first three months of the Flight's existence, i.e.:- November and December, 1943, and January 1944. It has not been submitted before because the forms were not obtainable. Compilation is from notes made as short and regular intervals. Facts and figures of formation and equipment are available from the Orders and Organisation, Armaments and Equipment Files. The phase of the Flight's development are best studied under the various geographical headings, which, at the time of writing, are three in number:-
R.A.F. REGIMENT DEPOT., Secunderabad, INDIA. This Flight originally bore the number 4449 and most of the training supervised by myself and 989630 Sgt Farnham, (now with 4442 Flight). This continued through the last half of September and for the first half of October 1943. I, F/LT. H.F. Homer., 127613, was posted Officer Commanding 4448 A.A. Flight, R.A.F. Regiment, w.e.f. 12/Oct/43 by authority of A.H.Q. Signal P.539 of 15/Oct/43. I had interviews with F/LT. Gilchrist, S/Ldr. Gardiner, and W/Cmdr. Kennedy and obtained permission to switch the numbers of the Flights on the Official Formation Parade. 1305384 Sgt Jones was posted to the Flight together with Three corporals:- Cpl Tute, Cpl Hardy, and Col Stephenson. These were probationary postings but I had no cause for demanding any changes. Cpl Barcley was picked later by Sgt Jones. As Lac's Reed, Cundy, and Hunt fell out of the Flight through accident, unfitness and illness

respectively, their places were taken by L.A.Cs Hillman, Donovan and Heath, all fit and recommended men.

The last two weeks of October were spent kitting the men out, drawing weapons, ammunition and equipment, and carrying on with weapon and field training. Sgt Jones and three of the corporals volunteered for permanent toughening up and twelve gunners followed suit; this entails training over whatever type of country in which we may find ourselves. My idea in calling for the volunteers, which I intend leading myself, is an attempt to get a good Flight spirit going from the start. The two initial outings over the desert and hills around Secunderabad were gruelling and successful. On October the 30th, the whole Flight went out in attack formation and moved very well over rough and difficult country. The sections showed that they can move well by bounds and get into final assault on time. One move involved considerable rock climbing in full battle order which tested fitness, endurance and nerve.

The men march well and easily in Flight or Ack/Ack formation. Drill is up to standard, marksmanship good and weapon training a little over average. Football and swimming standards are good. Welfare outings for tea, swimming and a visit to Hyderabad Bazaar were organised and general behaviour was good, turn out smart.

POLICY

My general policy is based on making all ranks efficient, happy and fit. Once attained, this standard will be maintained. Physically I ask nothing of the men that I am not able to do myself and I take every opportunity to let them see that I can do it as well if not better, than the best of them.

CRITICISM

The posting of officers and sergeants to Flights by number might well detract from efficiency. Sgt Farnham was sad indeed at being posted away from the Flight and myself; I experienced difficulty in leaving the Depot with the Flight I had worked with there: Sgt Jones was not happy when I switched the numbers of the Flights. It is pure luck that he has now settled down and that we work well together.

THE FIRST JOURNEY. SECUNDERABAD/CALCUTTA/DUM-DUM.

A routine Indian train journey which went well. At Nagpur, we were held up for 24hrs during which I organised ablutions on the station, hot meals in the town, games, reading & writing facilities at a canteen, a swimming party to a tank outside the town and parties to visit the zoo and museum. The moving of kit and equipment on Howrah Station was carried out with smartness, efficiency and in a willing spirit. Nothing was lost. All were abed at Dum-Dum by 22.30.

POLICY.

Sgt Jones, a glutton for hard work, backed me up in splendid fashion in my policy of trying to provide the men with adequate meals, keeping them cheerful and free from constipation. In shifting and man-handling baggage and equipment, we lent a hand and did not merely supervise. This kept the men at it with a will.

CRITICISM.

Before leaving Secunderabad, I warned both the guard and Flight Runner, 1251060 L.A.C. Shelton, to call me should the Flight "T" Waggon be detached from the train. This was not done, with the result that I arrived at Nagpur on the Grand Trunk mail some twelve hours before the Flight. The R.T.O. and the Station Master, both most helpful and kind to me, did not seem to work in harmony with each other. This is not common to Nagpur alone. To quote from my note:-

"I contacted the R.T.O. at Nagpur at 09.30hrs and ran into some personnel of 4447 Flight who were making the journey without an officer and were twenty four hours behind schedule. I arranged for them to leave at 21.05 and was assured that my own Flight would travel on that night. A visit to the Assistant Station Master confirmed this view but at 20.00 this confirmation was cancelled although 4447 Flight got away. 4448 Flight was promised the Bombay Mail at 10.00hrs the next morning. At 09.00hrs. the next morning (Nov 2nd '43) the R.T.O. was astonished to find us still in Nagpur. Both he and another Assistant Station Master refused me the Bombay Mail and said that we would proceed on the 21.05 that night. This was so but the train started two hours late and arrived in Calcutta four hours and forty minutes late."

4449 A.A. Flight training at Secunderabad and posted to Cholavarum (November)

No.4449 A.A. Flight was formed and located in the first instance at the R.A.F. Regt. DEPOT SECUNDERBAD, where personnel had taken part in a training course (3 weeks duration) which included instruction on Browning MGs, Bren Guns and a certain amount of Field Training. 118205 F/O WRIGHT was given command of the Unit and the following personnel posted to fill the N.C.O. vacancies

1035419	A/SGT CRUMBLEHOLME	H.J.	GUNNER V
1464759	A/CPL ATTERBURY	H.E.	GUNNER V
1358575	T/CPL FIELD	A.E.	GUNNER V
1355684	T/CPL MADAMS	W.T.	GUNNER V
1472070	T/CPL NEIGHBOUR	J.G.	GUNNER V

A certain amount of equipment was collected, but deficiencies included Conversion Sets for Browning MG's.

No.1508224 LAC. WHITBY CA and No.1144902 LAC PICTON were selected to attend Units Armourers Course at No.5 S. of T.T. and proceeded on 27th Oct 1943.

On the 3rd Nov. 1943 the Flight received orders to move to CHOLAVARUM. Entrainment took place at 09.00hrs 5th Nov. 1943 and the Unit duly arrived at CHOLAVARUM at 23.00hrs.

4450 A.A. Flight posted to Sigiriya, Ceylon (November)

Formation of 4450 AA Flight R.A.F. Regt.

Movement of 4450 AA Flight on posting to R.A.F. Station Sigiriya, Ceylon.

War Establishment of an Anti-Aircraft Flight – No. India/664

May, 1943.

Appendix "B" to War Department Letter No. 3106/593/Org. A.F. dated 21st April, 1943.

Establishment No. India/664 (E.C.)   ROYAL AIR FORCE.

War Establishment of an Anti Aircraft Flight, Royal Air Force Regiment.

PART I – PERSONNEL.

SUMMARY.

	F/Lt.	F/O.	Total.	W/O.	F/Sgt.	Sgt.	Cpl.	A.C.	Total.
Flight Headquarters	1	–	1	–	–	1	1	1	3
Anti Aircraft Flight	–	–	–	–	–	–	3	30	33
	1	–	1	–	–	1	4	31	36

Flight Headquarters.

	F/Lt.	F/O.	Total.	W/O.	F/Sgt.	Sgt.	Cpl.	A.C.	Total.
R.A.F. Regiment	1	–	1						
V. Gunners (a)						1	1	1	3
	1	–	1			1	1	1	3

Anti Aircraft Flight.

	F/Lt.	F/O.	Total.	W/O.	F/Sgt.	Sgt.	Cpl.	A.C.	Total.
V. Gunners (b							3	30	33
							3	30	33

Policy:-

18 L.M.G's, 20 Sten Machine Guns and 17 rifles

Remarks:-

(a)	Include for:-	
	2nd i/c Flight	1 Sgt.
	Reserve Section Commander	1 Cpl.
	Signaller	1 A.C.
(b)	Include for:-	
	3 Sections (each)	
	Section Commander	1 Cpl.
	Gunners	6 A.C.s
	Spare Gunners	3 A.C.s
	Signaller	1 A.C.

PART II - MECHANICAL TRANSPORT.

Prime Movers 'A'		Prime Movers 'B'	
Nil.		Cycle Motor	1
		Vans 15 cwt.	4
			5

Other Vehicles 'A'		Other Vehicles 'B'	
		Bicycles	7

TOTAL PRIME MOVERS 'A' AND 'B'	=	5
TOTAL OTHER VEHICLES 'A' AND 'B'	=	7

Formation Order No.385

3218/44/Org.   SECRET   Air Headquarters, India.

Dated 6th May,1943.

FORMATION ORDER NO.385.

FORMATION OF ANTI-AIRCRAFT FLIGHTS, R.A.F. REGIMENT.

IMFORMATION.

1. It has been decided to form the following Anti-Aircraft Flights
   of the R.A.F. Regiment, at the R.A.F. Regt., Depot (India),
   Secunderabad, with effect from 26th April 1943.

   The Flights will be mobile but for the time being will be located
   at Secunderabad.

       (i)   No.4355 A.A. FLIGHT R.A.F.R. (now No.4405 A.A.
            FLIGHT R.A.F.R.
       (ii)   No.4356 A.A. FLIGHT R.A.F.R. (now No.4406 A.A.
            FLIGHT R.A.F.R.
       (iii)   No.4357 A.A. FLIGHT R.A.F.R. (now No.4407 A.A.
            FLIGHT R.A.F.R.
       (iv)   No.4358 A.A. FLIGHT R.A.F.R. (now No.4408 A.A.
            FLIGHT R.A.F.R.

EXECUTION.

Establishment.
2. The Flights will work to Establishment India/664.

Function.

3. To provide for ground defence (primary role ground to air;
   secondary role, ground to ground), at airfields or establishments
   of the Air Forces in India.

Control.

4. The Flights will be located in accordance with directions issued
   by Air Headquarters, India (C.D.O), from time to time, and will
   come under the operational control of the A.O.C. responsible for
   the area in which they are located.

<u>ADMINISTRATIVE ARRANGEMENTS.</u>

<u>Personnel.</u>

5. Air Headquarters, India (P. Staff) and B.P.O. will post personnel to implement the establishments in conjunction with arrangements to be made with C.D.O., Air Headquarters, India.

<u>Administration.</u>

6. The Flights will be allocated a Group by Air Headquarters, India in accordance with instructions to be issued. The Group will assume administrative control of the Flight which will be exercised thro' a unit, to be nominated by Administering Group in respect of:-

> Accommodation,
>
> Rations,
>
> Accounting,
>
> Discipline,
>
> Medical arrangements,
>
> Welfare,
>
> Security and Works.

<u>Equipment.</u>

7. Initial equipment will be drawn through S.H.Q., Secunderbad. Subsequent issues will be drawn under arrangements to be made by the Administering Group, who will also be responsible for nominating the Unit to carry out the equipment Accounting for the Flights.

<u>General Instructions.</u>

8. Detailed instructions on the following subjects will be issued by sections of Air Headquarters, India, as shown:-

> Returns,   )
>
> Stationery,   )   G.R.& P.
>
> Sanction for Office equipment)
>
> Office allowances   )
>
>
> Initial issue of Forms & Pubs.   (Equip. staff.
>
> Issue of pack-up of Stationery)
>
> Intercommunications   -   C.S.O.

Medical arrangements   -   P.M.O.

Pay issue and Accounting   -   Command accounts.

Correspondence.

9. Correspondence will be addressed, whilst the Flight ate at Secunderabad:- Royal Air Force, Secunderabad.

Air Vice Marshall
Air Officer i/c Administration

Formation Order No.430

3218/44/Org.   SECRET   Air Headquarters, India.

Dated 7th July,1943.

FORMATION ORDER NO.430.

FORMATION OF ANTI-AIRCRAFT FLIGHTS, R.A.F. REGT.

INTENTION.

1. To form the following Anti-Aircraft Flights of the R.A.F. Regt., at the R.A.F. Regt., Depot (India), Secunderabad, w.e.f. 12th July, 1943.

   The Flights will be mobile and in the first instance located at Secunderabad.

(1)	No. 4417 A.A. Flights, R.A.F. Regt.
(2)	No. 4418 A.A. Flights, R.A.F. Regt.
(3)	No. 4419 A.A. Flights, R.A.F. Regt.
(4)	No. 4420 A.A. Flights, R.A.F. Regt.

EXECUTION.

Establishment.

2. The Flights will work to Establishment India/664(E.C.).

Control.

3. The Flights will be located in accordance with instructions issued by A.H.Q., India (C.D.O), from time to time, and will come under the operational control of the A.O.C. responsible for the area in which they are located.

Function.

4. To provide for ground defence (primary role ground to air; secondary role, ground to ground), at airfields or establishments of the Air Forces in India.

ADMINISTRATIVE ARRANGEMENTS.

Personnel.

5. A.H.Q., "P" Staff and B.P.O. will post personnel, in accordance with Establishment requirements, and in conjunction with A.H.Q.(I) (C.D.O.).

Priority.

6. The Flights are allocated priority "C".

Administration.

7. R.A.F. Regt. Depot (India), Secunderabad, will be responsible for the issue of instructions relating to the under-mentioned headings, in respect of Flights whilst located at Secunderabad, but on proceeding to new Stations this responsibility will be assumed by the administering Group:-

> Accommodation,
>
> Rations,
>
> Pay issue and Accounting,
>
> Medical,
>
> Welfare,
>
> Security and Works Services.

Equipment.

8. Initial equipment will be drawn through S.H.Q., Secunderbad. Subsequent issues will be drawn under arrangements to be made by the Administering Group, who will also be responsible for nominating the Unit to carry out the equipment Accounting for the Flights.

General Instructions.

9. Detailed instructions on the following subjects will be issued by sections of Air Headquarters, India, as shown:-

> Returns,   )
>
> Stationery,   )   G.R.& P.
>
> Sanction for Office equipment   )
>
> Office allowances   )
>
>
> Intercommunications   )   C.S.O.

Correspondence.

10.   Correspondence will be addressed: R.A.F., Secunderabad.

Signed

Air Vice Marshall,
Air Officer i/c. Administration,
Air Headquarters, India.

Distribution.

As per Formation Orders.   7/7/43.

Formation Order No.493

3218/44/Org.   SECRET   Air Headquarters, India.

Dated 7th September,1943.

FORMATION ORDER NO.493.

FORMATIONS OF NOS.4439-4450 A.A. FLIGHTS, R.A.F. REGT.

INTENTION.

1. To form the following Anti Aircraft Flights of the R.A.F.
   Regiment, at the R.A.F. Regiment, Depot (India), Secunderabad,
   w.e.f. 31st May, 1943. The Flights will be mobile and in the first
   instance located at Secunderabad.

                No. 4439 A.A. Flight - R.A.F. Regiment.
                    4440   "   "   "   "
                    4441   "   "   "   "
                    4442   "   "   "   "
                    4443   "   "   "   "
                    4444   "   "   "   "
                    4445   "   "   "   "
                    4446   "   "   "   "
                    4447   "   "   "   "
                    4448   "   "   "   "
                    4449   "   "   "   "
                    4450   "   "   "   "

EXECUTION.

Establishment.

2. The Flights will work to Establishment India No./664(E.C.).

Control.

3. The Flights will be located in accordance with instructions
   issued by A.H.Q., India (C.D.O), from time to time, and will come
   under the operational control of the A.O.C. responsible for the
   area in which they are located.

Function.

4. To provide for ground defence (primary role ground to air;
   secondary role, ground to ground), at airfields or establishments
   of the Air Forces in India.

ADMINISTRATIVE ARRANGEMENTS.

Personnel.

5. A.H.ir Headquarters, "P" Staff and B.P.O. will post personnel, in accordance with Establishment requirements, and in conjunction with A.H.Q.(I) (C.D.O.).

Administration.

6. R.A.F. Regiment Depot (India), Secunderabad, will be responsible for the issue of instructions relating to the under-mentioned headings, in respect of Flights whilst located at Secunderabad, but on proceeding to new Stations this responsibility will be assumed by the administering Group:-

       Accommodation & Rations,

       Discipline,

       Pay issue and Accounting,

       Medical,

       Security,

       Defence,

       Welfare,

       Works Services.

Equipment.

7. Initial equipment will be drawn through S.H.Q., Secunderbad. Subsequent issues will be drawn under arrangements to be made by the Administering Group, who will also be responsible for nominating the Unit to carry out the equipment Accounting for the Flights.

Priority.

8. The Flights are allocated priority "C".

General Instructions.

1. Detailed instructions on the following subjects will be issued by sections of Air Headquarters, India, as shown:-

       Returns,   )

       Stationery,   )   G.R.& P.

       Sanction for Office equipment)

       Office allowances   )

      Intercommunications   )   C.S.O.

Correspondence.

2. Correspondence will be addressed:-

      R.A.F. Station, Secunderabad.

Signed

Air Vice Marshall,
Air Officer i/c. Administration,
Air Headquarters, India.

Distribution.

As per Formation Orders.

Formation Order No.2943 and 2944 Squadron (R)

COPY

218/44/ORD.   SECRET   AIR HEADQUARTERS, INDIA.

Dated 18thMay, 1943.

FORMATION ORDER No. 394

FORMATION OF NO.2903 & 2904 SQUADRONS, R.A.F. REGIMENT.

FORMATION

It has been decided to form No.2903 and 2904 Sqdns. R.A.F. Regiment with effect from 10th May, 1943. The Squadrons will be Mobile and in the first instance located at R.A.F. Regiment Depot, SECUNDERABAD.

EXECUTION

Establishment.

The Squadrons will work to establishment India/663, copies of which have already been issued to all concerned.

Control.

The Squadrons will be located in accordance with directions issued by Air Headquarters, India for time to time, and will come under the operational and administrative control of the A.O.C. responsible for the area in which they are located.

Function.

To provide ground defence (Primary role ground to ground, - secondary role ground to air) at aerodromes or establishments of the Air Forces in India.

ADMINISTRATIVE ARRANGEMENTS

Personnel

Air Headquarters, India (P. Staff) and B.P.O. are to post personnel to implement the establishments in conjunction with Air Headquarters, India (C.D.O.).

Accommodation

Accommodation is available at Secunderabad to implement the Establishment in full.

Equipment and Equipment Accounting

Initial equipment will be drawn through S.H.Q. Secunderabad. Subsequent issues will be made under arrangements with Controlling Group, who will be responsible for nominating a Unit to carry out the Equipment Accounting for the Squadrons.

H.Q. R.A.F. Regiment Depot, will be responsible for the issue of instructions relating to the undermentioned headings, in respect of the Squadrons whilst located at Secunderabad but on proceeding to new locations the responsibility will be assumed by the Controlling Group.

Pay issue and allowances.

Medical.

Welfare.

Security

Works Services.

General Instructions.

Detailed instructions regarding the following will be issued Sections of Air Headquarters, India as shown:-

Returns	)
Stationery.	)
Sanction for Office equipment	) G.P-& P.
Office Allowances	)
Initial issue of Forms & Pubs	) Equipment
Issue of Pack up of Stationery	) Staff.
Inter communications	- C.S.O.
Medical	- D.M.O.
Pay issue & Accounting	- Command Accounts.

Correspondence

Correspondence will be addressed, whilst the Squadrons are located at Secunderabad.

Royal Air Force,

SECUNDERABAD.   Xxxxxx

Distribution

As per Formation Orders.

Air Vice Marshall,

Air Officer i/c Administration

Amendment to Formation Orders

EXTRACT FROM

218/43/Org.   S E C R E T   Air Headquarters, India.

                                                              Dated 5th June 1943.

Amendments to Formation Orders

Nos.   85 - 96

No. 96.5/6. Formation Order No. 394. No. 2903, 2904 RAF Reg.Sqdns.

Delete Nos. 2903 and 2904 and substitute Nos. 2943 & 2944.

                                        Signed   xxxxxx

                                        Air Vice Marshall,

                                Air Officer i/c Administration,

                                    Air Headquarters, India.

No.221 Group - Supporting British Army IV Corps

Overview

The Regiment units protecting the flying squadrons of No.221 Group and the A.M.E.S. (radar) sites spent the first part of 1943 in transit, following training at Secunderabad. Many forward landing strips weren't ready for the units coming to protect them and co-protecting aerodromes with detachments awaiting their call to the Depot, sometimes brought additional administration burdens.

The A.A. flights immediate task was to ensure that the defence plan and the sighting of the Gun Pits were optimised, in contrast the field squadrons spent most of the year training, developing the skills that Field Marshall Slim, recognised the allies lacked, readying themselves for the post Monsoon campaign.

No.221 Groups' main role was to support the British Army IV Corps and on average had around seven operational flying squadrons, including for example, No. 42 Squadron, with Mk V Bristol Blenheim's, No.110 Squadron, with Vultee Vengeance, Dive Bombers and Hawker Hurricanes.

During May, No.4408 A.A. Flight was in transit to the advanced landing ground at Imphal. With only a slight shunt of one its rail carriages at a siding near Calcutta, it wasn't long until the flight took control of the Gun Posts at the A.L.G. By the end of June, the resident gunners of No.76 R&R Party were instructed to move to the Depot at Secunderabad, to start their Regiment training. No.2943 Field Squadron, in transit to the aerodrome at Jessore, was able to collect four 15 cwt trucks and some welfare items, including a gramophone, football, books and games and managed to persuade the central store to part with a stationery pack-up, which was proving hard to get from normal sources.

The next three months saw No.4408 A.A. Flight settling in at Imphal, even building the Gun Posts themselves, as no labour was available, mainly out of bamboo, as that was the only material at hand. No.4418 A.A. Flight arrived at Imphal in August and the three sections were deployed to nearby A.M.E.S. sites. In September, with No.4418 A.A. Flight settled into their routine, there was still no sign of their four allocated 15 cwt trucks and motorcycle, although they were able to loan vehicles from a Wing H.Q. for the short-term, petrol rationing was also causing a bit of a headache. The Defence scheme for the aerodrome was approved and No.4408 A.A. Flight had completed the construction of ten Gun Posts, of which they could only man 5.

No.4416 A.A. Flight arrived at the aerodrome at Kumbhirgram, after quickly settling in, gained early agreement with the Garrison Engineer to construct additional cookhouse, latrine and ablution accommodation. The aerodromes' Gun Posts were jointly manned with the gunners from No.42

Squadron defence detachment, who were soon despatched to the Depot at Secunderabad. Some of the Gun posts had to be closed down as a result, however No.4417 A.A. Flight arrived to fill in the resource gap. Although both flights were working well together, a significant number of men where either on courses, detailed for other duties or sick, making manning all Gun Posts difficult. On the 8th September L.A.C. Scrase (No.4417 Flight) passed away in hospital, having suffered from Weil's Disease. O.C. No.4416 conducted the burial service at Silchar Cemetery, as there was no padre or minister available.

Operational at the Jessore aerodrome, No.2943 Field Squadron had now completed and taken over the Guard Room, Equipment Store and Armoury buildings and the sergeants moved into their new mess and quarters. Away from the squadron, a number of N.C.O.'s and men were now attending a range of courses, including Drill & Weapons training, Camouflage, Signals and Weapons Armourer. A Battle of Britain address was conducted by the unit O.C. on the squadrons parade ground.

The last three months of the year saw the units continue with their settling in, awaiting and sustaining their vehicles, the occasional pass over of Japanese bombers and reconnaissance planes, some key inspections and the continuation of routine training.

In October the Lewis Guns of No.4408 A.A. Flights were replaced with Twin Brownings, and during the full moon periods all Gun Posts were manned, 24 hours a day. The defence of the A.L.G. was assessed by S/Ldr. Last and was not only satisfied with the measures taken, but stated that the Gun Posts were the best camouflaged in the whole of Bengal. November saw several Air Raid Red warnings, one formation of 16 Army 99 bombers, escorted by 6 "OI" fighters, bombed the landing ground from 18,000ft, with no damage to or casualties suffered by the unit. A football league had been set up, in December, between all Regiment units within the Imphal area, with team strips being supplied by Welfare and boots being bought by the men. All the flight was able to have Xmas Dinner over Christmas and Boxing Day, thanks to No.155 Squadron, who also gave a concert, which the flight attended.

The newly completed assault course at Jessore Aerodrome was tested by No.2943 Squadron Demonstration Squad and soon became an integral part of the 'Backers-Up' training package. The Squadron paraded for Lord Louis Mountbatten, Supreme Commander, S.E.A.C. who inspected and spoke to all of the paraded men. In early November the squadron was instructed to move to the aerodrome at Palel. Being responsible for all the station patrols, the squadron soon took over the complete ground at Palel, with one flight in tented accommodated close to the landing strip.

Instructions arrived late in December for the squadron to collect seven armoured observation vehicles from Calcutta and to send one flight on detachment to Tamu.

Routine operations at the aerodrome at Kumbhirgram, for both No.4416 & 4417 A.A. Flights, were becoming frustrating, as the Gun Posts, even after several verbal confirmations that work would be started and materials obtained, were still in an unsatisfactory state. The domestic site was also criticised for its standard of cleanliness following an inspection, but actions were confirmed and both flights also agreed to set up a joint canteen and committee. The first Vultee Vengeance (dive bombers) aircraft of No.45 Squadron arrived and soon became operational, following the arrival of No.110 Squadron to the aerodrome. The flight's vehicles were withdrawn to be used by the flying squadrons, which immediately reduced the mobility of the A.A. flights, this coupled with over half the flights men away on courses, other duties or sick, put the efficiency and effectiveness of the units at risk. November saw the first air raid, with 18 bombers in two equal formations, with a small fighter escort bombing the aerodrome. The Gun crews re-acted quite well, but the attack height of 18,500ft, was disappointing, as they were too high for the crews to engage. Although most of the bombs dropped short, one bomb dropped just 4 yards from a Gun Post, not quite finished luckily only damaged the camouflage. By the end of November all but one of the Gun Posts were complete and the aerodrome split between No.4416 A.A. Flight, taking the northern and No.4417 A.A. Flight, taking the southern sectors. With unit vehicles now at the allotted numbers, the mobility of the units was tested and recorded that H.Q. was cleared within 48 seconds of the alert and all Gun Posts manned within 4 ½ minutes. Xmas dinner was well received and highly successful and by the end of the year work was to commence on a new domestic site.

In November, No.4418 A.A. Flight moved from the A.L.G. at Imphal, to the aerodrome at Ukhrul Road, where it spent the rest of the year settling in. Training consisted mainly of rifle range activities, which paid off, as the unit beat the local R.A. unit, winning two bottles of rum. The flight also built their own Canteen, celebrating its opening with a New Year's party.

Following the release of No.4448 A.A. Flight from the Depot at Secunderabad, the unit entrained to the airfield at Dum-Dum, where it quickly got into the routine of a training programme, taking advantage of the jungle environment and river crossing opportunities, for all those not on Gun Post duties. The flight was instructed to move to the aerodrome at Manipur Road and entrained with several other units, including a contingent of 130 American officers and men enroute to China. The conditions throughout the journey were very poor and only made slightly bearable by some of the units pooling its food allocation. The state of the domestic site at the aerodrome was poor and with no water and condition of the latrines, dysentery was inevitable. A new site was found and the rest of the month was spent building a new domestic site and starting the work on the Gun Posts.

The table and map below show the units protecting No.221 Group as at the end of 1943, with 16 Officers and 510 Airmen distributed between 8 key locations.

R.A.F. Regiment Units in 221 Group R.A.F. – December 1943

Area	A.A. Flight	Field Squadron
Imphal	**4408**	
Ukhrul Road	**4418**	
Sapam	4440	
Palel	4430, 4444	**2943**
Dimapur	**4448**	
Silchar	4445	
Kumbhirgram	**4416, 4417**	
Rayjeswapur	4434	
Establishment Numbers	10 A.A. Flights = 10 Officers and 360 Airmen	1 Field Squadron = 6 Officers and 150 Airmen

(Note units in bold included in this book)

Map showing the location of R.A.F.R. Units as at 31st December 1943

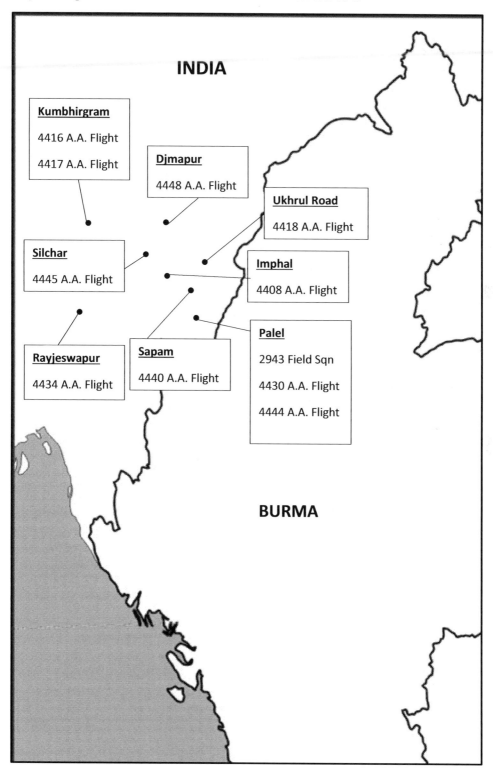

INDIA

Kumbhirgram

4416 A.A. Flight

4417 A.A. Flight

Djmapur

4448 A.A. Flight

Ukhrul Road

4418 A.A. Flight

Silchar

4445 A.A. Flight

Imphal

4408 A.A. Flight

Rayjeswapur

4434 A.A. Flight

Sapam

4440 A.A. Flight

Palel

2943 Field Sqn

4430 A.A. Flight

4444 A.A. Flight

BURMA

(Author adapted - http://d-maps.com/carte.php?num_car=126&lang=en)

Operational Diaries

May
4408 A.A. Flight – In transit via Calcutta to Imphal

Flight arrived Calcutta, F/LT GRIERSON reported to S/L LAST at H.Q. 221 Group R.A.F. and received instructions to proceed with 8 airmen to 170 WING SILCHAR to collect M.T. vehicles allotted to Flight. Coach shunted into siding at Howsah Station on instructions of Movement Control to wait further orders.
F/LT. GRIERSON reported to Movement Control, Lower Circular Road, Calcutta the following day.
S/L LAST Group Defence Officer H.Q. 221 Group R.A.F. visited Flight at Howsah Station and took over 9 Motley Stock A.A. Mountings as they were incomplete. Move to Transit Camp carried out.
F/LT. GRIERSON and 8 airmen left Calcutta for SILCHAR.
Remainder of Flight under SGT. LEASTER left Calcutta for Imphal.
F/LT. GRIERSON and party arrived at 170 Wing H.Q. SILCHAR. Informed that two 15 cwt Chevrolet trucks Nos. 136294 and 135148 were being held by No.42 Squadron at Kumbagham.
F/LT. GRIERSON admitted to 23 C.C.S. SILCHAR with acute appendicitis.
Main Party with Sgt. LESTER arrived MANIPUR ROAD

June
4408 A.A. Flight – Arrived at the Advanced Landing Ground at Imphal

Main Party left for Imphal A.L.G.
Main Party arrived Imphal A.L.G. F/O JENKINS DEFENCE OFFICER to No.76 R&R Party took charge.
Flight No. changed to 4408, Authy. A.H.Q. Signal 024 of 4.6.43.
Gunners of No.76 R&R Party left for R.A.F.R. Depot Secunderabad. 4408 Flight took over the manning of the Gun Posts.

2943 Field Squadron – In transit to Jessore

The first party reached JESSORE at 1730 hours on 12 June '43 and F/O S.J. CLARK immediately went sick.

F/O's H.E.M. LEWSEY and F.N. HALLAM after a busy day getting the camp organised, met the 1730 hours train at JESSORE expecting the arrival of the second party. However, only S/LDR T.F. RYALLS, wearing the appropriate rank as O.C. Squadron, put in an appearance: he explained that owing to faulty arrangements F/O's H.W. FREEMAN and A.E. COLLEDGE together with the remainder of the party would not be arriving until midnight.
The second party arrived
Having received information from A.H.Q. BENGAL regarding availability of Squadron transport F/O's HALLAM and LEWSEY left for M.T.S.U. CALCUTTA with volunteer drivers to pick up same.
Group Captain J.L. WINGATE, O.C. 175 Wing visited the Camp.
F/O's LEWSEY and HALLAM returned from CALCUTTA with four 15 cwt Chevrolets driven by squadron personnel. A few items of welfare were also brought back, including a gramophone, 2 footballs, 50 books and some indoor games.
F/O. S.J. CLARK returned to duty from 47 B.G.H. CALCUTTA.
Wing Commander FOWKE, C.D.O. A.H.Q. visited us.
Six A.C's proceeded Base H.Q. CALCUTTA to attend No.1 Field Cookery Course. Auth: H.Q.B/S/10/5/7/AIR, dated 10/6/43.
F/O's COLLEDGE and HALLA proceeded 313 M.U. to pick up stationery pack-up. 313 M.U. refused to supply the pack-up as A.P.E.S. Delhi had not authorised them to do so. They went on to the Central Stationery Store, Calcutta and persuaded them to part with a parcel of stationery.
The official postings of N.C.O's and airmen arrived from B.P.O., but the posting of officers is still awaited.

July
4408 A.A. Flight – Settling in at Imphal

F/O JENKINS left for R.A.F.R. Depot Secunderabad.
F/O PACKMAN arrived to take over pending section of F/LT GRIERSON.

2943 Field Squadron – Operational at Jessore

S/LDR T.F. RYHLLS proceeded CALCUTTA to visit C.D.O. A.H.Q. BENGAL and G.D.O. 221 Group.
41 men left for No.4 Hill Depot, CHAKRATH on attachment
Wing Commander STEWART, S.M.O. 221 Group paid a visit and inspected the Camp.
S/LDR T.F. RYHLLS returned from CALCUTTA bringing back the much needed stationery pack-up, a typewriter, and a wireless set for the airmen's canteen.
S/LDR F.W.J. LAST, 221 Group Defence Officer & F/LT CAMPBELL 221 Group Camouflage Officer, paid us a visit.
Information received that F/O H.E.M. LEWSEY had been granted the Acting Rank of F/LT & would be second i/c. Squadron and i./c No.4 Flight.
F/LT PRATT (S.M.O. 175 Wing) lectured the Squadron on health and hygiene. Amendment No.1 to Establishment No. India 1663 received. It was decided to mark off a portion of the camp area to be used as a Demonstration Area for Hygiene and Sanitation.
Air Commodore ROWLEY, A.O.C. 221 Group accompanied by Group Captain WINGATE visited the camp.
Work on Demonstration Area for Hygiene & Sanitation commenced.
Guard Room, Equipment Store and Armoury buildings completed and taken over. Sergeants moved into their mess & quarters.
Telephone installed in Guard Room.
Squadron Headquarters Offices completed and occupied.
O.C. Squadron accompanied by Commanding Officer 175 Wing inspected the Station Defences from the air.
E.T. Room opened. S.M.O. 175 Wing lectured Squadron personnel on V.D.
S/LDR LAST, 21 Group Defence Officer paid us a visit.
Five 15 cwt. trucks arrived.
S.M.O. 221 Group visited and inspected the Camp.
3 N.C.O's and 13 A.C's proceeded 221 Group for a Signals Course. Auth: 221G/S/810/4/DEF.

4416 A.A. Flight – In transit arriving at Kumbhirgram Aerodrome

Departure from BEZWADA and arrival at WALTAIR of Flight.
Departure from WALTAIR, arrival at and departure from KHURDA ROAD.
Arrival at HOWRAH (CALCUTTA).
Arrangements being made for departure from HOWRAH.
Departure from HOWRAH.
Arrival at SANTAHAR where transfer to metre gauge took place.
Departure from SANTAHAR and arrival at ferry.
Crossing of ferry and arrival at AKHAURA.
Departure from AKHAURA and arrival at destination KUMBHIRGRAM. Copy of report on the journey is attached herewith (APP "C").
Flight sorting out living quarters and efforts being made to establish co-operation between unit and 42 Squadron who are already located on the aerodrome.

August
4408 A.A. Flight – Constructing Gun Posts at Imphal

F/LT. GRIERSON returned to Unit.
F/LT. GRIERSON reported to Group Captain H.S. BROUGHALL, M.C. D.S.O.O/c 170 WING RAF.
Visited OC 3rd Gwalior Inf. and inspected Guards on Aircraft, Petrol Dumps, Ammo. Dumps, Armoury & M.T. found satisfactory.
Visited 383 A.M.E.S. Wiring of Perimeter not satisfactory.
Inspected Gun Posts at A.L.G. only
Visited 355 W.U.
Contacted 114 C.R.E. Imphal to obtain materials for construction of Gun Posts, informed that no materials were available except bamboo which would be ready in a few days.
Applied to H.Q. 170 WING for labour on Gun Posts, none available.
Lecture on Security given by 170 Wing Security N.C.O.
Visited 857 A.M.E.S.
Quantity of Bamboo attained, work on the Gun Posts commenced by personnel of Flight.
Visited H.Q. 256 SUB. AREA
Visited H.Q. 241 L.A.A. Battery

Visited 383 A.M.E.S. Triple Pannest Fence now erected around perimeter.
Two Gun Posts now completed.

2943 Field Squadron – Operational at Jessore

Inoculation & Vaccination of Squadron Personnel.
Aircraft of 215 Squadron crashed S.W. of runway. Guards supplied.
Fifing party supplied for funeral of victims of aircraft which crashed the previous day.
O.C. Squadron attended Conference with A.A.D. where Squadron's role in Defence Scheme decided upon.
Wing and Squadron M.T. drivers lectured on Map Reading by O.C. Squadron.
1544605, LAC. Stobbs, R. died in 47 B.G.H. CALCUTTA from M.T. malaria.
LAC. STOBBS, R. buried with full military honours at the Military Cemetery, CALCUTTA, Grave No.L.79. Rev (S/LDR.) J.E. MILLER was the officiating chaplain.
Atabrine, Malaria Suppression treatment was instituted for the whole Squadron.
Rev. (S/LDR.) HUTTON conducted C of E services in Squadron Canteen.
Rev. (S/LDR.) CORNER (C of S)paid us a visit.

4416 A.A. Flight – Manning Gun Posts and constructing Domestic site at Kumbhirgram

O.C. Flight attended a board held on the aerodrome to review the finding s of the last board. The result was a recommendation to cancel the previous findings and substitute a much more simple report. This mainly in view of the decrease on the number of garrison troops.
Garrison Engineer agreed to construct additional accommodation including new cookhouse, ablutions and latrines on the RAFR domestic site, and to repair existing buildings. The new buildings were sited.
Obtained loan of motor cycle from 42 Squadron for use of the O.C. Flight.

A detailed inspection of domestic site revealed so much "hidden" dirt, it was decided that there be in future a "Duty Fatigue Squad" for maintaining proper cleanliness in this area. Followers in limited numbers only are available.
Gun Posts now being manned by members of this Flight jointly with members of 42 Squadron R.A.F.R. Detachment.
Work started by Garrison Engineer labourers on domestic site, 62 Squadron RAFR Detachment left for CALCUTTA.
O.C. Flight left for CALCUTTA to clear up points od Organisation and Administration with Group Defence Officer and to collect Stores.
Signs of Malaria becoming prevalent. Strict instructions issued for prevention of this disease.
O.C. Flight had long interview with Group Defence Officer (221 Group) and many points were cleared up. Some stationery forms and equipment was collected.
More forms collected from Govt. India Central Forms Store and taken to RAF Transit Camp ready for journey back to unit base.
O.C. Flight left CALCUTTA for KUNBHIRGRAM. Forms and equipment being brought by two airmen on a later train.
Work started on new cookhouse.
O.C. Flight returned form CALCUTTA.
42 Squadron Detachment RAFR despatched first party to CALCUTTA en route for SECUNDERBAD. This entailed closing down No.6 and 7 gun posts temporarily.
O.C. Flight had interview with O.C. 181 Signals Wing regarding A.A. protection of units of that Wing, with particular references to RAJYESWARPUR. It was found necessary to withdraw the guard from that station pending the arrival of more RAFR and in the meantime H.Q. 221 Group were advised it being suggested also that an A.A. Flight be posted to the SILCHAR area for A.A. protection of these units.
Second party of 42 Squadron RAFR Detachment left for CALCUTTA.
Final party of 42 Squadron RAFR Detachment left for CALUCTTA.
Arrival of 4417 Flight RAFR (o/c F/Lt. H.E. Hardy) to supplement this Flight on the airfield.
No.6 gun post re-opened. Decided not to re-open No.7 owing to new building in course of erection masking field of fire.

4417 A.A. Flight – In transit to Kumbhirgram

Arrived HOWRAN Station. Off-loaded baggage and proceeded to Transit Camp. Guards detailed for baggage.
F/Lt. HARDY reported to 221 Group Defence Officer – S/LDR. LAST.
Departure from CALCUTTA on journey to KUMBRIRGRAM, ASSAM, via GOALUNDO, CHANOPUR and SILCHAR.
Arrived at R.A.F. Station, and contacted Local Defence Officer Commander. F/LT. WILSON, Officer Commanding No.4416 A.A. FLIGHT. Accommodation not quite completed.
Unit personnel detailed for duties in conjunction with No.4416 FLIGHT

4418 A.A. Flight – In transit for Imphal

The Flight left the Depot, Secunderabad on 23rd August 1943, for Imphal, Manipur State. The move was carried out smoothly and without difficulty. On arrival the sections were deployed in accordance the following:- To 583 A.M.E.S. - H.Q. Section   No.1 Section To 857 A.M.E.S. - No.3 Section To 885 A.M.E.S. - No.2 Section and Sgt. Stone. All sections were comfortably settled as above on 1st September, 1943.

September
4408 A.A. Flight – Nearly fully operational at Imphal A.L.G.

First aircraft of 155 Squadron arrived.
Visited by Col. SHIVSHARAN Officer Commanding 3rd GWALIOR INFANTRY.
Visited by Capt. BENSON from 256 SUB. AREA.
Wiring at S.H.Q. completed.
Six gun posts now ready.
Escort returned from 39 E.P no guns or mountings available.
Defence scheme for airfield finished and approved by Capt. BENSON of 256 SUB. AREA.

Necessary fitting for Browning Guns ex. 155 Squadron obtained from 170 WING and work commenced on assembling.
Ten gun posts completed, five being manned.
One Cpl. And six airmen ceased attachment to 383 A.M.E.S. and 355 W.U. and returned to Unit.

2943 Field Squadron – Operational at Jessore Aerdrome

Sgt. Lewesdaw, A.S. and Cpl. Flemming, S.G. proceeded to RANCHI to attend Drill & Weapon Training Course. A.H.Q. Bengal letter HQB/S/151/13/AIR dated 11.8.43. Officers' and Sergeants' mess grants received.
"Action Stations" practice alarm carried out. Personnel at Action Stations in 3 minutes.
Service at Wing Headquarters on anniversary of the fourth year of the war.
Routine Orders No.85 showed F/O H.W. Freeman as posted to No.4406 A.A. Flight and F/O G.B. Chambers as posted from No.4406 A.A. Flight to this Squadron w.e.f. 6.8.43. No posting notes yet received.
Air H.Q. Signal A.209 6/9 received stating F/O A.E. Colledge to proceed to BAIGACHI on attachment to 136 Squadron w.e.f. 8.9.43.
A.H.Q. India posting note received stating F/O G.W. SPURR posted to this unit ex. R.A.F.R. Depot, SECUNDERABAD as replacement to F/O S.J. CLARK w.e.f. 21.8.43. Auth: 1015/19/137/P.2. 30.8.43. Signal received ex R.A.F.R. Depot, SECUNDERABAD to the effect that F/O SPURR was sick and would be proceeding to this unit when fit.
Practice Alarm with collection of arms carried out. All personnel at their posts with rifle and Sten Gun in 6 minutes.
F/Lt. Lewsey lectured Wing and Squadron M.T personnel on Map Reading.
Backers Up Training commenced.
Battle of Britain Ceremony O.C. unit gave suitable address to Squadron on the parade ground.
Posting authority received from A.H.Q. India advising the posting of F/O H.W. FREEMAN to 4406 A.A. Flight, F/Lt. vacancy due to F/O G.B. CHAMBERS from 4406 A.A. Flight to this unit Posting note marked "Delayed in Transit".

Rev S/Ldr. Hutton held open air C of E Service.
F/O F.N. HALLAM gave Security lecture. Subject "Security of Information" One sergeant and two corporals proceeded to B.H.Q Calcutta on No.4 Short Camouflage Course. Auth: HQ.B/1705/8/P.3 18.9.43..
Four LAC's proceeded School of Technical Training, AMBALA on Armourers Course. Auth: HQ. Bengal signal M.854 23/9.
F/O G.B. CHAMBERS arrived on posting ex 4406 A.A. Flight.
F/O G.B. CHAMBERS proceeded A.H.Q. Bengal for interview with A.O.C., Bengal Command.

4416 A.A. Flight – Operational at Kumbhirgram

In company with 4417 Flight, 9 fresh gun posts were sited – in 3 blocks of 3 gun posts in each block.
A fourth block of 3 gun posts was sited. This completes the siting of new posts. Alternative positions will be constructed in suitable places.
Garrison Engineer approached regarding labour and material for construction of new posts; this promised in near future.
Saw Heavy A.A. regarding warning system, also the possibility of ground to ground fire by these guns was discussed.
The new cookhouse started working also the billet in use as a temporary dining room was opened.
A short simplified "Backers Up" training programme was started for the Squadron covering Rifle, Bayonet, Sten & Grenade.
The Superintendent of Police, Silchar, visited the unit to discuss the employment of specially trained police on the airfield for security work.
O/C 4417 Flight left for CALCUTTA, and O/C this unit had to conduct the burial service of an airman of 4417 Flight who died in hospital, this was due to the fact that no padre or minister was available.
Reminded Garrison Engineer about labour for construction of new gun posts - promised for two days time.
Defence Officer 221 Group arrived mid - day. Afternoon spent in conference.

Group Defence Officer inspected R.A.F. Regt. quarters and installations in morning. Afternoon Group Defence Officer accompanied by O/C Flight visited H.Q. 181 Wing where it was arranged that the O/C Flight should site 3 gun posts in the near future. 94 E.P. was then visited where it was arranged that O/C 4416 Flight should act as Liaison Officer between the E.P. and any fresh R.A.F.R. Units entering the district until such units should have had time to settle down.

Group Defence Officer left for CALCUTTA by air.

Construction of new gun posts started.

Personnel question getting serious - too many men being told off for courses at a time. There are now 4 men from this Flight away on courses, another two detailed as escorts for M.T. and other equipment and two on sick leave.

Visit of Camp by S.M.O. 221 Group. Camp untidy and sanitary arrangements not up to required standard; Garrison Engineer to be consulted. F/Lt. Hardy (4417 Flight) returned from CALCUTTA.

Arrival of 4430 and 4434 A.A. Flight at BADARPUR where O/C 4416 Flight met them to hand over some equipment.

O/C 4416 Flight organised transport to convey 4434 Flight to RAJYESWARPUR, and took O/C that Flight to H.Q. 181 Wing before going on to RAJYESWARPUR.

4417 A.A. Flight – Operational at Kumbhirgram

No.42 Squadron, having provided facilities and links for belting the Browning ammunition, all available men are now employed on this work. Lecture of "R.A.F. Regiment" given by F/LT. HARDY to aircrews of N.42 Squadron, at S/LDR. GEE's request.

F/LT. HARDY toured the Station area, in company with the Local Defence Commander - purpose, siting permanent gun emplacements.

Conference with local Defence Commander concerning Defence Plan. F/LT. HARDY officially reported arrival of Unit to W/CDR. WEBSETR, O.C. No.42 SQUADRON, who had returned from leave.

F/LT. HARDY assisted local Defence Commander to complete Defence layout.

A man was attached to Station Sick Quarters for a "refresher" course in First Aid, Treatment of Drinking Water and treatment of Bacterial Cases, etc. in case the Unit is posted at any time to a location remote from a C.C.S. or Sick Quarters.

1446658 L.A.C. SCRASE, who was admitted to 25 C.C.S. on 8th Sept. 1943 and transferred to 23 C.C.s. on 13th Sept. 1943, died from WEIL'S DISEASE and was buried in SILCHAR Cemetery.

F/LT. HARDY proceeded to CALCUTTA on Temporary Duty to arrange for early shipment of Unit M.T. which was urgently needed, together with various Stores items.

Arrival of Group Defence Officer - S/LDR. LAST, on inspection tour.

Departure of Group Defence Officer.

Two men detached from Unit for 3 weeks Course at No.1 S.T.T. AMNBALA, on instruction from A.H.Q BENGAL - signal (M854 dated 23.9.43.).

1546784 L.A.C. ASHWORTH arrived from the Depot as a replacement for L.A.C. SCRASE (Deceased).

F/LT. HARDY returned from CALCUTTA.

Generally speaking, the Unit health for September was poor. There were 16 admissions to hospital, due mainly to recurrent malaria.

4418 A.A. Flight – Nearly fully operational at Imphal

GUN POSTS:

No.1 Section completed during September 3 Gun Posts and have since 21st September manned one.

No.3 Section have completed 3 Gun Posts and manned one since 20th September.

No.2 Section have manned one post with twin Lewis guns since 1st September. No new posts have been constructed by this section owing to the pending move of the A.M.E.S. to a new site.

In the matter of materials for gun posts, furniture for headquarters etc., the Army units in Imphal under 4 Corps have been most helpful and given the Flight their full co-operations.

TRANSPORT:

On 9th September, two Chevrolet 3 tonners and one Norton M/c were procured from 181 Wing Advanced Headquarters at Imphal on loan. Four Chevrolet 15 cwt and one Indian M/c were allotted by 329 M.U. on 9th

September but have not yet arrived. Petrol rationing in the area is proving to be a great handicap but the work is proceeding favourably in spite of it. Ration for October is 50 gallons.

COURSES:

Two airmen left the Unit to attend am M.T.M. course at Calcutta commencing 4th October 1943. Two airmen left to attend an armament course Ambala commencing 1st October 1943.

ENEMY ACTIVITY:

During the month four 'alerts' were sounded on but no enemy aircraft approached nearer than at approx. 30,000 feet. All 'alerts' were in daylight round about midday.

VISITORS:

The Flight has not been visited by anyone during the month.

October

4408 A.A. Flight – Operational at Imphal Aerodrome

Three pairs of Browning Guns assembled & harmonised.
Guns taken on the range for firing tests, F/Lt., GRIERSON & fifteen men fired, guns found to be very accurate.
Three pairs of Browning Guns assembled and harmonised, F/Lt., GRIERSON & sixteen men fired, guns again found to be accurate.
Browning Guns fitted on gun posts, Lewis guns taken down.
Gun Posts manned full 24 hrs for Full Moon Period.
Read Warning, Army 97 passed over 25,000ft. (Reconnaissance).
End of Full Moon Period, Crews stand down.
F/Lt., GRIERSON visited Captain BENSON at 256 SUB. AREA.
Squadron Leader LAST, 221 Group Defence Officer, arrived A.L.G. on tour of inspection.
Sqdn. L/dr. LAST, inspected gun posts on A.L.G.
Sqdn. L/dr. LAST left for inspection of Palel, with F/LT. GRIERSON
Sqdn. L/dr. LAST left for inspection of 383 A.M.E.S. & 857 A.M.E.S. with F/LT. GRIERSON.
Lord LOUIS MOUNTBATTEN arrived.
Lord LOUIS MOUNTBATTEN left.
Sqdn. L/dr. LAST left.

General AUCHINLECK arrived.
General AUCHINLECK left.
Visited by Captain BENSON of 256 Sub Area, sighted new defensive positions for the Garrison Troops.
Squadron Leader LAST expressed himself as being satisfied with the measures taken for the defence of the Air Field and stated that the Gun Posts were the best camouflaged he had seen in the whole of Bengal.

2943 Field Squadron – Operational at Jessore Aerdrome

S/Ldr. F.W.J. LAST, 221 G.D.O. & F/LT. CAMPBELL visited the unit.
Assault Course completed. 2943 Squadron Demonstration Squad went over the course followed by Backers-Up.
Rev. (S/Ldr.) Carver held open air undenominational service.
Wellington aircraft of No.99 Squadron crashed and exploded west of runway. All night guard supplied,
F/LT. A.E.M. LEWSEY injured in an explosion at Wing Armoury. Firing Party supplied for funeral of the victims of the crash which occurred the previous day.
Nine men from the newly arrived L.A.A. Battery commenced to receive instruction with this Unit in Infantry and Weapon training.
F/O G.W. SPURR Arrived.
Backers-Up taken over Assault Course.
A.H.Q. Bengal signal A.9 16/10/43 received stating F/O COLLEDGE to cease detachment with 136 Squadron and return to this Unit forthwith. Two 15 cwt. trucks returned to 329 M.U. & 1-3ton lorry (4 wheel drive) collected as per amendment No.3 to Establishment No.663 (H.Q. 221 Group letter 221G/4605/1/ORG. dated 9/9/43 refers).
Squadron personnel paraded at 175 Wing H.Q. when LORD LOUIS MOUNTBATTEN, Supreme Commander, S.E. ASIA COMMAND inspected and spoke to all personnel.
Tentage arrived from 313 M.U. Authority for collection HQB/S/2320/E.6 dated 8/10/43.
No.4439 A.A. Flight arrived Jessop and settled into this Unit's Camp by 0500 hours.

A.H.Q. Bengal's letter to 329 M.U. reference HQB/S/2450/9/E.1 dated 25/10/43(copy to this Unit) authorised collection of 1 Jeep and 2 Motor Cycles.

4416 A.A. Flight – Operational at Kumbhirgram

Special inspection of domestic site showed insufficient care being taken regarding general cleanliness; measures taken to enable much higher standard of hygiene to be attained. Gun-Posts under construction in unsatisfactory sate owing to lack of suitable material, and also to lack of labour. The Garrison Engineer explained that the latter was due to a/ the periodical change of labour force and b/ the Peya keeping the Coolies away.

Drivers from 4430 and 4434 A.A. Flight tested, passed, and sent to CALCUTTA to collect vehicles for their Flights.

F/Lt. Kerswill (4434 Flight) left for CALCUTTA, O/C this Flight holding watching brief in his absence on RAJYESWARPUR.

Meeting of all available men from this and 4417 Flight, and decided to start our own Canteen, Committee elected.

O/C this unit visited RAJYESWARPUR, everything as satisfactory as could be expected.

Saw Garrison Engineer regarding Gun-Post construction, he is going to make special effort to obtain speedy completion of these posts. First aircraft of 45 Squadron arrived.

In company with F/LT. Hardy, O/C this unit went to SILCHAR to purchase canteen goods. Canteen opened same night, and all personnel highly appreciative.

All transport withdrawn for use of 45 Squadron. This leaves both Flights with one 15 cwt truck which is actually an Army issue to the local Defence Commander (O/C 4416 Flight).

In view of the continued unsatisfactory progress on the construction of gun posts, and the failure of verbal requests to have any effect, wrote to the Garrison Engineer asking for immediate completion of the work.

First Aircraft of 110 Squadron arrived. 45 Squadron commenced operations.

Lack of transport proving very acute. In event of alarm emergency orders are in operation, but 100% efficiency is impossible.

Lecture by M.O. on new Malaria Suppressive Treatment.

All R.A.F. Regiment personnel on this station commenced this Suppressive Treatment - Atabrim - 4 tablets - 1 ½ grams each per week, 2 each day, on two consecutive days. Gun posts at South end of strip almost completed, 42 Squadron moved to their new Headquarters; this is going to make the borrowing of a Typewriter very difficult.

O/C Flight visited H.Q. 181 Wing. Position satisfactory and Defence Training Instructors there are very much appreciated.

Interview with M.T. Officer, 221 Group and our serious difficulties explained. He agreed and is going to make every effort to help us.

Cpl. Lawes, 4417 A.A. Flight returned to the station from CHITTAGONG where, he informs us, two vehicles of each Flight have been for over a fortnight and as no assistance of any kind is coming from either R.T.O or R.A.F. Authorities, it is likely to be at least another fortnight before these vehicles can be put on rail. Cpl. Drummond of 4416 A.A. Flight was left in charge of the vehicle, while Cpl. have reported to his unit. A combined report will be made by these two N.C.O.'s in due course (will be an appendix).

Inspection of RAF Regiment camp by Medical Officer, produced a satisfactory report, except for certain obvious and avoidable points in connection with the cookhouse and latrines.

Enquiries having showed that it is possible to get 15 cwt trucks from CHITTAGONG to this station by road, Sgt. Horton and a reserve driver are today going to CHITTAGONG and the vehicle will be brought up by road.

Another airman left the unit today to go on a course -this makes over 22% of the unit away on courses. Another 11% are away on other duties and 13% sick - a total of 47% almost being away. This effectively prevents any possibility of leave or 48 hour passes being granted.

All gun posts at South end of strip finished except for the concrete settings for the mountings.

The first of our vehicles arrived from CHITTAGONG by road 2, 15 cwt trucks and 1 motor cycle, very welcome in view of the difficulties under which we have been working.

4417 A.A. Flight – Operational at Kumbhirgram

Inspected domestic site with F/LT. WILSON. General cleanliness was below standard. Measures taken to improve condition.
Two men sent on M.T.M. Course.

F.LT. HARDY spoke to the L.D.C. about the slowness of gun pit construction and was informed that the Garrison Engineer had been approached on the subject. Main reason appeared to be difficulty in obtaining sufficient labour.

One man sent on a Field Cookery Course.

It was decided to open a R.A.F. Regt. Canteen for the use of personnel from No's 4416 and 4417 A.A. Flights.

The L.D.C. informed F/LT. HARDY that he had seen Garrison Engineer who had promised to make a special effort to hasten the completion of the gun pits.
Aircraft of No.45 Squadron arrived.

R.A.F. Regt. canteen opened.

Both A.A. Flights are now deprived of M.T, which has been withdrawn for use by No.45 Squadron.

The L.D.C. informed F/Lt. HARDY that he had written to the Garrison Engineer stressing the urgency to completion of the gun pits, and that no action had resulted from his previous requests.

Received copy No.5 of Defence plan.
Arrival of No.110 Squadron.
Operations commenced, Gun crews warned to keep an extra sharp look out.

In view of the lack of M.T., F/LT. HARDY discussed with the L.D.C. the impossibility of putting the complete Defence Plan into operation, if required.

All available personnel given lecture by S.M.O. F/LT. GOLD, on Suppressive Treatment of Malaria.

Supply of Atabrine tablets received from S.M.O. Suppressive Treatment commenced to counter high rate of malaria casualties.

No.42 Squadron moved into their new headquarters away from the R.A.F. Regt. site. This make the loan of a typewriter most difficult.

CPL. LOWE rejoined Unit from CHITTAGONG. He informed both Flight Commanders that M.T. vehicles, together with guns and stores had been at CHITTAGONG for two weeks. Apparently the R.A.F. authorities not the R.T.O at CHITAGONG had provided any assistance so far as onward transmission was concerned, and there is no indication as to when these urgently needed vehicles or stores are likely to arrive. A report will be submitted to H.Q. No.221 Group, later. Two men sent in A/C Recognition Course.

The R.A.F.R. domestic site was inspected by the newly arrived Medical officer for No.45 Squadron. Everything was satisfactory, apart from one or two unavoidable points regarding the Cookhouse and Latrines.

Having checked the possibility of the convoy at CHITTAGONG continuing the journey by road, SGT. HORTON and a spare driver from No.4416 Flight are proceeding to CHITTAGONG to bring the convoy trough.

One man sent of Field Cookery Course.

In view of the possible construction of dispersal areas across the R.A.F. Regt. site, F/LT.HARDY had a discussion with the L.D.C. concerning new site, and location of R.A.F. Regt. M.T. bays.

Suggested changes in the disposition of Infantry in the event of an attack on this station, led to a discussion between LT/COL. D.C. BRANFOOT, Officer Commanding Infantry unit, the L.D.C. and F/LT. HARDY.

The Adjutant of No.110 Squadron approached F/LT. HARDY with regards to Defence role of ground personnel of No.110 Squadron. He was referred to the L.D.C. who explained their positions.

F/LT. HARDY agreed to supervise personal instruction in Unarmed Combat, as soon as the Adjutant could arrange for instruction.

All personnel on Unit strength made thoroughly conversant with layout of area, with particular reference to roads, tracks, ferries etc. Lecture by F/LT. HARDY.

Arrival of M.T. vehicles and stores from CHITTAGONG.

November
4408 A.A. Flight – Operational at Imphal A.L.G.

Armoury moved from 155 Squadron Headquarters, to 28 Squadron Headquarters.
Armoury moved from 28 Squadron to 155 M.T. Section.
Visited by Col. Bramfoot, S.S.O. Kumbrigram.
Air Raid Warning, RED?
Formation of 16 Army 99 Bombers escorted by 6 "OI" Fighters, bomber Airfield from 18,000ft. No damage or casualties was suffered by this Unit.
Air Raid Warning, RED. No enemy aircraft sighted. All clear 09.30.
Wing Commander Fowke, Command Defence Officer arrived on tour of airfield.
Wing Commander Fouke, with F/Lt., GRIERSON inspected Gun Posts.
Wing Commander Fouke, with F/Lt., GRIERSON left for 383 A.M.E.S.
Wing Commander Fouke left.
Air Raid Warning, RED. [Reconnaissance].
Major Nicholson, Officer Commanding "C" Company, 27 Mahrattas visited Headquarters.
S/Leader LAST, 221 Group Defence Officer, arrived.
F/Lt., GRIERSON left for CALCUTTA, S/Leader LAST took over Flight.
Flight started on Defence Training Courses, for periods of six & a half days.
Assault Course started and under construction.

2943 Field Squadron – In transit from Jessop to Palel Aerodrome

1 Jeep and 2 motor-cycles arrived ex 329 M.U. Authority A.H.Q. BENGAL's letter reference H.Q.B/S/2450/9/E.1. dated 25/10/43.
Visited by GROUP DEFENCE OFFICER who expressed satisfaction with the efficiency of the Squadron.
Assault Course gone over by personal of Squadron followed by an exercise. Commanding Officer and Squadron Officers took part and Wing photographer, who was present, was able to tale many realistic photos.

A simple church service was held under the shade of a mango tree by Rev (S/LDR) HUTTON.
A.H.Q. BENGAL signal (0/829. 7/11) received informing Squadron of move from JESSORE to PALEL.
Movement Order No.88, dated 11/11/43 received from O.C. R.A.F. Movements, BENGAL.
F/O. G.W. SPURR & 23 B.O.R's left site to catch 1057 train to Calcutta in accordance with Movement Order.
7 B.O.R's (M.T. personnel) with 5 - 15 cwt trucks loaded to capacity and 1 motor cycle as escort, left by road for Barrackfore Race course Sidings in accordance with Movement Order.
S/LDR. T.F. RYALLS admitted 47 B.G.H.
Information received from S.M.O. 175 Wing that F/LT. H.E.M. LEWSEY would be unfit for duty in a forward area and would be posted N/E Sick. Telephonic instructions received from 221 Group Defence Officer that F/OF.N. HALLAM was to assume command of Squadron forthwith.
F/O G.B. CHAMBER and 30 B.O.R's left by 10.57 train for CALCUTTA in accordance with Movement Order.
F/SGT. PEDEN E.D. and 29 B.O.R's left by 10.57 train for CALCUTTA in accordance with Movement Order.
F/O A.E. COLLEDGE and 27 B.O.R's left by 10.57 train for CALCUTTA in accordance with Movement Order.
F/O F.N. HALLAM and 19 B.O.R's left by rail and 10 B.O.R's (M.T. party) left by road in accordance with Movement Order.

4416 A.A. Flight – Operational at Kumbhirgram

Received word that out other two vehicles are en route for CHITTAGONG, so sent an airman to meet them to bring the vehicles by road.
The two vehicles arrived late evening by road after uneventful journey. This completes delivery of our allotment.
Work started on the taxi - track which runs through the R.A.F. Regt. area. More than half our buildings will have to come down.

Raid at Imphal and our warning system revised - should be more satisfactory.

First Air Raid - 18 Bombers - believed Army 97 and 6 Fighter escort - Fighters not identified. Warning 09.01 bombs dropped 09.12 in pattern type. Dispersal apparent target but bombs fell mainly short, only about 100 yards of dispersal area being hit. Height 18,000 feet. No damage to RAFR personnel or property.

Check up showed one bomb dropped 4 yards from one of the new gun posts (not quite completed) doing no damage to the post except destroying some of the camouflage.

Picked out prospective new site for RAFR camp - split domestic area and H.Q. area owing to lack of space. Saw Admin Officer 168 Wing re. this, arrangements to be made with G.E. Satisfactory promises were also made by that officer regarding employment of a follower (cookhouse) by the Wing, to be detailed to the Flight, and about a better supply of water.

An unofficial stand-by warning 1.38 but this did not develop.

o/c Flight visited RAJYESWARPUR taking with him stores and correspondence for the R.A.F.R. units there. Called at SILCHAR strip on return journey but F/LT BATES not there. Got our own men om concreting new gun posts.

First of new gun posts completed and guns mounted - quite satisfactory. Sent LAC MYERS to CALCUTTA for parts for Brownings and mountings.

Two more of new posts opened -appear very satisfactory.

Obtained Pioneer Corps labour to finish heavy construction of the Gun Posts. One more post completed.

No labour available. Five more posts finished off using RAFR labour.

All possible posts finished - making 11 in all. LAC MYERS returned from CALCUTTA with information that Browning spares must be obtained from 170 Wing.

After some trouble got Garrison Engineer to make efforts to arrange for labour to finish off remaining gun posts.

All but one of the new gun posts completed and guns mounted. Airfield divided - North end 4416 Flight, South end 4417 Flight. 9 Posts

fully manned with 3 emergency posts ready for manning at immediate notice.

4417 A.A. Flight – Operational at Kumbhirgram

M.T. vehicles and Motor Cycle sent to Station M.T. section for thorough overhaul.
All stores received from Calcutta examined and deficiencies reported to L.D.C.
Information received concerning movements of enemy a/c into Burma.
Inspection of gun pits, guns, and construction work on new gun positions.
F/LT. HARDY contacted Garrison Engineer about difficulties in mounting twin Brownings on Motley Stork mountings. Latter agreed to have work done immediately.
Air Raid warning received. 18 bombers apparently Army 99's, with small fighter escort approached in two formations of 9 from the N.E.
Attack delivered from height of 18,500ft. Men on gun posts re-acted quite well, but were disappointed in being unable to engage the enemy. F/LT HARDY accompanied the L.D.C. on tour of inspection immediately after raid. No casualties or damages to R.A.F.R. personnel or site. Report and Postagram sent to H.Q. No.221 Group by L.D.C. for both Flights.
Signal received A.H.Q.(B) for F/LT. HARDY to report to the C.V.A.R.I.S. RABCHI for course on Aircraft Recognition Instruction.
Air Raid Warning received. No sign of raider. F/LT HARDY left for RANCHI.
4417 A.A. FLT. R.A.F.R. comes under S.E. Asia Command.
Air Raid Alert. 20 enemy a/c reported 100 miles SOUTH – heading towards Station. No sign of enemy. No warning sounded.

4418 A.A. Flight – Operational at Ukhrul Road A.L.G.

F/Lt JEFERSON SMITH – Denist – visited the Flight and during the ensuing fortnight treated all No.1 Section and H.A. and No.3 Section in a surgery improvised in a bullock shed.

C.O. visited No.3 Section at BURRI BAZAAR on these dates and found the section in order

Sixteen enemy bombers and 4 fighters were seen over the area travelling from NE to SW. Bombs were heard dropping at Aerodrome IMPHAL. AA guns (Army) opened up when a/c were about 15.000ft but results were nil. During the month 6 other warnings were sounded but no activity followed.

TRAINING

Four Firing practices Have been held during the month when twin brownings were fired by all personnel of No.1 Section & H.Q.

COURSES

Four airmen returned to the Unit from COURSES as follows:-
a/c/ recognition LAC Buffet "F" LAC Barham "F"
M.T.M. LAC Parbles Result not notified LAC Brace - Course not taken due to illness.

WELFARE

Comprehensive pack-up together with Radio arrived from 234 Group

Wing Commander J.L. FOWKE visited the Flight and expressed satisfaction with the Flight in general.

LAC SIMMS has formed the nucleus of the Flight First Aid Room which has proved its worth.

No visits to No.2 Section but Sgt STONE visited Flight H.Q. on 23rd Nov.

Night Patrols were started at each V.P.

SPORT

The Flight team drawn from No.1 and 3 sections drew against 857 AMES and beat 383 AMES 3 - 0.

Badmington is being taken up enthusiastically by No.1 Section and a tournament is under consideration.

REPORT BY WING COMMANDER J.L. FOWKE (CDO)

   (a)   Personnel satisfactory

   (b)   Sgt STONE recommended for F/Sgt

   (c)   High malaria rate at Dimapur

   (d)   Arms, Equipment and M.T. satisfactory

   (e)   Training not attempted with section so widely dispersed

   (f)   Gun posts - 3 at each V.P. Design good.

4448 A.A. Flight – In transit at Dum Dum Airfield

At Raipur (11.00 of 4/Nov/43), Jharsuguda (21.00 of 4/Nov/43) and at Kharagpur (14.00 of 5/Nov/43) we were told that had a message been wired ahead a hot meal would have been prepared and served gratis to the men. I suggest that officers be informed of the existence of such facilities.

The main problems here were to equip the Flight to full scale in preparation for a forward move, at the same time keeping up the Depot standard of training. This plan was held to in the main but there were diversionary influences as will be shown.

A routine daily programme was drawn up and carried out which included drill, weapon training revision and patrol and field work, around the airfield. I gave the men two lectures a week, one on map-reading and the other on topical subjects such as "the German Man in the Street". 1931 to 1938 and "The British Empire; What it is and Why". On three occasions (Nov: 12-18-25) I took a party over the Assault Course at Alipore. Squadron Leader Hallet, Intelligence Officer of 224 Group, came to see a demonstration on one occasion when some of us completed the circuit twice. Following these periods, it was my habit to take the men to the lakes, in South Calcutta, for swimming and instruction. This led to our attempting, on Dec: 1st, an exercise in water-crossing in the large tank opposite the Farm on Dum-Dum Airfield. Referring again to my notes:- TRAINING FOR RIVER CROSSINGS.

A section in full battle order, myself and Sgt Jones, crossed a large tank in front of the Farm. First went a pair of scouts covered by two L.M.Gs. A raft then took No.1 L.M.G. and crew ready to fire over the heads of the scouts and covered by No.2 L.M.G. More riflemen and sten-gunners followed and then No.2 L.M.G. with crew. The bridgehead was established and enlarged whilst the was used for loading stores, ammunition and finally my Indian motor-cycle.

Weak swimmers used two petrol cans tied one each end of a bamboo pole. The raft was constructed out of odd pieced of timber and wood gathered in the vicinity and lashed for support to five oil drums. Twine and creepers were used to effect this.

There were no mishaps although 1140754 L.A.C. Bland found swimming in full kit with rifle was too much for him so he turned back and tried again with the petrol-tins-bamboo support. He made a successful and plucky crossing. All ranks agreed that much was learned from this exercise.

L.A.C. Hughes from Photographic Section, A.H.Q.B. attended and took pictures, a set of which accompany this record if they could be made obtainable.

Firing on the range with rifle, Lewis, Browning and Sten-gun was held weekly.

Apart from the more active and advanced forms of training which I have recorded in some detail, the bulk of the routine fell upon corporals, pressure of administrative work causing both myself and Sgt. Jones to devote all too little time to it. The fact that they did not fully live up to their rank is borne out by an order that I issued which is dated 1/Dec/43, a copy of which was handed to each corporal following a lecture I gave to them on "Administration". This unfortunately became the start of a weakness in the Flight which is still apparent as will be shown later when I deal with it more fully.

There were two more factors which did not help us:- "The dual administration of 4448 Flight which No.1 Flight (Sgt. Murdoch) who were waiting to go to Secunderabad and were a representative detachment of gunners, pre-depot vintage. It was obvious that one of the two Flights would influence the other so I warned 4448 that they were to set an example. All not on gunpost duty then started the training programme together. But this did not last long. From the very first, it was obvious that the Commanding officer, Wind Commander Marvin, held different ideas to mine as to the policy and function of the Royal Air Force Regiment:-

1. My appointment as Gas Officer was promulgated in D.R.Os. but cancelled on authority of Squadron-Leader Last of 221 Group.

2. My billet was three miles from the airfield but I moved into another on Nov: 10th and when this was taken over by S.H.Q. I moved into an N.C.Os billet near to my office.

3. On Nov. 10th I was elected Mess Secretary and my protest overruled although I was seldom able to spare the time to take more than one meal a day there. I resigned on Nov. 18th on receipt of "Stand-By Movement Order".

4. Jobs such as erecting perimeter wiring, Station M.T. Compound wiring and providing Fire Picquets and guards for prisoners who were digging slit trenches for civilian use outside the Control Tower, were all allocated to my men. Some I refused and the others were carried out by No:1 Flight whose Snr: N.C.O. Sgt Murdoch did not seem what I would call "R.A.F. REGIMENT MINDED".

4448 Flight continued the training programme above as I refused to let them do more than half a day's wiring a week under the head of Field Engineering.

MISCELLANEOUS EVENTS.
I took the Station Church Parade at which the general bearing and turn-out of the R.A.F. Regiment Detachment was very marked in contrast to that of Station personnel. They put up a really good show which drew comment in the Officers Mess.
I helped to take a Japanese prisoner off an incoming plane and sent Cpl. Stephenson as an R.A.F. representative in the guard which conducted him to the Prisoners of War Camp.

December
4408 A.A. Flight – Operational at Imphal A.L.G.

F/Lt., GRIERSON, arrived took over Flight from S/L., LAST.
Squadron Leader LAST and F/Lt., GRIERSON visited Headquarters, MAHARRATAS for siting board. Two Defence Training Instructors arrived.
Three Bren Guns for Flight, arrived.
Group Captain HARRIS, Air Command, S.E. Asia, and Wing Commander FOWKE C.D.O. Third Tactical Air Force, arrived.
Group Captain HARRIS, Wing Commander FOWKE, Squadron Leader LAST & F/Lt., GRIERSON inspected Gun Posts.
Bren Guns assembled and taken on Range for firing practice.

Two Bren positions constructed on West of A.L.G.
Eight Tents brought from SAPAM for Flight.
Six Tents brought from SAPAM for new Flight.
Ten Tents erected. Strip visited by A.O.C. in Chief, Air Chief Marshal Sir Richard Peirse, K.C.B., D.S.O., A.F.C., on the 14th, of December, 1943.
Maj. General STRATEMEYER arrived in a Liberator.
Maj. General STRATEMEYER left.
The general health of the Flight is good, football matches have been played with, 155 S.H.Q. 221 Group Gunners, (A football league as been arranged between all the Regiment Flights and Squadrons in the Imphal area) and this Flight has high hopes of winning the league. Strips have been received from the Welfare and Football Boots are being bought from S/L., LAST at Rs 9/8/-. Work was so arranged that one half of the flight had a Christmas Day off & the other half Boxing Day. All the flight were able to present at the X'mas Dinner, which was indeed a tribute to 155 Squadron. A good time was had by all. A full gathering of the flight attended a concert given by 155 Sqdn.

2943 Field Squadron – Following move Operational at PALEL, with one Flight detached to TAMU

Took over station patrols. Aircraft dispersal, P.O.L Dumps, Ammunition Dumps and essential installations covered.
GROUP CAPTAIN HARRIS (C.D.O. S.E.A.A.C.) accompanied by WING COMMANDER FOWKE (C.D.O. A.H.Q. BENGAL) and SQUADRON LEADER LAST (G.D.O. 221 GROUP) visited and inspected the Squadron and Camp.
Camp organised into Camp Areas and each Flight made self-supporting.
Final party, which left JESSOP by road on 27/11/43.
Letter received from Advanced H.Q. 221 GROUP, reference 211G/S/801/DEF. dated 9/12/43 to effect that, at a between COL. ELLIOTT - O.C. 256 Sub-Area and Group Defence Officer on 9/12/43, it was agreed that the ground of PALEL was to be taken over by this Squadron completely w.e.f. 20/12/43 on final move of the company of MAHRATTAS to SAPAM.
A.O.C. in C. S.E.A.A.C. visited the station and enquired as to the Squadron's well-being.

S/LDR. T.F. RYALLS returned to duty from 47 B.G.H. CALCUTTA.

F/O G.B. CHAMBERS left for CALCUTTA by air to arrange collection of seven Armoured Observation Vehicles on instructions from H.Q. 221 Group.

One Flight moved to tented accommodation near to landing strip for aerodrome patrols.

Xmas day and a good time had by all in the existing circumstances. S/LDR. LAST (G.D.O. 221 Group) paid a visit and addressed the Squadron personnel regarding movement of one Flight to TAMNU which was to take effect from 27/12/43.

F/O A.E. COLLEDGE and 38 B.O.R's left by road for TAMU in accordance with Movement Order.

S/LDR. T.F. RYALLS (O.C. Squadron) visited the detachment at TAMU, returning the following day.

4416 A.A. Flight – Operational at Kumbhirgram Aerodrome

Two Defence Training Instructors arrived on the Station for use as directed by 168 Wing; o/c this unit asked to arrange programmes.

Sited 3 more gun posts on South side of main dispersal area with intention that these be manned by Squadron personnel in the event of an alarm. Adjutant 45 Squadron consulted and principle agreed upon.

F/Lt. Taylor (S.E.A.A.C.) arrived by mail plane on tour of inspection G/Capt Harris and W/Com Fawke also called for a shirt while on their way further forward.

o/c/ Flight took F/Lt. Taylor to RAJYESWARPUR and SILCHAR to visit RAF Regt units in these stations.

Emergency test of emergency gun crews - all crews clear of HQ in 48 seconds and all guns manned for firing in 4 ½ minutes. F/Lt Taylor left of conclusion of inspection.

Garrison Engineer informed us that one of the billets must be pulled down to make way for taxi track. Saw Wing Admin Officer and new site for domestic area approved. Plans drawn up giving proposed layout of this area and submitted to 168 Wing for approval.

One of the new posts sited on 3 Dec ready for cementing.

Second of new posts ready for cementing. Air Raid Warning at 17.20 hours for 10 minutes only. Some slight amendment to Air Raid Warning to meet circumstance during non-working hours is necessary.
S/Ldr Last (G.D.O. 221 Group) arrived by air on tour of inspection.
O/C Flight accompanied S/Ldr Last on inspection of some posts and a visit to 94 E.P. and 4445 A.A. Flight.
S/Ldr. Last left by air. Arranged with Defence Training Instructors that they report to this unit periodically to report progress and discuss any problems.
Saw Defence Training Instructors and arranged for regular reports from them.
Arranged with 110 Squadron for two posts on watch tower after obtaining permission from o/c 168 Wing.
Work commenced on Wing HQ. gun posts.
Air Raid Warning 10.41 to 10.54 but no enemy aircraft sighted.
Excellent work done by 1513640 LAC SYMINGTON and 1393139 AC1 HIRST (both Gunners) in preparing the Christmas dinner and supper – menu attached as appendix.
Re-sited two of the Wing HQ gun posts owing to fresh constructional work over-riding previous siting.
Gun Posts in 45 Squadron dispersal area finished – cement to dry out then posts ready to be manned by their personnel.
Practice A.A. fire by Heavy and Light A.A. at 14.10 and 20.20 hours. Night practice interesting from point of view of the barrage possibilities.

4417 A.A. Flight – Operational at Kumbhirgram Aerodrome

Unit visited by C.D.O. – GROUP CAPTAIN HARRIS, accompanied by W/COMDR. FOWKE and F.LT. TAYLOR, the last named remaining on the Station. The C.D.O. with W/CDR. FOWKE departed the same day.
Departure of F/LT. TAYLOR.
Two 15 cwt. M.T. vehicles delivered to the Unit, this completing the M.T. establishment.
Air Raid Warning sounded. All Clear sounded. No events.
Arrival of S/LDR. LAST- G.D.O. F.LT HARDY returned from Course.

Discussion with G.D.O.
Departure of G.D.O.
Air Raid warning signal given by Heavy A.A. All Clear sounded. In the absence of the L.D.C., F//LT HARDY contacted Operations Room, who stated that an unidentified aircraft believed to be American, had passed overhead
The first XMAS DAY to be celebrated by the men as one Unit. All men on gun post duty ....in view of a possible attack to-day. Dinner highly successful.
The L.D.C. informed F/LT. HARDY that the Garrison Engineer had stated that work was about to commence on the new domestic site for the R.A.F. REGT.

4418 A.A. Flight – Moved to and now operational at Ukhrul Road Airfield

4 Air raid warnings were sounded during the month but no enemy activity was observed.
TRAINING As training other than range practices has been done during the month. At the range rifle firing has been carried out four times , each man firing 40 rounds. A high standard of shooting is recorded by some 10 or 12 members of the Flight, and the remainder of the Flight reached a good average mark. The Flight rifle team beat the local R.A. Unit in a shooting match by 16 points, in a possible 240. A prize of two bottles of rum was given by L.J. Hills R.A. and F/LT Ferrier-Jones.
WELFARE The Flight has during the month built its own Canteen from bamboo straw and an old tarpaulin, at a cost of Rs22. The building is a complete success and a Flight party was held in it on New Years Eve as an opening ceremony. Sq/Ldr. F.W.J. Last G.D.O. 221 Group, F/Lt. S.M. Rigg M.O. 181 Wing, F/LT Jefferson Smith Dental Officer M.F.H. were in attendance and a most enjoyable evening was spent by all. No.3 Section won the evenings darts competition and a prize of Rs 30 was donated and presented to the team by Sq/Ldr Last. Sq/Ldr Last also presented the prize for the shooting competition referred to under training. The mail is now coming through satisfactorily.

Football is being played with great enthusiasm and the month's results are as follows:-

Beat 857 AMES 6 - 1

Draw 383 AMES 1 - 1

Lost ARMY team 1 - 3

Lost ARMY team 0 - 1

MEETINGS

At the General Flight meeting held on 21.12.43 a Canteen Committee was elected as follows:-

President F/Lt R.T. Ferrier Jones

Secretary Cpl J.T. Nash

Treasurer F/Lt R.T. Ferrier Jones

Members

No.1 Section LAC Haylett

No.2 Section LAC Robertson

No.3 Section LAC Shingleton

CHRISTMAS FARE

The Flight enjoyed an excellent day at Christmas. The Catering was in the hands of R.A.F. Station and all credit is due to them for the efficient manner in which the whole thing was organised. Dinner consisted of Duck and Christmas Pudding in addition to numerous other good things.

No leave was taken this month.

VISITORS

F/LT F Copeland of 4430 A.A. Flight

Sq/Ldr F.W.J. Last (G.D.O.) 221 Group

G/C Harris A.H.Q. Delhi

W/C J.L. Fowles. Bengal Command

F/LT S.M. Rigg 181 Wing

F/LT Jefferson Smith M.F.H.

4448 A.A. Flight – Operational at Manipur Road Airfield

I was present in a gunpost during the two-wave raid on Calcutta. One wave of enemy aircraft appeared for a time to be approaching Dum-Dum but this did not transpire and we observed the bomb bursts and heavy Ack ack fire from the direction of the Hooghly River. The men's demeanour was excellent.

PERSONALITIES.

A Tribute must be paid here to Sgt. Jones and L.A.C. Shelton who, during this period, worked hard and cheerfully often for ten and eleven hours a day. The latter even went into Calcutta twice a week for type-writing lessons and attended the S.H.Q. Orderly Room for instruction in administration and the general duties of a clerk.

2.A./ THE SECOND JOURNEY. DUM-DUM/ CALCUTTA/ MANIPUR ROAD.

I visited Sealdah twice at 18.30 and 23.00. Equipment was neatly sorted and stacked: Cpl. Tute had put guards on and all was in order. Most of my day was spent in getting clear of S.H.Q. and checking that all was packed up and got away to the station. The Sikh Temple case, in which I was the Investigating Officer, was, I hope, finally closed and a last revision of it took up most of the morning.

REVEILLE at 04.00hrs: left Dum-Dum Airfield at 05.25, arrived at Sealdah 06.00. A good breakfast was put on. Additional cookhouse equipment has been acquired and crated, my view being that 4448 Flight's need will be greater than Dum-Dum's. On the station the movement was supervised by F/Sgt. Gordon. He was most helpful and the men worked well together on the loading. They seemed to appreciate Sgt Jones and myself lending a hand.

Also in the special were the ground personnel of 42 & 5 Sqdns: and about 130 U.S. officers and Snr: N.C.Os enroute for China. The train pulled out at 09.15 instead of 07.30. B.O.Rs. were very crowded. I shared a compartment for two with three officers. O.C. train was F/Lt. Evans, the M.O. of 42 Sqdn: O.C. U.S. Army Detachment was Capt Leonhardt and O.C. 5 Sqdn: was their M.O. F/Lt.Skene. I worked for full co-operation between units but was not entirely successful. However after a midday meal out of tins, the following arrangement was made:- No.42 Sqdn: 4448 Flight and the Americans pooled rations, the cooking was done by Cpl Gray of 42 Sqdn: and my two LACs. Hookham and Littlewood. The American rations provided a variety for our men, and the Americans were pleased as they had no cooks in their party. No.5 Sqdn: had a F/Sgt and other cooks but preferred not to join the pool.

We arrived at Santanar at 16.00 and an excellent meal was put on and cooked at the end of the platform. No.5 were on the track at the other side of the train. All ranks of the pool were most happy at the result and personnel mixed well at work and during the long evening on the bare, fly-blown and evil-smelling station platform. We slept on the train and performed miracles of ablution.

Again all equipment was moved, first on to the platform, then into a truck and a coach of the narrow gauge railway. Again 48 Flight worked as a team. This was commented on by two R.A.F. officers and one American. I detached Cpl Tute and LACs Donovan, Hill, and Langan who volunteered to stay with the equipment and live in the truck. The R.T.O. routed them by rail to a ferry across the river directly through to Dimapur. Rations were drawn and were in charge of LAC Hill. Good meals were again enjoyed by the pool and included tea, coffee, bacon, beans, bully, beet, sweet corn, veinna sausages, potatoes, jam, marmalade, butter, biscuits, and canned fruit.

A day of waiting and start-time rumours. Food and morale still excellent. Moved off at 21.00. Earlier times given were 16.42 and 23.50.

Arrived at Tista Mukh Ghat in the early hours. De-trained at 08.00hrs. No ablutions. Good meal at the side of track. Orders came to move into Transit camp on bank of the Bramaputra. F/Lts Evans & Skene asked me to march all B.O.Rs off. I agreed, called the Snr N.C.Os together and called a parade for 10.00 4448 Flight turned out in full marching order and headed the column, leaving bed-rolls under a guard. The squadrons tried to carry too much. The move was completed and 48 Flight marched like the Guards. This was commented on by other officers. I got the squadrons there but it was hard going over half a mile of railway lines and dusty embankment. Finc dust and a hot sun.

On arrival we found the transit camp had not been notified. The Indian Officer and English Sgt: (Army) in charge were quite incompetent and non-co-operative. After three hours haggling, we (the O.C's parties) managed to clear three lines of tents and install our hot, dirty and weary men. We saw to it that they got a meal and left them to an after-noon round the pump wash-themselves and their clothes. Many personnel of 221 Group were in the camp and had been there for five days. We were told that our stay might well prove of many days so in the afternoon we made our way to the river bank an interviewed the Movements Officer, Lieut Fletcher, in his office on a barge. After discussion of our different reasons for demanding priority, he told us that we should move off at 05.00hrs the next day. This order was cancelled indefinitely at 20.00hrs: by Major, i/c/ Transit Camp. I cleaned down under a pump and slept on the floor of a tent after seeing the men are alright. During the night I suffered somewhat from the cold as I had sent my camp kit on with Cpl Tute and had only a Dhurrie and ground sheet for bed.

At 09.00 we were given 40 minutes notice to leave the Transit Camp and make our way to the point of embarkation on the bank of the Bramaputra. Again I was asked to take charge of the marching but this time each man had to carry his all. Again 4448 Flight rose above the circumstances and marched away from them all. The distance was something more tha three-quarters of a mile along a railway embankment some two inches deep in fine dust. A steady breeze blew across oy and soon both head and tail of the long column was lost to view beneath an eight foot cloud of dust. The stink from native camps did not help.

I left the Flight alone and stayed with the Squadrons, encouraging the weaker all I could and taking in turn now and again with a tin-trunk or rifle. On arrival I sorted the crowd out into it's component parts. The Americans had come separately and in good order but I was caught in a cross fire of ball feeling between the Squadron. This came to a head at embarkation time when I was forced to step in and secure proper accommodation for my own men.

Once aboard the meals were again organised on the train, No.5 still standing aloof. Owing to the danger of queues causing lists, all were served under the supervision of myself and Lieutenant Gallagher of the U.S. Army.

On board the Vulture all day, we sailed yesterday at 15.00hrs, making steady progress up to Bramaputra. From flat bare paddy to country gradually changed to hills with mountains in the distance. The men were in good spirits and had a sing-song last night. F/Lt Evans and

myself were woken up at 02.00 and had to shift from their deck spaces
some forty R.A.F. men so that a chain of coolies could come on board
to coal up the ship. Meals continued good and plentiful.

An R.T.O. Sergeant woke F/Lt Evans and myself at 02.15 to say that
we had arrived at Pandu and were to disembark at 05.00 and spend the
day in a rest camp.

Hot breakfast would be provided. We decided to disembark at 07.00
after giving the men a mug of gun-fire tea at 06.00. This was done.
48 Flight moved off the ship and stored their webbing and bedrolls
under voluntary guards. The Americans entrained straight away and
our time as given as 17.55. The Squadrons were dealing with their
equipment individually so I fell in the Flight and marched a good
half mile to the Rest Camp; reporting to the cookhouse. The sergeant
in charge had not been informed of our arrival by the R.T.Os. office
so the men were forced to wait for a meal. 48 were served first.
They were dismissed until 15.00 and either rested, bathed or went
climbing in the adjacent hills. I had a most welcome meal in the
Officer's Mess Basha. Instead of a rest however, F/LTs Skene and
Evans informed me that the R.T.O. had ordered that the train be
loaded at the siding half-way between the railway station and the
rest-camp. This would not have been so bad for my men but was
distinctly rough on the Squadrons who carried considerable
quantities of this and that. So we decided to go down and interview
the authorities at the station and the river.

In all we saw four captains and a Major and were treated to the
worst display of inefficiency and non-co-operation that has ever
been my misfortune to witness. By the time we returned for a late
tiffin at the camp the situation was unchanged. In the afternoon,
after having a look at the train and the siding, another attempt was
made to persuade the authorities to let us load in the station but
to no avail. It seemed that everything would have to be man-handled
for almost half a mile. Fortunately F/LT. Skene contacted an officer
and arranged to telephone to borrow a three tonner. Loading started
at 16.30 and was still in progress at 19.00 when the train was
started. 48 Flight had been early away with their kit and were all
aboard but one of the Sqdns: were unable to load all their kit and

personnel. F/LT Evans was left behind as well. The men were disgracefully crowded as were the officers as at the last minute an Indian Army unit was allotted much accommodation. At the first stop, a captain informed me and those with me that our compartment had been reserved by the R.T.O. at Pandu for a Colonel who was going through to Manipur Road. I informed him that he would have to find me other accommodation as I could not be separated from my unit. He was not helpful. The Colonel heard the discussion and immediately offered to take two R.A.F. Officers in with him. None being willing I was approached and agreed to move back into the compartment. This was done, the train waited for another to bring F/LT Evans and so an unsatisfactory day drew to a close. But my men were still singing in their dark and crowded coach and I congratulated them on their moral as I said good-night. Food for all was cold "bully" and biscuits.

At 10.00 we arrived at Manipur Road and I contacted W/O Sheppard of 113 Squadron who took me straight out to the strip in a jeep. Accommodation was in old Bashas and the floors, doors and entrance steps were in bad condition. There was no water and the latrines were disgusting. However, faute de mieux, we moved in with two three-tonners kindly lent by the Squadron. A hasty meal was prepared and eaten before detailing working parties and contacting Cpl Tute at Dimapur rail-head. All equipment was off-loaded and brought to the camp. I visited 885 A.M.E.S. which is half a mile from the strip. Contact was made with F/O Harper, the O.C., and Sgt Stone of 4418 A.A. Flight whose section I relieved.

At 08.30 I climbed into the back of a 3 ton lorry at the A.M.E.S. and went to Imphal, a distance of nearly a hundred and forty miles across the Naga Hills. It was an amazing journey and took eight hours. Before leaving the Flight were allotted tasks on the camp-site - erection and equipping a cook house, ablutions, canvas water trough, repairs to billets and general settling in.

I found Squadron-Leader Last in camp and got a warm welcome followed by a most welcome meal. I rendered him a full report of 48 Flight's activities.

After breakfast and a talk in Squadron-Leader Last's office, I returned to Dimapur by car with F/Lt. Riggs M.O. and F/Lt. Ferrier-Jones of 4418 A.A. Flt. When I returned to my camp, Sgt Jones reported that all was well and the men behaved and worked well. The latrine situation was bad however, and the cold at night camp up through the bamboo floor.

At 10.00hrs the M.O., F/LT. Rigg, came round, inspected the camp and condemned it out of hand. Dysentery, it seems, was not a possibility but a certainty. A new site was found on a bluff overlooking the run-way and orders were given to stand by for a move directly the M.O. obtained the authority for drawing tents from the army. A start was made on the assembly of guns and mountings. Billets were still in need of repair and I ordered work to be continued. I went to Dimapur in the afternoon and collected some equipment for 113 Sqn: bought 5 ½ doz eggs in the bazaar to supplement rations, failed to buy ducks and geese or to find a dhobi. At the 153 Sqdn. Area H.Q. I interviewed the S.S.O. and the D.A.Q.M.S. for various reasons but nothing concrete resulted. Among other things I tried for Christmas rations and a beer issue.

No.1 Section was put on to dhobi, the remainder working on preparations for the move. Five Army signatures having been obtained on the authority to draw tents, I went myself to Ordnance and collected them. They are splendid jobs of the square marquee type and I allotted them as follows:-

1/. Orderly Tent & O.Cs. quarters.

2/. Ration Stores & Cooks quarters.

3/. N.C.Os. quarters (and Armoury Stores pro tem).

4/. Men's quarters.

5/.   Ditto.

The men are crowded but I hope the quarters will be only temporary ones.

No.1 Section paraded at 07.30 in full marching order for inspection and moved down to 885 A.M.E.S. to start a week of manning two gunposts by da and doing patrols by night. Mountings and guns were moved yesterday. I went again t Area H.Q. and saw Captain Gasper. He was interested to learn our role on the defence plan of the airfield. I also reported the change of camp sites and tried again for beer. LAD Goode & LAC Ford reported back from the aircraft recognition course at Alipore. Both obtained a "B" pass.

Movement to the new site was started in the morning and by dusk the tents had been erected, the water tank and cookhouse put into operation and all equipment moved in. Work started on a proper field latrine.

All hands turned to with a will and, apart from another abortive visit to the S.S.O., I spent the day supervising and taking a shift myself at all the jobs of work. These included the digging of the latrine, the moving and proper siting of the 500 gal. water-tank, the building of a field oven in the cookhouse I (which consists of two pieces of corrugated iron supported on six uprights), various drains and nullahs were dug or cleared out and many other items such as getting the stores and office organised, contacting various authorities for drawing water purifying tablets, squared timber, charpoys etc etc. Little or nothing however was obtained.

MANIPUR ROAD.

My policy for the first six weeks at Manipur Road Dec: 15th to Jan:31st falls under four main headings:-

1/. To get a full quota of proper gunposts into operation around the strip.

2/. To make the camp-site habitable and as pleasant as possible.

3/. To keep the men fit and happy by means of good sanitation and plenty of sport.

4/. To maintain the paper work so that administration should not fall behind.

The camp-site is cleared jungle on the edge of the strip itself and has been occupied by some four hundred men of the Indian Pioneer Corps who folded their tents and left nothing but debris.

No.4416 A.A. Flight – Movement Order No.1

SECRET   MOVEMENT ORDER NO.1   APPENDIX "A"

4416 A.A. Flight. R.A.F. Regiment

The intention is to carry out the move of the above-named unit, nominal roll as per Appendix "A commencing on the 21st July 1943, to Kumbhirgram (Silchar) as detailed below.

1. Personnel to be moved are 1 B.O. and 36 B.O.R.s and will be accommodated as follows:-

    (a)   1 B.O. in train service.
    (b)   36 B.O.R.s in reserved third class bogie.
    (c)   Luggage in sealed E.V.P. wagon.

2. Times as arranged by H.Q. 11 M.C. & M.F. Area are as follows:-

(a)	Secunderabad	Dep 10.05	21st July 1943
(b)	Bezwada	Arr 19.00	21st July 1943
		Dep 00.15	22nd July 1943
(c)	Waltair	Arr 11.35	22nd July 1943
		Dep 23.50	22nd July 1943
(d)	Khurda Road	Arr 12.28	23rd July 1943
		Dep 20.55	23rd July 1943
(e)	Howrah	Arr 17.10	24th July 1943

3. Ice and Camel Cisterns will be collected from R.T.O. Secunderabad before entraining, 45lbs of bread and 180lbs of ice will be collected from Waltair and Khurda Road.

4. Movement Control, Calcutta have been asked to arrange the move from Calcutta to destination, and contact will be made with them immediately upon arrival to Howrah.

5. Rations will be drawn for 14 days for 37 men, and will be divided into 14 parcels, each parcel to contain a complete days rations for the whole party. The preparation and issue of the rations will be done by 546 LAC Jones, 540 LAC Symington, and 927 LAC Debenham. Water arrangements will be made en route.

6. Arms and ammunition will be carried by each man, 17 rifles and 20 Sten Guns being taken on individual charge. Rifles to have 50 rounds and Sten 35 rounds per gun.

BAGGAGE.
All kit and baggage is to be clearly marked with the owners name and number. The unit number or destination will not be marked on any article. All baggage will be neatly stacked outside Hut 19 by

07.45 on the 20th July 1943, and will be loaded by the baggage party on to the transport at 08.30 that day. The lorry will make a second trip being loaded up by the Guard Party who will take with them 24 hours rations and remain with the railway truck over-night. Arrangements for weighing the baggage will in charge of Cpl. Drummond assisted by members of the guard Party.

The Baggage party will consist of :-

T/Cpl.	Adams
LAC	Flynn
LAC	Davies
LAC	Debenham
LAC	Ewen
LAC	Fretwell
LAC	Herring
AC1	Hirst
LAC	Narduzzo
LAC	Paynter
LAC	Peachey No.1 Section

The Guard Party will consist :-

T/Cpl.	Folwell
LAC	Debono
LAC	Gray
LAC	James

O/C Flight will proceed with the first load to collect Warrants and Credit Notes from R.T.O. Secunderabad. Transport requirements will be made to S.H.Q. 658 at least 24 hours before time required.

Dress as detailed in Appendix "C"

<u>Discipline</u>   Halts.
No one will leave the train without first obtaining the O/C's permission, and then only if properly dressed. No Minerals or Ice Cream may be purchased en route. During the hot hours of the day sun blinds if fitted should be used. From dusk to dawn, long sleeved shirts, slacks and anti Mosquito ointment should be used.

Appendix "B"

Date	Time	Details
19.7.43	08.00 Hours	Check Paybooks, Identity Cards & Discs
19.7.43	09.00 Hours	Collect Ammunition
19.7.43	11.00 Hours	Medical inspection
20.7.43	07.45 Hours	Baggage to be stacked outside Hut 19
20.7.43	07.50 Hours	Baggage Party to parade.
20.7.43	08.15 Hours	All equipment and stores to be ready for loading (with baggage) on the lorry. The guard party will draw 24 hrs rations
20.7.43	08.30 Hours	Load Lorry
20.7.43	17.30 Hours	O/C Flight will proceed to Secunderabad R.S. to see to the sealing of E.V.P. and to inspect guard.
21.7.43	06.30 Hours	Breakfast
21.7.43	07.45 Hours	Roll call and inspection.
21.7.43	08.00 Hours	Clearance chits and inspection of vacated Quarters
21.7.43	08.15 Hours	Final Parade.
21.7.43	08.30 Hours	Embark for Station
21.7.43	09.00 Hours	O/C Flight to contact R.T.O. with regard to Ice and fresh water.
21.7.43	09.30 Hours	Entrainment to be completed.
21.7.43	10.05 Hours	Depart Secunderabad.

Appendix "C"

Dress:-
Long sleeved shirts, sleeves rolled up, shorts, boots, putees, bush hat, water bottled filled. Respirators will be worn in the alert position in accordance with full marching order.

The Following kit will be carried :-

Further kit to last ten days should also be carried)

Large Pack :-	Blanket	Side Pack:	Small Kit
	Slacks		Towel
	Shorts (2 pairs)		Hussif
	Shirts (2)		Plate
	Vet		Irons
	Underpants		Mug
	Gym Shoes		
	Socks (3 pairs)		
	Hose Tops		
	Clean Towel		

No.4416 A.A. Flight – Nominal Roll

Nominal Roll

4416 A.A. Flight. R.A.F. Regiment.

F/O F.C. Wilson (104081) Officer Commanding

1350902	T/Sgt	Horton	A.
1306748	T/Cpl.	Royal	P.A.
988164	T/Cpl.	Drummond	J.
1303321	T/Cpl.	Folwell	H.V.
957750	T/Cpl.	Adams	J.L.
1341564	LAC	Anderson	A.
1316891	LAC	Beechey	E.D.
1510884	LAC	Curle	H.
1515550	LAC	Davies	R.E.
1239927	LAC	Debenham	L.W.
1352770	LAC	Debone	H.
1529782	LAC	Devereaux	P.R.
1343061	LAC	Ewen	J.
1000613	LAC	Flynn	W.P.
1551900	AC1	Forest	
1106476	LAC	Fretwell	S.
1533675	LAC	Gray	H.
1446393	LAC	Herring	R.A.
1393139	AC1	Hirst	W.T.
1095423	LAC	James	W.G.
1418546	LAC	Jones	W.T.
1086179	LAC	Kime	J.E.
1431555	LAC	Monaghan	J.
1003237	LAC	Myers	R.D.
1470896	LAC	Narduzzo	C.A.
1322032	LAC	Neville	J.A.
1046957	LAC	O'Neill	M.S.
1307113	LAC	Paynter	F.G.
1322572	LAC	Peachey	W.G.
1342098	LAC	Rendall	D.J.
1428277	LAC	Steadman	E.C.
1513540	LAC	Symington	K.
1553283	LAC	Thomson	T.
1109050	LAC	Will	A.G.
1249768	LAC	Wright	G.
1557804	AC1	Black	A.

No.4416 A.A. Flight – Xmas Menu December 1943

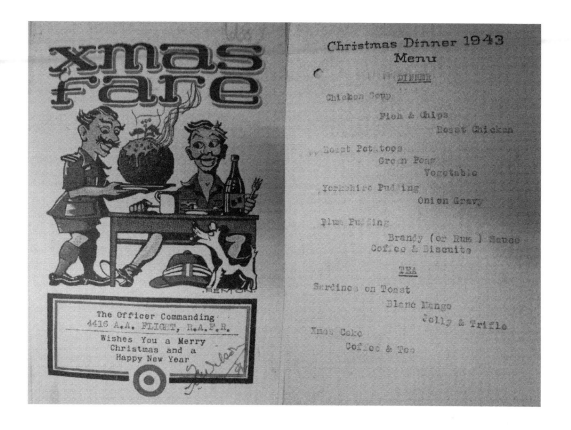

No.4448 A.A. Flight Photograph 1943

No.4448 A.A. Flight – Crest

Group 222 - General Reconnaissance

Overview

There was a disappointing start in July for No.4413 A.A. Flight as it arrived at Madras Central Station, with delay and little in way of food and drink for the men, following denial from the transport staff there that any signals had been received of the unit's movement. This was short lived and following a stop at Colombo Fort, where the men were given a hot meal, the unit moved to its final destination south of the island of Ceylon, at an airfield at Koggala.

Near the end of the month, the flight commander was instructed to take control of all Ground Defence personnel staff at the airfield and organised the men into three separate flights (4413, "A", "B").The next three months began with local training, directed by the flight commander, for all Ground Defence staff stationed at the airfield,. Nine Gun Posts were now fully manned, with each flight taking on the duty on a week's rotation. Those men not on duty would undertake programmed weapons and field training, the enhancement of the defence of the station and the occasional trip to the cinema.

A couple of "Yellow" Air Raid warning were received, where all main and auxiliary Gun Posts were manned, but no action was taken, as either the aircraft were too high or not seen.

November saw the arrival of No.4450 A.A. Flight, stationed in the middle of the island, at the airfield near Sigirya. Unlike the airfield at Koggala, Sigirya had no previous Ground Defence, with dense jungle giving little or no ground to air visibility, except for the runway. With no equipment or vehicles, the unit was seriously stuck and action was urgently needed to get them out of this unacceptable situation.

December was a mixed month, as sadly for No.4413 A.A. Flight, L.A.C. Partridge drowned whilst bathing and was later laid to rest, at the Dadulla Cemetery. At the Sigirya airfield, No.4450 A.A. flight, finally got started clearing, siting and constructing its Gun Posts.

The map and table below show the units protecting No.222 Group as at the end of 1943, with 4 Officers and 148 Airmen distributed between 4 key locations.

Map showing the location of R.A.F.R. Units as at 31st December 1943

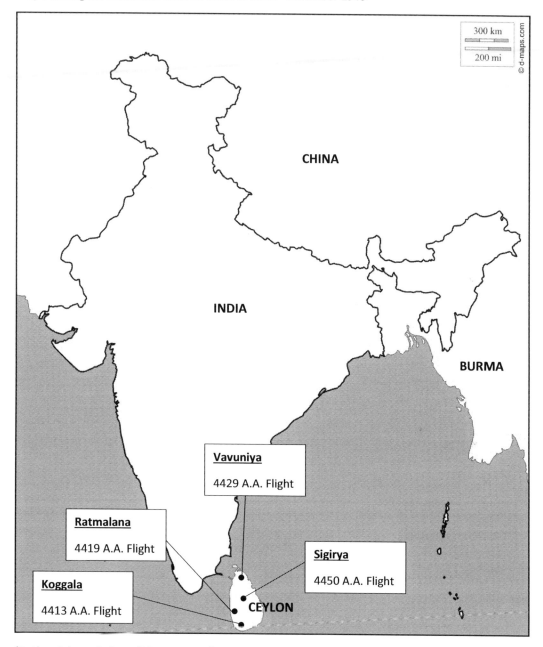

(Author Adapted - http://d-maps.com/carte.php?num_car=32142&lang=en)

R.A.F. Regiment Units in 222 Group R.A.F. – December 1943

CEYLON (Now Sri Lanka)	A.A. Flight	Field Squadron
Koggala	**4413**	
Ratmalana	4419	
Vavuniya	4429	
Sigirya	**4450**	
Establishment Numbers	4 A.A. Flights = 8 Officers and 148 Airmen	Nil

(Note units in bold included in this book)

Operational Diaries

July
4413 A.A. Flight – Entrained from Secunderabad, en-route to Koggala Airfield

Arrived Central Station, MADRAS. R.T.O. intimated he had no notice of our arrival and denied having received Signal from Movements Control, SECUNDERABAD sent off 13.6.43. This caused little inconvenience as it only allowed just over two hours to unload kit and reload at Egmore Station. No tea or a little bread was available. Left MADRAS at 13.55 having had only a very scratchy meal.
Arrived TRICHINOPOLY where bread was issued by R.I.A.S.C.
Left TRICHINOPOLY.
Arrived DHAMUSHKODI. R.T.O. was very helpful. Left at 12.00.
Arrived TALAIMANNAR by Ferry. Left by railway 16.05.
Arrived COLOMBO FORT. Loaded all kit on lorries and proceeded to ECHELON BARRACKS where men were given a hot meal. P/O. R.H. Christie Miller then called at H.Q. 222 Group and interviewed Movements Control, 'P' Staff and the Ground Defence Officer. During the afternoon orders were issued for us to proceed to R.A.F. COLOMBO with kit and stores. This was completed by 10.45.
Left COLOMBO FORT en route KOGGALA. Arrived KOGGALA HALT 08.45. Men were given a hot meal and then unloaded kit and stores.
P/O. R.H. Christie Miller interviewed by Station Commander in the forenoon instructed to await return of F/O. UPHILL before taking over Gun Posts as the Flight had left the Depot without an issue of Browning Guns. Personnel were given a day's rest during which time they saw Station Medical Officer and gave their particulars to Station Orderly Room and Pay Accounts.
Weapons Training commenced.
Route march and inspection by Station Commander, G/Capt. R.L. MILLS.
Day of rest.
Training as per programme.
Weapons Training Continued.
Four Gun Posts taken over by 4413 A.A. Flight. P/O. R.H. Christie Miller instructed by Station Commander, G/Capt. R.L. Mills to take

charge of all Ground Defence Personnel at KOGGALA. This was done and three separate Flights were made i.e. A.A. 4413,'A' Flight, 'B' Flight. One flight will man gun posts for one full week, while the two remaining flights are given instruction in Field Training and Weapons Training. 4413 A.A. Flight took over Station guard. Weapon Training was also continued according to Programme.

Ministry of Information Film attended by all personnel. Four Gun Posts manned, Weapons training continued in the afternoon.

August
4413 A.A. Flight – Operational at Koggala Airfield

DAY OFF. Rest of men off gun post duty. GUN POSTS MANNED.

Gunners already stationed at Koggala, started new training under the direction of Pilot Officer R.H. Christie Miller. Five new Gun Posts taken over by 4413 A.A. Flight, making total of nine gun posts manned in all.

GUN POSTS manned. Weapon training continued for remainder of men.

COMMANING OFFICERS' PARADE. Very complimentary remarks made about No.4413 A.A. Flight. GUN POSTS manned. Weapon training continued for remainder of men.

GUN POSTS MANNED. Remainder of men continued weapon training and field training.

A" Flight manning gun posts. Remainder of men continued Weapon and Field training.

A" Flight manning gun posts. Remainder of men on Route march.

A" Flight manning gun posts. Day of rest for remainder of men. During this day R.A.F. Form 540 was completed for the month of July, signed by F/Lt. Christie Miller and duly sent to Headquarters, No.222 Group, R.A.F. CEYLON.

A" Flight manning gun posts, remainder of men training.

"A" Flight manning gun posts, remainder of men training and organised sports in the afternoon.

Pilot Officer R.H. Christie Miller appointed the rank of FLIGHT LIEUTENANT w.e.f. 31.7.43. Authority:- AIR H.Q. Signal P.712 dated 16/7/43.

1540670 L.A.C. COMRIE, D., appointed to the rank Acting Corporal (PAID) w.e.f. 31.5.43. Authority:- B.P.O. Draft Note BPO/2001/2/A.2 dated 21st July, 1943 promulgated on P.O.R. 1/43 dated 8th August, 1943.

Station guard taken over by 4413 A.A. Flight.

"A" Flight manning Gun Posts. Remainder of men on Weapon training and Field training, including range firing.

"A" Flight manning Gun posts. Remainder of men training. Khaki battle dress being altered, if possible, by Camp Tailor, on the authority of the Station Equipment Officer. NEW DINGHY provided for use of men manning Gun posts. One Sergeant and one Corporal arrived from Secunderabad. Sent to Kalamitiya as Instructors.

"B" Flight manning Gun posts, having taken over from "A" Flight. Remainder of men on training. Half of personnel attended cinema show as per instructions issued on Daily Routine Orders. (Ministry of Information films).

"B" Flight manning Gun posts. Remainder of men on Route March. Half of personnel attended Cinema show.

"B" Flight manning Gun posts. Day off - rest for remainder of men.

"B" Flight manning Gun posts. Remainder of men on Field Training and Weapons Training. Station guard taken over. 48 hrs leave sanctioned and roster made out, which is now in operation. Rest leave at Radella starts 19.8.43, 5 men proceeding. Two men proceeding on part annual leave 20.8.43. 4 men detailed to help backers up at Kalamitiya for one week.

"B" Flight manning Gun posts. Remainder of men on Field Training and Weapons Training. Demonstration by No.148 L.A.A. Battery, Royal Artillery of Bofor gun firing.

"B" Flight manning Gun posts. Remainder of men on rifle range. Cricket match played against Maintenance. Football match played against Marine Section. All men showing keened for sport.

"B" Flight manning Gun posts. Remainder of men on Field Training & Weapons Training.

No.4413 A.A. Flight manning gun posts having taken over from "B" Flight S.H.Q.R.A.F. Regiment. Remainder of men on Field Training and Weapons Training.

No.4413 A.A. Flight manning gun posts. Remainder of men on route march and followed by Foot inspection.
No.4413 A.A. Flight manning gun posts. Day off for men off duty.
No.4413 A.A. Flight manning gun posts. Remainder of men on Field Training & Weapons Training. Also started wiring outer fencing due to barbed wire being down.
No.4413 A.A. Flight manning gun posts. Remainder of men on barbed wiring.
No.4413 A.A. Flight manning gun posts. Remainder of men on barbed wiring. Pilot Officer R.H. Christie Miller promoted to the rank of F/O on probation (W) w.e.f. 12/11/43. Authority:- London Gazette dated 16/4/43. Khaki Battle dress sent in for alterations by men of No.4413 A.A. Flight proved absolutely unalterable, owing to the extremely large sizes. The Station Commander has reported same to Officer Commanding R.A.F. Regiment Depot, SECUNDERABAD.
No.4413 A.A. Flight manning gun posts. Remainder of men on rifle range and barbed wiring. Squadron Leader Ball visited Koggala and with F/Lt. Christie Miller proceeded to Kalamitiya where "Backers up" are training.
"A" Flight manning gun posts, having taken over from No.4413 A.A. Flight. Remainder of men on Field Training and Weapons Training, also barbed wiring. Half of personnel attended Cinema show in accordance with Daily Routine Orders. (Ministry of Information films).
"A" Flight manning gun posts. Remainder attended M. of I. films in accordance with D.R.O's. Wiring was completed during the afternoon.
"A" Flight manning gun posts. Remainder of men on day of rest.
"A" Flight manning gun posts. One section on firing range, rest of men on Field Training and Weapons training. Afternoon spent on barbed wiring. Station guard taken over by No.4413 A.A. Flight.
"A" Flight manning gun posts. Remainder of men on Field Training and Weapons Training, also Unarmed Combat.

September

4413 A.A. Flight – Operational at Koggala Airfield

R.A.F. Regiment manning gun posts, ('A' Flight), remainder of men on Field Training and Weapon Training.
'A' Flight, R.A.F. Regiment manning gun posts. Remainder of men on Field Training and Weapon Training.
'B' Flight, R.A.F. Regiment manning gun posts. Remainder of men on Commanding Officer's Church Parade. Kit Inspection taken by F/Lieut. Christie Miller.
Route March. 'B' Flight, R.A.F. Regiment manning gun posts.
'B' Flight, R.A.F. Regiment manning gun posts. Day of rest for the remainder of men.
'B' Flight, R.A.F. Regiment manning gun posts. Remainder of men on Field Training and Weapon Training.
'B' Flight, R.A.F. Regiment manning gun posts. Remainder of men on Field Training and Weapon Training. 975468 LAC. Barrett R. Gunner being Medically Boarded at 35 British General Hospital for Tuberculosis. Relief applied for from R.A.F. Regiment Depot, Secunderabad.
'B' Flight, R.A.F. Regiment manning gun posts. Remainder of men on Field Training and Weapon Training, and Range Firing.
'B' Flight, R.A.F. Regiment manning gun posts. Remainder of men on Field Training and Weapon Training. Practice Air Raid Warning. All Personnel stood to.
No.4413 A.A. Flight, manning Gun Posts. Remainder of men on Field Training and Weapon Training. Half of personnel attended Cinema Show as per instructions D.R.O.s.
No.4413 A.A. Flight, manning Gun Posts. Remainder of men on Field Training and Weapon Training. Afternoon spent in Barb-wiring outer defence of Station.
No.4413 A.A. Flight manning Gun Posts. Day of rest for remainder of men.
No.4413 A.A. Flight manning Gun Posts. Remainder of men Field & Weapon Training.
No.4413 A.A. Flight manning Gun Posts. Remainder of men Field & Weapon Training. All men have been detailed to attend Gas Lectures.

S.H.Q. Ground Gunners manned Gun Posts in the early morning. 4413 A.A. Flight R.A.F. Regiment attended the Commanding Officer's Parade, which was in commemoration of the 'Battle of Britain'. Remainder of men on Field Training and Weapon Training. A Practice Air Raid was carried out during the afternoon.

No.4413 A.A. Flight manning Gun Posts. Remainder of men Field & Weapon Training.

'A' Flight, R.A.F. Regiment manning Gun Posts. Remainder of men on Field Training and Weapons Training.

'A' Flight, R.A.F. Regiment manning Gun Posts. Remainder of men on Route March. A part of the afternoon was spent in the cleaning of all Barrack Huts in which R.A.F. Regiment personnel are billeted, and beds were laid out in the sun.

'A' Flight, R.A.F. Regiment manning Gun Posts.

Orders given by S/Ldr. Admin that all auxiliary Gun Posts were to be manned. This was completed at 08.32 hours. 20 Gun Posts were manned in all, this was due to the 20th September, 1943 being Japanese Aviation Day and it was felt that an attack might be made in view of this.

Yellow Warning received. All Station Defence personnel stood to.

Red Warning received. Syren sounded.

Aircraft overhead. Later identified as Japanese. This aircraft was not seen owing to bad visibility, nothing further occurred until 'All Clear' at 2312.

All Gun posts stayed until 0130 hours 20th September when auxiliary posts stood down.

Auxiliary Gun crews returned to their Posts. All Posts fully manned during night. Nothing to report,

All Gun Posts duties back to normal. 'A' Flight, R.A.F. Regiment manning Gun posts.

'A' Flight, R.A.F. Regiment manning Gun posts. Remainder of men cleaning all Guns and Gun emplacements. Afternoon spent in Barbed Wire outer Defence of Station.

'A' Flight, R.A.F. Regiment manning Gun posts. Remainder of men on W/T. and Field Craft. Range Firing in fore-noon.

'B' Flight, R.A.F. Regiment manning Gun posts having taken over from 'A' Flight. W/T continued for remainder of men.
'B' Flight, R.A.F. Regiment manning Gun posts. Remainder of men visited Cinema to see Ministry of Information Film, as per instructions D.R.O.s. Afternoon spent in Barbed wiring defences.
'B' Flight, R.A.F. Regiment manning Gun posts. Remainder of men attended a Church Parade.
'B' Flight, R.A.F. Regiment manning Gun posts. Remainder of men on Field Training and Weapon Training.
'B' Flight, R.A.F. Regiment manning Gun posts. Remainder of men on Field Training and Weapon Training.
'B' Flight, R.A.F. Regiment manning Gun posts. Remainder of men on Field Training and Weapon Training.
'B' Flight, R.A.F. Regiment manning Gun posts. Remainder of men on Field Training and Weapon Training. Men attended a Lecture on Burma in Station Cinema.

October
4413 A.A. Flight – Operational at Koggala Airfield

R.A.F. REGIMENT manning Gun Posts. Remainder of men on Field Training and Weapons Training.
R.A.F. REGIMENT manning Gun Posts. Remainder of men on Field Training and Weapons Training.
R.A.F. REGIMENT manning Gun Posts. Remainder of men on Field Training and Weapons Training.
R.A.F. Regt. manning Gun Posts. Remainder of men on Field Training and Weapons Training.
R.A.F. Regt. manning Gun Posts. Remainder of men on Field Training and Weapons Training. F/Lt. Christie Miller proceeded to Kalamatiya on an inspection of training carried out by instructors detailed from R.A.F. Regt. Depot, Secunderabad.
R.A.F. Regt. manning Gun Posts. Remainder of men on Field and Weapons Training.
R.A.F. Regt. manning Gun Posts. Remainder of men on Field and Weapons Training.

R.A.F. Regt. manning Gun Posts. Remainder of men on Field and Weapons Training.
R.A.F. Regt. manning Gun Posts. Remainder of men on Field and Weapons Training.
R.A.F. Regt. manning Gun Posts. Remainder of men had the day free for rest.
R.A.F. Regt. manning Gun Posts. Remainder of men on Field and Weapons Training.
R.A.F. Regt. manning Gun Posts. Remainder of men on Field and Weapons Training.
R.A.F. Regt. manning Gun Posts. Remainder of men on Field and Weapons Training. An Air Raid Warning Yellow was received at 1100 hours, lasting one hour, all posts stood to. At 1200 hours the ALL CLEAR was received and normal routine was then carried out.
R.A.F. REGT. manning Gun Posts. Remainder of men on Field Training and Weapons Training.
R.A.F. REGT. manning Gun Posts. Remainder of men on Field Training and Weapons Training. 1351849 L.A.C. SOPER arrived here from Secunderabad on posting to make up the strength of 4413 A.A. Flight, deficient owing to 975468 L.A.C. BARRETT being found unfit.
R.A.F. REGT. manning Gun Posts. Remainder of men on Field Training and Weapons Training.
R.A.F. REGT. manning Gun Posts. Remainder of men had day free for rest.
R.A.F. REGT. manning Gun Posts. Remainder of men on Field Training and Weapons Training.
R.A.F. REGT. manning Gun Posts. Remainder of men on Field Training and Weapons Training.
R.A.F. REGT. manning Gun Posts. Remainder of men on Field Training and Weapons Training. The two men L.A.C. Robinson and L.A.C. Marshall, chosen by F/Lt. Christie Miller as the Armourers for this Flight, have proceeded to Secunderabad on an Armourers' Course, in accordance with the signal sent through R.A.F. Station, KOGGALA.

R.A.F. REGT. manning Gun Posts. Remainder of men on Field Training and Weapons Training.
R.A.F. REGT. manning Gun Posts. Remainder of men on Field Training and Weapons Training.
R.A.F. REGT. manning Gun Posts. Remainder of men on Field Training and Weapons Training.
R.A.F. REGT. manning Gun Posts. Remainder of men paraded on Church parade.
R.A.F. REGT. manning Gun Posts. Remainder of men on Field Training and Weapons Training.
R.A.F. REGT. manning Gun Posts. Remainder of men on Weapon and Field Training.
R.A.F. REGT. manning Gun Posts. Remainder of men on Weapon and Field Training.
R.A.F. REGT. manning Gun Posts. Remainder of men on Field Training and Weapons Training.
R.A.F. REGT. manning Gun Posts. Remainder of men on Field Training and Weapons Training.
R.A.F. REGT. manning Gun Posts. Remainder of men on Field Training and Weapons Training.
R.A.F. REGT. manning Gun Posts. Remainder of men had day free for rest.

November

4413 A.A. Flight – Operational at Koggala Airfield

During the month training was carried out as per attached training programmes. Gun Posts were manned in accordance with latest instructions from Headquarters, No.222 Group.   On 12th November, 1943, Air Raid Warning received T 001 HOURS. All Gun posts manned. All Clear sounded at 0200 hours.   F/Lt. R.H. Christie Miller proceeded on Ceylon Army Command Battle course.

4450 A.A. Flight – Settling in at Sigiriya Airfield

Movement of 4450 AA Flight on posting to R.A.F. Station Sigiriya, Ceylon.
Arrived at R.A.F. Station Sigiriya to take up duties of R.A.F. Ack Ack Defence. No previous Defence by R.A.F. in existence. Dense jungle surrounding and little or no visibility from ground to air except for runway.
Equipment practically nil. 674 Action taken.
Lack of Transport proving a serious handicap. Action taken.

December
4413 A.A. Flight – Operational at Koggala Airfield

Gun Post duties were carried out throughout the month by No.4413 A.A. Flight in accordance with Group Headquarters instructions. Training was carried out as per enclosed training schedules. On the afternoon of the 30th November, 1943, 1450246 L.A.C. PARTRIDGE, L.C. was drowned whilst bathing off the foreshore. His body was recovered on the 1st December, 1943, and he was buried in Dadulla Cemetery on the 2nd December, 1943. Request has been made for an airman to be posted to the Flight in order to bring the strength up to establishment. F/Lt. Christie Miller returned from Ceylon Army Command Battle course on the 9th December, 1943.

4450 A.A. Flight – Constructing Gun Posts at Sigiriya Airfield

Normal Routine Training carried out.
Replacement arrived ex. Secunderabad – L.A.C. Millar.
Gun Posts sited & construction commenced.

No.4413 A.A. Flight -Training Programme 6th – 11th September 1943

TIMES.	0645-0715	0845-0930	0930-1015	1030-1115	1115-1200	1400-1445	1445-1530	1530-1630
MONDAY.	P.T.	DRILL	RIFLE LOADING AND UNLOADNG	GRENADE CHARACTER-ISTICS AND STRIPPING	BROWNING NAMES OF PARTS	LECTURE BY F/L CHRISTIE MILLER MESSAGE WRITING	APPLICAT-ION OF FIRE METHOD OF SEARCHING GROUND	RIFLE LYING POSITION
TUESDAY.	P.T.	DRILL	RIFLE 1ST LESSION IN AIMING	GRENADE THROWING STANDING POSITION	BATTLE DRILL	APPLICATION OF FIRE STUDY OF GROUND	STEN GUN MECHANISM AND STRIPPING	TALK ON AERODROME DEFENCE SCHEME
WEDNESDAY.	P.T.	DRILL	GAS DRILL	FIELD EXERCISE		BROWNING HARMONISATION AND BREECHING UP		STEN GUN LOADING UNLOADING AND HOLDING
THURSDAY.	P.T.	DRILL	BAYONET FIGHTING	UNARMED COMBAT	BROWNING MECHANISM	RIFLE LYING POSITION BEHIND COVER	BROWNING GENERAL DESCRIPTION	LECTURE BY F/L. CHRISTIE MILLER
FRIDAY.	P.T.	DRILL	RIFLE HIOLDING, AIMONG AND SIGHT SEEING	STEN GUN FIRING POSITIONS	LECTURE BY F/L CHRISTIE MILLER OPERATIONAL ORDERS	RIFLE AND KIT INSPECTION		
SATURDAY.	P.T.	DRILL	ROUTE FOOT	MARCH AND INSPECTION		GRENADE THROWING LYING POSITION	BROWNING MECHANISM	BROWNING LOADING AND UNLOADING

No.4413 A.A. Flight -Training Programme 13th – 18th September 1943

TIMES.	0645-0715	0845-0930	0930-1015	1030-1115	1115-1200	1400-1445	1445-1530	1530-1630
MONDAY.	P.T.	DRILL	RIFLE SIGHT SEEING	STEN GUN LOADING UNLOADING AND HOLDING	BROWNING LOADING UNLOADING AND SIGHT SEEING	AIRCRAFT RECOGNITION	GRENADE THROWING DIFFERENT POSITIONS	DEFLECTION SHOOTING
TUESDAY.	P.T.	DRILL	BAYONET FIGHTING	FIELD EXERCISE DEFENCE AND ATTACK		BROWNING MECHANISM	LECTURE MAP READING F/L CHRISTIE MILLER	JUDGING DISTANCE
WEDNESDAY.	P.T.	DRILL	RIFLE CLEANING BEFORE AND AFTER FIRING	BATTLE DRILL	BATTLE ORDER TAKING UP POSITIONS	LECTURE THOMPSON SUB. MACHINE GUN	BROWNINGN AMES OF PARTS	AIRCRAFT RECOGNITION
THURSDAY.	P.T.	DRILL	RIFLE LYING POSITION	RIFLE APPLICAT-ION OF FIRE	UNARMED COMBAT	DEFLECTION SHOOTING	FIELD SIGNALS	BROWNING GENERAL DESCRIPTION
FRIDAY.	P.T.	DRILL	RIFLE MECHANISM AND TRIGGER PRESSING	STUDY OF GROUND	GAS DRILL	LECTURE MAP READING F/L CHRISTIE MILLER	RECOGNITION DIFFICULT TARGETS	RIFLE SIGHT SEEING ELEVATION AND DEPRESSION
SATURDAY.	P.T.	ROUTE MARCH						FOOT INSPECTION

Group 224 – Supporting Indian XV Corps

Overview

No.2941 Field Squadron was the first field squadron to leave the Depot and spent April at a temporary camp site at Agartala aerodrome. Although the site was not suitable for permanent occupation, the men were employed as 'pioneers', clearing overgrown jungle and doing their best to settle in. Following a visit from the Group Defence Officer, however, plans were drawn up for the occupation of a new permanent camp. Volunteers were sought to take on the roles of clerk, cooks, butchers and medical orderlies, who were not part of the establishment, but essential to its self-sustainability. A comprehensive training programme was devised by the squadron commander, which would continue in earnest for the rest of the year, to bring the unit up to its self-proclaimed status as "Special" squadron.

In contrast, No.2942 Field Squadron arrived at the aerodrome at Comilla and found their allocated accommodation in excellent condition with buildings on three sides of a square and bashes on the fourth for the Ack-Ack flight. The men quickly recovered from their journey and were cheerfully settling into patrolling and guarding the aerodrome.

For the men of No.2941 Field Squadron, training hours in June were revised to take on board changes in the climatic conditions, with reveille at 05.15hrs, the first of three sessions starting at 06.30hrs, finishing with compulsory games at 17.15hrs. The first session was carried out in P.T. kit, with rifles and later sessions, in kit applicable to the training carried out, only one free day was allowed and even Church Parade was substituted for a training session. Training at squadron level was proving difficult, as around 20 men were classified as unfit and awaiting replacement, an average of 20 men were off on the Hill Party at Shillong and a similar number of men, on average, were away on a variety of training courses. On top of this, there were still deficiencies in the number of vehicles and a lack of essential equipment, such as signalling apparatus, prismatic compasses, Bren Guns and discharge cups etc.

At Comilla, No.2942 Field Squadron was joined by the resident detachment of gunners from No.607 Squadron, who had returned for the Hill Party at Shillong and they immediately took over the anti-aircraft Gun Posts duties on the aerodrome. Even though the weather was poor, the training programme was making good progress, with grenade throwing at the newly dug pits and Rifle and Bren Gun firing at the local range. On a rain sodden pitch, a local football match with the Operations Room took place and the field squadron won 9 goals to nil, supporting the commanders view that the physical condition of his men was extremely good.

One of the first new units, No.4402 A.A. Flight was quickly operational at the Dohazari airfield, working with the resident ground defence flight from No.60 Squadron, who had recently been given their orders to move to the Depot for Regiment training. Heavy downfalls of rain during the month reduced the activities of the men to billet cleaning, repair of the domestic site, routine cleaning and maintenance of their Lewis Guns. By mid-June all the aircraft had been withdrawn and even the dummy aircraft had been removed, so with a number of the Gun Posts being waterlogged, alternative sites were recce'd and sited. Authorisation had been received from No.224 Group Headquarters confirming employment of two Cooks, two Sweepers and one Water Carrier and although temporary, greatly reduced the difficulties previously mentioned by the flight commander in his letter to H.Q.

Four days of continuous heavy rain had made the roads impassable around the airfield at Cox's Bazaar, however, the Gun Pits were standing up well, with the ideal monsoon pits being those that have a raised base, with the bottom half the pit wall being bricked. On the 4th June 1943, all of the new flights were renumbered, with the original designation of No.4353, the now No.4403 A.A. Flight, was struggling with the weather and lack of serviceable vehicles, which meant that a significant amount of time was being wasted servicing the gun posts and transferring rations. The defence plan of the airfield was agreed and the present Gun Pits considered quite adequate for their role. The end of the month saw a period of fine weather and news that four vehicles had been allocated to the unit. A redistribution of Gun Post responsibility took place, following the arrival of No.4410 A.A. Flight, who were detailed to take over 8- Gun Posts from No.4403 A.A. Flight, on Signal Hill, 5042 A.M.E.S. and the Filter Room. The new flights training programme for the month, included aircraft recognition of Japanese Navy and Army fighters and bombers, Lewis Gun, V.G.O. Rifle and Sten Gun, elementary map reading, ring & aperture sighting and sessions of P.T.

At the Feni airfield, an Air Raid Alert one afternoon only saw half the Gun Posts of No.4404 A.A. Flight manned, if transport had been available, a further three Posts would have been manned. The first heavy rains of the Monsoon have meant that the gun crews have had to be withdrawn and following continuous rain most Gun Posts have been rendered unserviceable.

The resident Defence Flight, at the Chittagong Aerodrome, left for Regiment training at the Depot and No.4411 A.A. Flight moved in and took over the Gun Posts to the north of the aerodrome. No.4405 A.A. Flight, who were already operational covering the southern sector of the aerodrome, gained approval to erect a new build or occupy an existing one on the aerodrome, to provide a lock up for ammunition and duty gun crew accommodation. This would allow manning of the Gun Posts during heavy rains, when the perimeter roads became unserviceable. With no accommodation allocated to No.4407 A.A. Flight at Chittagong, they spent their first week at No.224 Group Transit Camp, where they "ate the bread of idleness". The unit though was soon operational at several sites, with No.1 Section manning the quadruple Browning Gun Post at No.378 A.M.E.S., No.2 Section manning two quadruple Brown Gun Posts at No.5029 A.M.E.S. and No.3 Section moved to No.879 A.M.E.S. No Gun Posts had been constructed at the latter site, so the men immediately got to work, building the first post. The flight commander took over another units Norton motor cycle, to help him maintain contact with his scattered units. This became near to useless, after heavy rain and therefore was able to loan a 3-ton Chevrolet lorry, to carry out vital transfers of stores and equipment between sites.

Throughout the month of July, the heavy rains of the Monsoon continued to disrupted the normal operations of the units. At the Argartala Aerodrome, No.2941 Field Squadron continued with its Jungle and Warfare Tactics training programme, combined with flight tactical route marches. The squadron was informed that it's flights would be attached to Army units and No.3 Flight was chosen to attend a 3-week training period, at the forward area of Imphal. The flight was bought up to strength and the squadron re-organised into 2 rifle flights and the Support Flight was used as a pool of non-effective or unfit men. The most common troubles of unfit men were found to be flat feet, appendicitis, ears, nose, chest and enlarged veins. The temporary unfitness of men was mainly caused by Malaria, skin and boils issues, sprains and stomach troubles.

Between the heavy rains, No.2942 Field Squadron, at Comilla Aerodrome, focused a little of its spare time on more domestic issues. A squadron magazine "Stand Easy" was started, with radio and football equipment received from Comforts. Later in the month the squadron presented its first Concert Party, a repeat show was performed at the end of the month, to R.A.F personnel and Nursing staff. The training programme continued with route marches & range work and the first cycle patrols started on the aerodrome.

Initially transiting at the R.A.F. Station at Chharra, No.2945 Field Squadron found the camp they were allocated appalling. The leaking huts had been used as cow houses, there were no sanitation or water supply, no cooking utensils and any furniture was destroyed or damaged. Despite this the squadron continued with it training programme.

No.4402 A.A. Flight spent time at the airfield at Dohazari constructing grenade pits, building the units oven, armoury work and tidying up the cemetery, making it quite presentable. Those men on parade where split into patrolling the aerodrome and keeping the local Natives in order. The flight moved to the aerodrome at Chiringa and although the roads to the aerodrome where in terrible condition, the men used planks, matting and a winch lorry to get the loads through to the new camp. A complete reconnaissance of the aerodrome found 18 Gun Pits, with only 4 unserviceable, the initial tasks of digging slit trenches and latrines were quickly completed. Six Gun Post tri-pods were sunk and gave complete field of fire for the whole aerodrome and were the maximum the flight could man. With 12 men on gun crew duty and a further 12 either in hospital, sick or on other duties, only 5 airmen were available to relieve the crews. With a commitment to undertake a 6-man night patrol of the aerodrome, the ability to man the six Gun Pits started to look unsustainable.

The defence plan of the airstrip at Cox's Bazaar was agreed and incorporated as part of the Major defence scheme for 26 Division. No.4403 A.A. Flight at last had authorisation to collect it allocation of vehicles and the establishment was increased to include a Cook, although it was still being argued that a Clerk was still required, to undertake the mountain of orderly room work. The C.O. of No.4410 A.A. Flight spent time during the month in charge of both No.4401 and No.4403 A.A. Flight, allowing the other commanders time to go on leave and undertake other duties.

The domestic camp of No.4404 A.A. Flight at the airfield at Feni had been completed and arrangements were no in place to construct 12 Gun Pits.

Gun Pits were still being constructed at the Chittagong Aerodrome, with 5 being completed by the beginning of the month. Following the theft of equipment from No.45 Squadron dispersal areas, search parties were organised, using all available Gunners from No.4405 A.A. Flight, where two Natives were apprehended and handed over to the R.A.F. Police. The flights Cookhouse and water supply were still out of order and had been so since March. Although plans have been submitted to Group H.Q., approval was still needed before work could take place. A 'Backers-Up' course took place, with two corporal instructors from the Depot. As all units taking part are presently quite dispersed, thoughts were expressed around having a training camp at the South of the aerodrome, which would ensure better attendance and reduced Tiffin times, whilst giving the Instructors their own store. The Gun Pits of No.3 Section, No.4407 A.A. Flight, were near completion and the arrival of four 5/15 cwt Chevrolet trucks, reinforced the need to have Gunners trained as drivers and in the skills of maintaining vehicles.

The rains of the Monsoon still caused disruption to the operational activities of units in August. In preparation for their move to Imphal, training continued for No.3 Rifle Flight of No.2941 Field Squadron at the Agartala aerodrome, including range practice with Rifle, Bren and Sten Guns. The remaining rifle flights continued with their training programme, including route marches, zeroing of Rifles, advanced handling of Bren Guns on fixed lines and bayonet practice. By the middle of the month No.3 Rifle Flight was entrained and on their way to Imphal.

At the aerodrome at Comilla, No.2942 Field Squadron received news confirming that the unit vehicles were at Calcutta and had been there since around mid-June, drivers were immediately to despatched to retrieve them. Several officers and N.C.O.'s of No.2941 Field Squadron visited the unit and had the pleasure of watching the squadron football team beat the R.A.F. Police, followed by entertainment at the Mess. The first practice "Stand To" was held and although most men were caught unawares, all were ready in 'Battle Order, within 7 minutes. All personnel were inoculated against Cholera and other inoculations were bought up to date.

The problems that No.2945 Field Squadron were facing at the R.A.F Chharra, were short lived, as a signal soon arrived ordering the squadron to move to the aerodrome at Feni. By the end of the month the whole of the squadron had arrived at Feni and eight 15 cwt trucks had arrived, allowing the squadron to recce and patrol the key areas of the aerodrome. No.4404 A.A. Flight were able to man on average 4/5 Gun Posts and 2 additional Gun Posts could be manned within a few minutes, even though the unit was 12 men below strength. A mock raid of the aerodrome was undertaken by Hurricanes simulating a bombing attack, which proved very useful and several lessons were learnt. Further surprised air raid warnings were sounded to help correct the previous days mistakes.

At the aerodrome at Chiringa, the first eight planes of No.261 Squadron arrived and dispersed along the air strips, as the taxi-tracks had not been complete. No.4402 A.A. Flight manned five Gun Posts, but due to the heavy rains, two crews had to be taken off, as the Posts had flooded, and the remaining planes arrival was delayed until there was a change in the weather. Near the end of the month, No.261 Squadron left the station and No.4402 A.A. Flights commanding officer took temporary responsibility of all the R.A.F. interests at the station.

No.4403 A.A. Flight, at Cox's Bazaar airfield became the only unit left to defence the strip, as the resident Gunners of No.136 Squadron detachment were ordered to the Depot to undertake Regiment training. Being practically up to strength and having recently started its suppressive Malaria treatment, Gun Posts were continually manned, and with 4 posts having quadruple Browning Guns, a heavy volume of fire could be directed at any hostile act. Sickness though, was clearly evident from airmen proceeding to the Hill Party at Shillong, where practically 50% of personnel reported sick on arrival. M.T. training for Regiment personnel had been adopted by No.224 Group, which would prove to be invaluable. The units allotted vehicles had been identified at Chittagong, however instructions were issued that they would not be released until after the Monsson.

The allocated vehicles for No.4405 A.A. Flight were collected and returned to the aerodrome at Chittagong, but because of the present conditions of the roads and tracks, the vehicles have to remain parked on the aerodrome, the only reliable vehicles for these conditions being four wheeled drives. All guns and ammunition were now kept on the aerodrome and guarded 24 hours a day. Practice firing of the quadruple Brownings of No.4407 A.A. Flight at No.879 A.M.E.S. resulted in trigger mechanism difficulties, with non-synchronisation between inner and outer guns. Orders for the redistribution of guns and mountings were received by Air H.Q., allocating the unit with 18 Brownings, twin mounted on Motley Stork frames.

With the tail end of the Monsoon now approaching, the month of September saw the training programme of No.2941 Field Squadron at Agartala Aerodrome in full swing, commencing with route marches and continuing with fieldcraft and weapon training, including range work with Rifles and Ben Guns. All flights practiced the siting of guns for Ack Ack defence of the camp area and ground protection. No.3 Rifle Flight returned from its forward area deployment with the Army and further deployments were cancelled. An increase in sickness was starting to be seen, in particular, the returning flight from the forward area of Imphal, had seen ten cases of Malaria being admitted to hospital.

With routine operations in place at the aerodrome at Comilla, No.2942 Field Squadron provided Officers and an armed flight to attend a special Church parade, in celebration of the 3rd anniversary of the "Battle of Britain". Success in sport saw the Squadron football team win the 'Benode Shield', in the Comilla League.

With a satisfactory inspection of No.4402 A.A. Flight, by the Defence Officer at the airfield at Chiringa, hopes were raised that soon more leave would be granted, as a number of men had not had any for the past 12 months. By the end of the month, No.4432 A.A. Flight had arrived at the airfield in support of its A.A. and general defence.

News was received at the beginning of the month of the Allied Invasion of Italy, which for No.4403 A.A. Flight, boosted morale up tremendously. At Chittagong Aerodrome confirmation had been received that Japanese Reconnaissance planes had flown over the area. Notification by the end of the month was given that the Japanese were now moving their aircraft to forward airfields and black outs were now enforced. During the month the flight apprehended two suspicious looking Natives, who were found to be in possession of the nominal rolls of the Bofor Gun personnel and another two Natives in possession of Bamboo, taken from the dispersal areas. Instructions for a sharp watch were given. No.4405 A.A. Flight were busy on the aerodrome siting and building their Gun Posts, whilst No.4407 A.A. Flight continued its firing practice at their respective A.M.E.S. sites, where they were still having difficulties with the trigger mechanisms of the quadruple Browning Guns. Log books were introduced for each Gun Post were all aircraft observed would be recorded. Gun Teams where now also being routinely moved to practice the mobility of the unit and to give the Gunners experience of new conditions. A comprehensive annual training scheme was issued to all units, which provided for a total of 216 periods of 40 minutes each, which would unlikely be achievable with current manning levels. The unit was ordered to move to the aerodrome at Agartala, and be in place no later than 16.00hrs on the 2nd October.

All eight Gun Crews of No.4404 A.A. Flight 'Stood Too' at Feni Aerodrome, following the siting of a twin engine enemy recce plane, flying in a north-easterly direction, at approximately 20,000ft, no action was taken. L.A.C. Trade Tests were held with five out to the ten AC's being recommended for promotion. Several airmen also proceeded to undertake external courses, four to Calcutta on separate M.T. and Camouflage courses and two to Ambala, for technical armament training.

With the end of the Monsoon, the month of October saw training for No.2941 Field Squadron at Argartala, focused on ground defence and attack, with several flight level exercises both day and night. The squadron also provided a Guard of Honour for the Supreme Commander, who's visit was cancelled. With the first Regiment unit to complete a move by road in India, No.4407 A.A. Flight arrived at the aerodrome at Agartala, without incident, although it was observed that complete mobility would be impossible if the units full scale of equipment had to be transported. The unit took over the L.A.A. Defence of the area around the main strip, with agreement of No.4401 A.A. Flight, manning borrowed Lewis Guns until replacement Browning Guns could be received.

A new syllabus of training for No.2942 Field Squadron was now in force at Comilla and carried out throughout the month. During the month the whole squadron, except the duty flight, attended a Mass Parade, for the visit of the Supreme Commander, Lord Louis Mountbatten.

Following an air raid near the airfield at Chittagong, men of No.4403 A.A. Flight searched the target area and found four unexploded bombs around the M.T. yard, barricades were erected and the R.E notified. No.4405 A.A. Flight took over the responsibility of No.4407 A.A. Flight, following their move. Splitting the unit into 3 Sections to defend separate A.M.E.S. sites.

The month of November training for No.2941 Field Squadron, at Argartala Aerodrome, started with flight fire and movement exercises, which continued throughout the month with Bivouac and bridge construction, range and grenade practice. Following the apprehension of two Natives earlier in the month, following several cases of sabotage, a special night time sweep (utilising all Regiment units) was undertaken of the whole site. A significant number of civilian were rounded up and brought into camp, where they were handed over to the Wing S.P.'s. Instruction was given to all Regiment personnel on the Re-arming and Re-fuelling of aircraft and soon took on these duties by flight, for a week at a time. Near the end of the month enemy aircraft were sighted at around 16,000ft above the airfield, but no bombs were dropped. Patrols were sent out following a report of descending parachutists, but nothing found. During the monthly waning moon period, all A.A. Gun Posts were fully manned. A raid by around 12 Type 99 aircraft, escorted by a small number of Type 01 Oscars fighters, bombed the airfield from about 20,000ft, destroying No.4407 A.A. Flight's Office, some huts and only slight damage to the runway, which was soon repaired. The camp barber was taken into custody and handed over, after telling an airman about an air raid, ten minutes before it happened.

By the end of the third week of November, No.2942 Field Squadron had moved, by road and rail from Comilla Aerodrome to the "Hay" forward airstrip near Ramu. Whilst at Feni Aerodrome, No.2945 Field Squadron continued developing it training programme, with a squadron level jungle exercise, taking place at the beginning of the month and the continuation of its monthly programme of night patrols at flight level, range practice and other routine training. A signal was read out by the C.O. giving warning that Japanese aircraft, including a new dive bomber, had been moved up within range of the airfield and that an attack was likely. T.O.E.T.'s (trade tests) were undertaken for the whole squadron, to bring all men to standard, in particular, to bring the A.C.1's up to L.A.C. standard. A squadron sports day was held, with running events up to 1 mile, walking, relay, tug of war, long and high jump, as well as cricket ball throwing. The tournament was won by No.1 Rifle Flight and a Concert was held in the evening entirely composed by the squadron, where the C.O. handed out sports day prizes. Volunteers were called to make a Composite Flight for special jungle training and once settled in, a larger force was set up and sent to attack this newly formed flight. Many lessons were learnt and the men found the experience both enjoyable and useful. Squadron personnel were deployed to crash sites during the month, guarding aircraft which included a Japanese Army 100 Recce plane and a Hurricane. An air raid near the end of the month by around 10 bombers and a fighter escort dropped their bombs at approximately 20,000ft, too high for the A.A. Guns, causing little damage.

At Chittagong airfield, both No.4403 and No.4405 A.A. Flights where on high alert during the waning moon period and although there were several air raids, there was no enemy action against the airfield or the A.M.E.S. sites.

The move to the airfield at Dohazari took less than 48 hours, following receipt of the movement order, for No.4404 A.A. Flight. The domestic site didn't take long to clean up, but the Cookhouse was not ready and it lacked water facilities, so immediate feeding of the men came from 167 Wing. No.4442 A.A. Flight arrived, lacking a flight commander and was taken under the wing of No.4404 A.A. Flight.

Three Gun Pits with quadruple Browning Guns were manned and by the end of the month three more pits were completed.

The new unit at the airfield at Cox's Bazar, No.4422 A.A. Flight, quickly settled in, with a number of men going on aircraft Re-arming and Re-fuelling courses. It wasn't long though until the flight commander was making a reconnaissance of the "Reindeer I" forward airstrip, with hints for a move at the end of the month.

At the Agartala Aerodrome, December would be a month of routine and progressive training for No.2941 Filed Squadron and the continual fulfilment of the new policy to undertake aircraft Re-arming and Re-fuelling activities. More exercises in boat building and river crossing were undertaken and an exercise against "Paratroops" was considered not to be a complete success, as the 'airborne' troops lacked an aggressive spirit, although the squadron's defensive position and mobile reserve were judged as good. Three crews were sent to Comilla to pick up the squadrons A.F.V.'s and on return, following preliminary trials, seemed satisfactory.

Detachments from No.2942 Field Squadron assisted in Re-fuelling and Re-arming R.A.F. and U.S.A.F. aircraft at Ramu and providing night patrols at Reindeer I and Lyon airstrips.

The flights out on recce in the surrounding area of the Feni Airfield had established an excellent camp and observed the various points at which the airfield could be observed. The continued training had now built No.2945 Field Squadron up to a good level of fitness and the use of the jungle camp for flight in defence and attack proved invaluable.

At the airfield at Chiringa, No.4402 A.A. Flight were now the only Regiment unit on-site, following the move of No.4432 A.A. Flight. By the end of the month the flight commander had received instructions to move to Joari.

No.4403 A.A. Flight, with the receipt of mountings and ancillary equipment, were now nearly fully equipped. An air raid warning at the beginning of the month, initially with no aircraft sited was later reported to have been 100 aircraft, 50 miles out to sea. Reports were received that Japanese Commando Raids could be possible at the Cox's Bazar airfield, resulting in all night patrols being doubled. The Supreme Commander, Lord Louis Mountbatten visited the station, who gave an informal talk to all men.

Several air raid warnings at Dohazari Aerodrome saw no action or aircraft for the Gun crews of No.4404 A.A. Flight. Liberator aircraft from No.159 and No.335 Squadrons landed at the aerodrome on their way to the first large scale raid on Bangkok. All Gun Pits were manned when a large formation of unidentified aircraft was seen but too high to recognise. They turned out to be the aircraft that bombed the aerodrome at Chittagong. Near the end of the month the quadruple Brownings were change to Twin Browning s and six Gun Pits are now manned.

The three sections of No.4405 A.A. Flight, defending No.378, 879 and 5029 A.M.E.S. on receiving their conversion kits, were now transferring to Twin Browning mountings and siting a new gun at each site.

The move of No.4407 A.A. Flight from Agartala to the landing ground at Parashuram, took place in the latter part of the month. The unit spent the rest of the month siting and digging in its Gun Pits.

At the "Reindeer I" airstrip, No.4422 A.A. Flight moved to its new positions, with No.1 Section manning 2 Gun Posts at the Northern end of the strip and No.2 Section manning 3 Gun Posts at the Southern end of the strip, close to their tented accommodation.

Although all units would have had to maintain normal operations on Xmas Day, it was still a day for celebrating. Most units would have had a formal meal, normally served by Officers and N.C.O.'s, with the men each having a beer, a tot of rum, cigarettes and a cigar. Larger units would have enjoyed a sports day and a concert.

The map and table below show the locations of each of the newly formed units as at the 31st December 1943.

Map showing the location of R.A.F.R. Units as at 31st December 1943

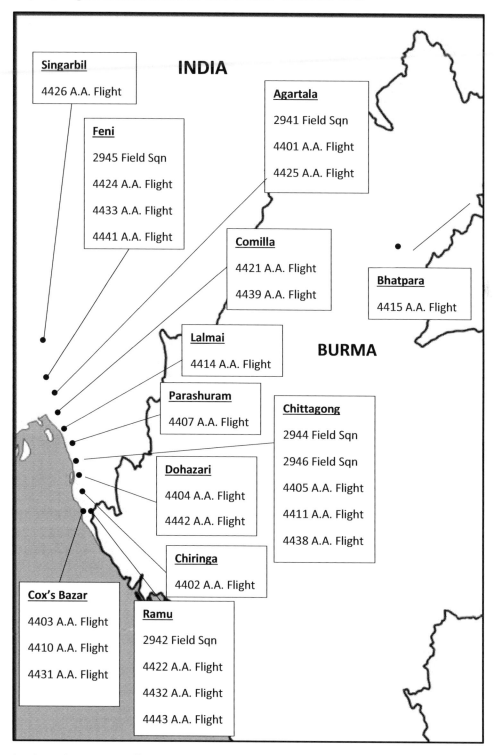

Singarbil
4426 A.A. Flight

INDIA

Agartala
2941 Field Sqn
4401 A.A. Flight
4425 A.A. Flight

Feni
2945 Field Sqn
4424 A.A. Flight
4433 A.A. Flight
4441 A.A. Flight

Comilla
4421 A.A. Flight
4439 A.A. Flight

Bhatpara
4415 A.A. Flight

Lalmai
4414 A.A. Flight

BURMA

Parashuram
4407 A.A. Flight

Chittagong
2944 Field Sqn
2946 Field Sqn
4405 A.A. Flight
4411 A.A. Flight
4438 A.A. Flight

Dohazari
4404 A.A. Flight
4442 A.A. Flight

Chiringa
4402 A.A. Flight

Cox's Bazar
4403 A.A. Flight
4410 A.A. Flight
4431 A.A. Flight

Ramu
2942 Field Sqn
4422 A.A. Flight
4432 A.A. Flight
4443 A.A. Flight

(Author adapted - http://d-maps.com/carte.php?num_car=126&lang=en)

R.A.F. Regiment Units in 224 Group R.A.F. – December 1943

Area	A.A. Flight	Field Squadron
Singarbil	4426	
Agartala	4401, 4425	**2941**
Comilla	4421, 4439	
Bhatpara	4415	
Lalmai	4414	
Chandpur	4409	
Feni	4424, 4433, 4441	**2945**
Parashuram	**4407**	
Chittagong	**4405**, 4411, 4438	2944, 2946
Dohazari	**4404**, 4442	
Chiringa	**4402**	
Cox's Bazaar	**4403, 4410**, 4431	
Ramu	**4422**, 4432, 4443	**2942**
Establishment Numbers	24 A.A. Flights = 48 Officers and 888 Airmen	5 Field Squadrons = 30 Officers 790 Airmen

Operational Diaries

April
2941 Field Squadron – Settling in at Agartala Aerodrome

> The Squadron was established in No.7 Camp, which was not suitable for permanent occupation, being a temporary camp adjacent to a Kutcha Strip to provide temporary accommodation for an incoming Squadron for a short period.

> Settling in and organising cooking facilities, water and fuel.

> Personnel employed in jungle clearing around buildings and throughout the camp, as the area was very overgrown. Cooks were called for and volunteers initiated to cooking mysteries, mason volunteers made field kitchens, ablutions and wells, and those not employed in jungle clearing became fuel cutters. For about a week the squadron became pioneers and eventually made the camp comfortable and sanitary – but the water supply question was always a problem. On 29/4/34 the Group Defence Officer visited the Squadron and plans were prepared for siting and erecting a new camp of a permanent nature for the resident R.A.F. Regiment Squadron. Arrangements were made for the Squadron to send leave parties to SHILLONG for 14 days.

May
2941 Field Squadron – Operational at Agartala Aerodrome

> The establishment does not provide for G.D. Clerk, Cook & Butcher, Armourers or Medical Orderlies and whilst the Cook & Butcher question could be dealt with by volunteer cooks – which meant taking men off training and off the fighting strength – the lack of a Clerk in the office and Medical Orderly for giving First Aid, was affecting the organisation of work. Several changes were made in trying to find two suitable A.C's for office duties and an untrained officer as Adjutant did not help matters. Eventually this difficulty was overcome to some extent and the Squadron Orderly Room gradually began to function. Lack of a Medical Orderly meant that personnel had to go sick for minor complaints or injuries and travel round trip of 6 miles to S.S.Q. daily. Efforts were made to obtain posting

of a Medical Orderly and although a posting was made it proved ineffectual. A Medical Orderly should be posted to the Squadron and until this addition is made to the establishment the organisation will always have a weak spot.

The first Hill party of 37 men and one officer left for SHILLONG on 3/5/43 for 14 days.

Training commenced as from 1/5/43 and it was soon evident that several men were unfit for Squadron work. The Sick Parade mounted up and a Medical Inspection showed that about 18 men had some form of complaint which incapacitated them from strenuous work. This matter was taken up with Group and arrangements made for a Medical Inspection of all doubtful cases and replacements to be obtained from the Depot for such unfit personnel. The C.D.O. BENGAL visited the Squadron on 6/5/43.

The VICEROY OF INDIA visited the Station on 8/5/43 and the Squadron provided a Guard of Honour, and personal guards throughout his visit.

It became very evident that the old spirit of the "Special" Squadron had been lost at SECUNDERABAD and the new 2901 Squadron had yet to identify itself. The change of officers, influx of new personnel and – to some extent – the very humid and relaxing climate at AGARTALA, were probably responsible for this lack of spirit and enthusiasm which had been so evident in the "Special" Squadron. Discipline had to be tightened and more drill training incorporated into the training programme before any improvement could be obtained, but a firm hand soon produced results.

On 13/5/43 No.2 Flight proceeded to SHILLONG.

Four 15cwt Chevrolet lorries and one Jeep were obtained from Group but the general equipment of the Squadron was still a feature affecting training. Bren Guns, discharger cups, cycles, motor cycles, M.T. vehicles and other equipment such as prismatic binoculars, compasses etc., were still unobtainable. The new camp was sited and work of erection commenced.

No.3 Flight returned from SHILLONG on 16/5/43 but their officer remained behind in hospital. The Adjutant F/O. REDINGTON, took over this Flight and from this time the Squadron was without an Adjutant at Headquarters and the Orderly Room staff had to run the organisation with the Commanding Officer doubling his job with that of Adjutant. Discipline throughout the Squadron was not yet up to a good standard and Officers i/c Flights had insufficient experience in man management to produce the best results. The old "Special" Squadron personnel wanted to get into action and cut more training and the new personnel, drafted to the Squadron at SECUNDERBAD, were, in several cases, physically not up to the work and in other cases, missing the easy life of an A.A. Flight. But improvement continued whilst attempts were made to get the unfit personnel replaced.

Petty thieving by native of surrounding villages was rampant and had been a source of trouble throughout the Station before 2901 Squadron arrived. Action was taken and villages raided. All property was recovered, suspect arrested and thieving completely stopped. A short lesson having been given, local inhabitants were reformed citizens.

A new system of training – lightest possible clothing and equipment for all tactical exercises – produced good results and before the end of the month the physical condition of the men- apart from those medically unfit – and stamina greatly improved and this improvement was reflected in better discipline. The weather remained very humid but late rains commenced towards the end of the month and helped to alleviate conditions.

The discipline strictures during the month had led to the reduction of two A/SGTs: to CPLs: and four A/CPLs: to L.A.C's, with a Temp: SGT: recommended for replacement and a Temp: CPL: for reduction to L.A.C. These reversions were necessary as the standard of N.C.O's was deplorable and those unfit and unsuitable for further training were reduced. An A/CPL: was promoted to A/SGT: and a L.A.C. to A/CPL. The vacancies were left unfilled. The shortage of officers, one away in hospital and one with the Hill Party, and the detachment of the whole Flight to SHILLONG, added to which an average of ten men in hospital and twelve men unfit for duty but present on the camp, made it impossible to carry out Squadron training. Training was concentrated on obtaining a better physical standard, improving discipline.

By the end of May, 2901 Squadron were becoming a Unit and the physical standards of all personnel, including officers, was improving. Organised games was a daily feature of training and helped considerably in fostering the competitive spirit.

A great improvement in all directions, physical, discipline, Flight organisation, Squadron administration and spirit de corps was evident by the end of the month and if equipment arrives and the unfit personnel are replaced, also an officer posted as Adjutant to replace P/O. BAXTER still in hospital, next month should show a progressive improvement. In April the Squadron were a collection of individuals, somewhat undisciplined – but by the end of May the Squadron was showing the form of a fighting Unit.

2942 Field Squadron – Settling in at Comilla Aerodrome

The quarters allotted to the Squadron proved to be excellent. They consist of an ex school, known as the Hundu Hostel which comprises single storey stone buildings set in 3 sides of a square round a large clean tank, (Mens accommodation and officers) with basha's on the fourth side for the Ack-Ack Flight. There is plenty of room and the whole forms one self contained compound. A small bungalow 50 yds up the road is used as the Officers Mess.

The remainder of the month of May was occupied in settling in, laying on guards and Patrols on the aerodrome which had to be reconnoitred, making local contacts with the adjoining Army Units, the Station Commander etc., and preparing and putting into operation a Training Programme.

The men rapidly recovered from the rigours of their journey and settled in cheerfully.

On 21st the C.O. and F/Lt Cattell went to Chittagong to contact the G.D.O. personally at 224 Group H.Q. and returned on the morning of the 23rd. On the 26th the G.D.O. S/Ldr Gordon visited the Unit and spent the night. The rest of the month was quite uneventfull.

June
2941 Field Squadron – Operational at Agartala Aerodrome

Training hours were revised to meet with climatic conditions and the following times laid down as standard for the rains period:-

Reveille - 05.15hrs: Breakfast -05.45hrs: First Parade - 06.30-08.30hrs

Second Parade - 09.00-11.30hrs: Tiffin - 12.30hrs: Afternoons Parade 15.00-16.00hrs: Compulsory Games - 16.15-17.15hrs:

This gives 6 ½ hrs training a day - including games. On route March or Field Exercise days the morning period is continuous and completed at 11.00hrs: The First Period of training 06.30 - 08.300hrs:is carried out in P.T. Kit, with Rifles only, and all work done in fast time. For the following periods dress varies according to training being done. One day a week is a free day for the Squadron, Sunday is an ordinary working day with a Church Parade substituted for one of the training hours.

The rains are late this year and consequently the climatic conditions are oppressive and not conductive to good conditions for training. The District is particularly for it's high humidity at this time of the year and in all my 23 years in the East I have never experienced such trying conditions. Training is, however, carried on normally and although a few cases of heat exhaustion occur, the men stand up to the conditions very well on the whole and only those who are not fit for Regiment duties fall out. No.2 Flight returned from SHILLONG on the 2nd and 24 men of No.1 Flight left for SHILLONG on the 3rd.

The Sergeant of No.2 Flight collapsed on Parade two days after returning from SHILLONG, and was admitted to Hospital. The SHILLONG Hill Parties have not been altogether an unmixed blessing as each party has left two or more men in Hospital at SHILLONG and on return to AGARTALA, the men feel the heat.

The weather changed and for a while it appeared that the rains had broken at last - but fine weather again set in and humidity was high and conditions trying again.

The Squadron took over Night Security Patrols on the Aerodrome and provided 21 men, 3 Patrols each with 6 men and 1 N.C.O., nightly. This somewhat interfered with training as the Patrols coming off duty had to be excused the first morning period of two hours.

P/O. BAXTER was still away in Hospital and a new Adjutant not yet arrived.

The BISHOP of ASSAM visited the Camp and took the Sunday Service.

Training in Flight Tactical Exercises has commenced and it is evident that officers require more training in handling their Flights. No.1 Flight returned from SHILLONG on the 18th: the weather has been very hoy and sticky during the week with only a little rain on one day.

Training on Jungle Warfare was intensified and the Commanding Officer took over this work himself as his 23 years jungle experience fitted him for this training. The work of the men improved and by the end of the month this form of training had shown great advancement. It was still not possible to train as a Squadron owing to the 20 or so medically unfit men still awaiting replacement, SHILLONG HILL Parties drawing on the strength and officers and N.C.O's not being up to establishment. Equipment was still deficient, vehicles, signalling apparatus, prismatic compasses, Bren Guns, Discharger Cups etc. Six men were sent to Calcutta for training as cooks and sixteen men on a Signals Course and these parties returned before the end of the month. Eighteen men of No.1 Flight and details of other Flights left for SHILLONG on 24/6/43. F/O. SUTTON was posted to the Squadron as Adjutant on 29/6/43.

2942 Field Squadron – Operational at Comilla Aerodrome

607 Squadron R.A.F.R. Detachment arrived from Shillong F/O. Chaffin (Adjutant 2902 Sqdn) admitted to B.M.H. Hospital. 607 Squadron R.A.F.R. det. take over Ack-Ack post on aerodrome, 12 Lewis guns sent to 224 Group to exchange for Brens. Reconnoitred existing A.A. Post on aerodrome.

Open range at Maynamati 4 clear days.

S/Ldr Hosking, President of District Court-Martial at Agartala. Visit of Brig. T Henry to Maynamati. He met all Unit Commanders at 09-00 hrs.

Visit of C.D.O. Bengal Command (W/C Fowke).
Took over additional Ack-Ack post on aerodrome making five. Should have manned 6 but A.A. Flight not strong enough owing to sickness.

L.D.C. appointed to Comilla. Major Tiffin of Border Regt.

Uneventful day, fired Sten guns.

C.O. went to Chandpur to collect stores. Stayed overnight.

F/O Chaffin returned from Hospital. Signal received that we are to be inspected by A.O.C. in C tomorrow. Concert by N Staffs Regt. Band.
Trying out new Training ground. F/O Hunter-Arnudel re-posted to 113 Squadron and joins our Mess.
Taking over another Gun post today, making 6 now manned on aerodrome. Fighter Ops Guard mounted last night. A.O.Cs. in C visit did not materialise.
2nd Shillong party leaves, the 1st party is remaining till 21st but P/O Budgen has been signalled R.T.U. F/O Chaffin and F/Lt Cattell proceed on 10 days leave, the first named on hospital recommended.
Band of N Staffs Regt gave concert in camp ground at 2-30hrs. Took over 20 Browning guns from 113 Squadron.
P/O Budgen returned 03-00 hrs from Shillong.
Church parade in camp. Wing Padre.
Note received that our transport (9 trucks) has now been allotted and to be collected from Calcutta.
Last few days have been quite uneventful, training has proceeded despite the weather and the Squadron is making very good progress. Tonight we played Op's room at soccer on a rain sodden ground and beat them 9-nil. The physical condition of the Squadron is extremely good.
Fired all 9 Bren guns (3 are on loan to the Army) with spare barrels at Maymanati today. Jorden is digging a Grenade throwing pit to be used next week.
Today the greater part of the Squadron is out at the Training ground throwing live bombs. The remainder has gone to the Range to fire rifle and bren guns.
There are only eleven AC1's in the Squadron, one being in hospital. The Remaining ten were Trade Tested today and eight passed for LAC.
The G.D.O. 224 Group, S/Ldr Gordon comes up tomorrow. Today nothing to report beyond usual routine.

4402 A.A. Flight – Operational at Dohazari

The Borderers arrived during the morning and established themselves in billets making their own cooking arrangements. Expected to take men of both Flights who were not on Gun Post duty on to range for further firing practice, but unfortunately a heavy down pour lasting throughout the morning rendered this impactable. Men were therefore detailed to clean up their billets, which were in a muddy condition and assist with Armoury work under LAC. Negus – (F/O. Homers Detachment). Orders arrived that F/O Homers Flight were to proceed to Secunderabad at less than 24hrs notice. Therefore four men were detailed from No. 4352 A.A. Flight to take over their vacated gun positions.

Training was again intended, but a further down pour caused it to be cancelled. Owing to more men having to be provided for gun post duty and men in hospital coupled with the fact that four men are on permanent 'other duties' namely, cookhouse, driver, office and water/bowser/ Canteen, the parade numbered only six men. These were given gun cleaning and repair work around the Cookhouse which had suffered because of the storm on the previous evening. F/O Homer's Flight left the station and this Flight took over the full defence duties.

Heavy rain again, Roads now practically impassable. Three to Thornycroft borrowed from P/O Hogshaw i/c Working Party for Defence duties. Additional canvas covers fixed over fires outside cookhouse, Cook is experiencing great difficulty in starting fires outside cookhouse during the Monsoon period. A general clean up of Armoury was also made and 80,000 rounds of assorted .303 was set aside to be taken to Base Ordnance, Chittagong, at earliest opportunity. This surplus ammunition was left with us by No.135 Squadron who passed through here recently.

Men were instructed on Sten Gun handling and later fired. First from the Stationery position and later while advancing. Tendency was to shoot low, but tis will no doubt be rectified with further practice.

Approximately 80,000 rounds of spare ammunition deposited temporarily in our armoury by 135 Squadron was today transferred to the Base Ordnance Yard at Chittagong by a party of eight men under

Sgt. Birtles. This comprised the entire parade for the morning except for 3 Corporals. These N.C.O's personally undertook the task of cleaning and checking our spare Lewis Guns, which are later to replace those weapons now in use on the Gun Posts.

The Lewis Guns were cleaned yesterday were this morning taken to the Gun Posts and the original guns returned to the Armoury for cleaning. Sgt. Birtles took the entire parade on the firing of the Sten Gun, and later Lewis Guns. The ammunition used for the Lewis was the "time expired" rounds returned from the Gun Posts. The Gun behaved exceptionally well during the practice.

The men on parade were this morning put on cleaning spare Lewis magazines, rain rendering other tasks impossible. At 11.30hrs twenty men of the Flight were taken to the R.A.M.C. Capt. And received Cholera inoculations. No. 1459625 LAC. Bligh was today posted to 308 M.U. Manauri, Nr. Allahabad.

This Flight is renumbered to 4402 A.A. Flight for No.4352 A.A. Flight re Headquarters letter 224G/6201/194/Org. date 6/6/43. Late last night another man was taken to Hospital with an attack of fever, while this morning one man was discharged with 14 days sick leave. The morning until 11.00hrs was spent in cleaning out the baggage etc. of men of No.60 Sqdn Def Flight (P/O Homer) who are either in Hospital, absent without leave or deserters. At 11.00hrs the remainder of the Flight were inoculated against Cholera.

Only 4 men were available for Parade this morning. These men were detailed to Chittagong to hand in the baggage etc. and firearms of P/O Homers men. N.C.O. did the routine armoury work for the day.

Existing posts were withdrawn this morning and alternative positions sited. Reasons for withdrawal was mainly the fact that all aircraft has now left, that even dummy planes have been removed and furthermore the posts were in a water logged condition. It would seem obvious therefore that if an attack did come it would be directed against the domestic camp. The new positions which will be started tomorrow are on the river bank, in two cases (Easily drained) with further posts to the North and N. West of the Camp. Two men of P/O Homer's Flight reported and collected kit this evening from stores. All men on Parade were detailed to Chittagong under Sgt.

Birtles to collect Beer rations goods for canteen, and went to 92 E.S. for Gum Boots etc. The letter received from Group by this Unit was answered by F/Lt. Gory as per appen (5).

A fatigue party started work this morning on the new gun posts and succeeded in marking out and digging to the depth of some 2'6" or 3' after 12.00hrs. The sticky heat rendered further digging in the open impracticable. The theft by local natives of four of our inner tent linings was also discovered and in the afternoon a party of eight men under Sgt Birtles scoured the villages and attempted to find some trace of them. Only one man was brought in, however who was in possession of a gun cover. Of the tent linings no trace could be found. The man will be interrogated as soon as possible. F/LT. Gory again visited Charinga, in preparation of the Flight moving down there.

F/Lt. Gory visited Chittagong this morning to lay certain matters before Group. The parade was put on to filling Lewis magazines which were then fired, each man getting ample practice. Guns were then stripped and cleaned and the party carried on with Gun Post construction. This morning P/O Homers two men left with their kit for Secunderabad. No.1297498 LAC Parker was admitted to Chittagong Hospital.

The new cook posted here from Group, 1059351 AC1 Jones. Commenced his duties this morning. Today also six men namely, LAC's Harrison, Ratcliffe, Summer, Wetherill, Sparks and White departed for the Hill Station. The morning was spent on Armoury work.

No. 1414408 AC Hawkins was discharged from Hospital and was given five days light duty. The parade was told off into fatigue parties and continued with the construction of the new gun posts.

The men on parade again worked on the gun post construction.

The entire parade was this morning taken on to the range for the firing of Sten Guns and rifles. Rifles were fired from 100yds on to an improvised target, much smaller than the regulation pattern. Even taking into account the smallness of the target, however, the firing of the rifles was rather erratic. Firing of Stens on the other had was quite good.

Very few men now remain who have not fired each weapon (i.e. Lewis, Sten, Rifle). Those who have not fired have either been on Gun Post duty, duty in Chittagong or Hospital when firing has been the duty of the day. These men will be taken to the range as soon as possible. The Group Padre held a Church Service at the Canteen. The Canteen General Meeting was held today to elect a committee etc. as per appendix 6.

The new gun posted were manned for the first time today. Men not on gun post duty erected a tent near each post for use of spare men during the heat of the day. Posts were inspected by F/Lt. Gory, who pronounced himself satisfied. A Letter was received today from BPO India reference BPO/2001/3/A2 dated 18/6/43 Confirming 1351199 T/Cpl Birtles Gunner's appointment to A/Sgt (Paid) w.e.f. 9/4/43 and the authority to be quoted is A.H.Q. India Phonogram P3/980 dated 15/5/43.

Advantage was taken of the absence of rain, to dig drainage channels from the gun pits. Only one post of the four is to any extent undrainable. The task was a larger one than was at first anticipated and will take some little time to complete. The usual morning P.T. was followed by a dip in the river, restriction by the M.O. now being removed.

Two men were sent to Calcutta this morning on duty, a further three men and the Cook went to Chittagong on Canteen duty and is attempt to procure stock for the Cookhouse.

Heavy rain fell during the night making the drainage of gun pits more than ever urgent. Accordingly we devoted all our available men to drainage work. As stated previously, the job is very difficult, more so now that the earth is soaked and liable to fall in our drainage holes.

Owing to heavy rain, which fell continuously from yesterday morning onwards outdoor tasks were rendered impossible. Accordingly the men were detailed to construct rough piping out of some old metal to provide support for the roof and sides of the gun post drainage tunnels, which are now completed. A complete check was also made on the rifle and sten ammo. (original issue). This was found to be in good condition.

The men this morning were given "refresher" lectures on the Lewis Gun. Results were quite satisfactory, each man being up to standard. AC1 Hawkins and AC1 Kitchen were also given an LAC Test. Both men satisfied the requirements of the examiner. Only two AC's now remain to be passed out. These men are at present o duty in Calcutta and will be given a test upon their return.

A regrettable incident occurred at 14.00hrs when 1234366 LAC Chapman was drowned while bathing in the river.

Witnesses to the incident in which LAC. Chapman lost his life had their statements taken and signed this morning. F/Lt. Gory drafted a letter of which copies were sent to HQ 244 Group.

AHQ India, BPO Bombay. Owing to heavy rain rations had to be fetched to camp by a fatigue party in a Sampan. Permanent arrangements to ensure arrival of rations are underway.

A fatigue party again went out to collect rations. Of the remainder two did armoury work while the rest under Sgt. Birtles went on patrol down the river to attempt to discover some sign of LAC Chapman's body. After proceeding a considerable way down the river, however, the patrol retired and reported that as yet no trace of it could be found. Later on however, a native arrived in camp at 11.30hrs and reported the body as located about ¾ mile away. A party again went out and the body was brought in and identified. The funeral was held almost immediately. F/Lt. Gory reading the Burial Service, in the absence of a Padre. A General Salute was given.

The usual fatigue party went to collect rations. Heavy rain again fell and prevented any outdoor activity. The remainder of the Parade, therefore was given a refresher on the Sten Gun, the lecture consisting mainly of questions and answers. No.166 Wing Defence Officer visited the station today.

The weather unexpectedly cleared this morning. Out of a Parade of 17 men, four stood by as Gun Crews, four went to fetch rations, four did armoury work and the remaining five were detailed to lay a net screen over the grave of LAC. Chapman, as a prevention against Jackals etc. The two men who went to Calcutta on June 19th returned today.

The weather being fine, a parade was held this morning, at which all personal weapons were inspected. Immediately afterwards billets were examined. Both weapons and billets were found satisfactory. Only two of our 4 gun posts are at present usable, owing to collapse of sides due to heavy rain. This Unit has been advised by No.224 Wing that four 15 cwt Lorries have been assigned to us, it is hoped that they will not arrive for some time, as the state of the roads at present would necessitate them being laid up for the monsoon period, and in all probability, being U.S. at the end of it. It has been found that the only vehicle of any use here at this time of the year is one possessing four wheel drive.

A further six men LAC's, Lawson, Aspden, Clarke, Kitchen, Parker and Naven, comprising our second Hill Party, left this station this morning. As the first one has not yet returned, this means that there are now 12 men absent from this Unit. After Supplying gun crews and ration party, therefore there were no men available for lecture or any other work.

Besides ration party, a party was also detailed thing morning to construct an improvised oven for the Cookhouse. Bricks and material were collected but heavy rain began to fall and work had to be stopped.

A letter 15th June '43 reference 224G/S 6200/61/Org has been received from Headquarters No.224 Group giving authorisation for the employment of the following by R.A.F. Flights:-

Cooks BJ Grade I - 1

Cooks BJ Grade II - 1

Sweepers 2

Water Carriers 1 } Total wages not to exceed Rps. 138 per Month.

The above are to be employed at nerrick rates of pay and are in temporary employment awaiting an official establishment for the enrolled followers.

This is a great help and solves some of the difficulties mentioned in this Units letter dated 10th Jan 43 and shown in appendix No.5.

4403 A.A. Flight – Operational at Cox's Bazaar

Weather – sporadic showers of rain. Canteen opened for unit.
224 GROUP DEFENCE OFFICER S/L GORDON visited the unit. General policy discussed with him. He was satisfied with and approved of the siting and construction of the gun pits.
Flight number now changed to 4403 A.A. Flight. AHQ Signal 023 dated the 4-6-1943 refers.
Very heavy rain for four days now, all low ground flooded to an extent of three to six inches, gun pits standing up well, ideal monsoon pit seems to be one built entirely of sandbags is bricked half way and sandbagged the remaining half. The base of the gun pit should be raised well above ground level with an outlet for the water that forms during heavy storms.
Roads impassable for vehicles, except the bamboo taxying tracks around the strips and even they are showing signs of wear and tear.
Our only vehicle a three ton Chevrolet keeps breaking down, M.T. pool here have only three vehicles serviceable so that no help can be extended from there. We have to waste man hours servicing the gun posts and bringing rations. Units coming forward should have their full complement of M.T. with them/
Weather fine. Made reconnaissance of the strip and country around with Brigade Major and Senior Administrative Commandant 26th Division, discussed and made an appreciation with a view to defence against attack by enemy ground troops. Conclusion reached was that an infantry company should be detailed to give support to the RAF in case of ground or airborne attack, but that no other special provisions need be made as the strip will be included in the general defence plan for COX'S BAZAAR. The present L.M.G. A.A. positions were considered quite adequate for their role.
Trained cook posted to the unit two days ago, already the standard of the food and consequently morale has risen a great deal.
Notified that a member of this unit is suffering with Cerebral Malaria (MT) at Shillong Rest Camp, and Dangerously ill. B.P.O. notified.
Informed by 224 GROUP DEFENCE OFFICE that four vehicles have been allocated to us, and to make arrangements to collect them from

Calcutta. M.T. pool here consented to provide drivers for this purpose.
Further communications from Group Defence Office stating that steps were being taken to collect and deliver the vehicles direct to units.
Weather exceedingly fine.
Unbroken period of fine weather.

4404 A.A. Flight – Operational at Feni

One Corporal and six airmen proceeded on leave to No.3 Hill Depot.
Air Raid Alert at 1445, lasting for half an hour. Four gun posts were manned, but had transport been available, it would have been possible to man another three posts. Against an establishment of four, the Flight is equipped with only one vehicle, which was out on duty at the time of the Alert.
Amendment No.97 to formation Order No.377. Authority for change of designation of Flight from No.4334 A/A to No.4404 A/A.
First signs of Monsoon. Heavy rains. All gun crews withdrawn.
One B.D.R. Cook attached to the Flight for duties.
Continuous rain. Most gun posts rendered unserviceable.
Ref. letter 224 G/S.6200/61/Org, authority to employ the following unenrolled followers, pending an establishment for enrolled followers. 1 Cook B.T. Grade I 1 Cook B.T. Grade II 2 Sweepers 1 Water Carrier} Total wages not to exceed Rs 138 per month. First Hill Party returns.
Second Hill Party proceeds.

4405 A.A. Flight – Operational at Chittagong

Work proceeding on gunpits.
New camp nearly completed - should be finished tomorrow with the exception of the Orderly Room & Armoury. 166 Wing Flight left for the Depot.

Moved the domestic quarters of North Camp extension today. OC Flight proceeded to Cox's Bazaar.
No.4411 A.A. Flight RAFR – F/O Hilsden in Command –moved into North Camp today & occupied the buildings vacated by 166 Wing Flight. OC Flight returned from Cox's Bazaar.
NIL.
Flight Canteen started on "slarcloldus" basis – initial capital Rs5 per man.
One Corporal and seven AC's detached to HQ 224 Group for squad duties. Heavy rain during the day prevented work on the gun posts.
Heavy rain – south end of runway under water. Nearly all gun posts and the approaches to same and all low lying ground underwater, making construction work very difficult. Guns were taken out of flooded gun posts and mounted on dry ground.
One .5 BROWNING pit and one quadruple browning pit finished & manned.
Heavy rain ceased but road to North Camp under water & breaking up rapidly. If this road becomes unserviceable for vehicles all water, rations and guns will have to be carried 300 yds to the camp.
Road to North Camp impassable. Both 30 cwt wheeled lorries became bogged last night. MES. Supplied coolies and sections of bamboo to build up the road. In the meantime all water for washing, cooking & drinking has to be rationed.
OC Flight contacted OC. 166 WING and requested that a hut be built on the aerodrome. The function of this hut would be to provide a "lock up" on the aerodrome in which guns and ammunition could be kept & at the same time provide sleeping accommodation for the next duty crews. This would prevent a reoccurrence of the difficulties of the last few days and in the event of the road becoming permanently unserviceable would ensure that the guns and ammunition would be in an accessible spot approachable by M.T. & that gun crews would be at all times during their tour of duty, within five or ten minutes distance (on foot) of their posts. OC Wing agreed to erect a building or use an existing building for this purpose.
Two more .5 BROWNING pits completed and manned.
NIL

4407 A.A. Flight – Operational at Chittagong and satellite A.M.E.S.

Unit's further movement to DOHAZARI was stopped at the "eleventh hour" by orders from No.224 Group allotting the Unit the role of A.A. Defence at A.M.E. Stations in the Chittagong Area, with H.Q. at No.5029 Holding A.M.E.S. This A.M.E.S. could not provide accommodation and had made no arrangements for reception.

The Flight was therefore located at No.224 Group Transit Camp where in effect, the "ate the bread of idleness" for a period varying from 3 to 7 days. O.C. Unit was accommodated at No.244 Group H.Q. and provided with a table in the R.D.F. Section as there was no room at No.5029 A.M.E.S., PAHARTALI.

No.1 Section (Cpl. Brooks and 10 gunners) moved to No.378 A.M.E.S., KATTALI. Taking over the manning of the existing Gun Post, equipped with quadruple Brownings Mk. II.

No.2 Section (Cpl. Brighton and 10 gunners) moved to No.5029 A.M.E.S., Pahartali, and took over manning of Nos.1 and 2 Gun Posts (Quadruple Brownings Mk. II) at Observation Hill, CHITTAGONG, i.e. the technical site.

Headquarters Section (Sgt. Burdett, CPl. Green and 1 Gunner) moved to accommodation at No.5029 Holding A.M.E.S., PAHARTALI.

Name of Unit changed from No.4357 Flight to No.4407 Flight (Air H.Q. Signal 24 dated 4.6.43).

No.3 Section (Cpl. Preston and 10 gunners) moved to No.879 A.M.E.S. This Station still being under construction, no gun posts had been constructed. In the absence of coolies labour, the Section got to work on the building of a first post in accordance with a drawing by the Flight Commander. The post originally designed for this Station was one of bamboo and earth only. The more massive type pf post was considered essential in view of the damage caused by rain and tide, especially in these Units located near the sea.

Standing Order No.1 (Orders for Gun Post Duty) issued.

Norton Motor Cycle taken over from No.5029 Holding A.M.E.S. for use by Flight Commander, owing to difficulties of maintaining contact with scattered Units.

Unit took over 3-ton Chevrolet from No.5029 Holding A.M.E.S. The provision of Unit transport became an urgent necessity when movement

of stores and equipment had to be carried out. The limitations of a motor cycle became plain when heavy rain put the roads in an appalling and often impassable condition.
Three gunners attended an R.A.F. Regiment Camouflage Course.
Amendment No.1 to Standing Order No.1 issued.
Weather during the middle of the month seriously interfered with outdoor works, especially the building of Gun Posts, in some cases subsidence occurring during heavy rain and high tides, but considerable headway was made during the fine spell towards the end of the month.
3-ton Chevrolet allotted to Unit on Transfer from Air H.Q. (Bengal) Signals. RAF letter written to No.224 Group, pointing out the lack of armouries at A.M.E. Stations, and emphasising the consequence difficulties of storage of ammunition and weapons, both for the Units themselves and R.A.F. Regiment detachments stationed there. (Ref.4407/S.202/Arm 3/7/43)

4410 A.A. Flight – Operational at Cox's Bazaar

Equip. 9 Twin Lewis and 9. Motley Stork Mountings returned to H.Q. 211 Group. Auth O.C. RAF.REGT. No.224, Group.
Arrived Cox's Bazaar.
Detailed to man 8 Gun Post on Signal Hill, 5042 A.M.E.S. and Filter Room. 4. Twin Lewis Guns, 4 V.G.O. taken over from F/LT. MEREDITH. O/C. 4403 A.A. FLT. RAF REGT.
Est. India 664 (E.C). Unenrolled followers. Cooks B.T. I -1, Cooks B.T. Grade II - 1. Sweepers 2. Water Carriers -1.
Org. Visit by F/LT. YATES, 166 WING DEFENCE OFFICER, RE: Defence Scheme of Cox's Bazaar.
Equip. Collected 12. Lewis Guns from custody of F/LT. MEREDITH. O.C. 4403 A/A FLT. RAF REGT. Which were delivered from H.Q. No.224, Group.
'C' - NIL -
'D' Training:- A/C Rec', Navy '0' Fighter, Navy '96 Heavy Bomber, Army '0' Fighter, Army '99' Medium Bomber. Arms:- Lewis Gun, V.G.O. Rifle, Sten Gun. Map Reading, :- Elementary.

Field Work.:- Building Gun Posts

P.T.

Sighting. Ring and Aperture.

July
2941 Field Squadron – Operational at Agartala Aerodrome

July opened the third month of training at Agartala, and Jungle Warfare Tactics combined with Tactical Movements of flights, were the main features outlined for training during July.
The G.D.O. 224 Group visited the Squadron. Twelve unfit personnel left for the depot at SECUNDERABAD, having already been replaced by a new draft from the depot.
The G.D.O. left for Base after observing Flight at work on Jungle Tactics.
Two new Sergeants arrived as replacements, Sgt: PHILIPS and Sgt: HOBDAY. The usual Squadron Parade and Church Service were held.
Heavy and continuous rain interfered with training and for two days inside work only was possible. A Tactical Route March of 12 hours duration was to have taken place, but weather prevented this being carried out.
Fast morning work covering the first two hours, 06.30 hrs: - 08.30 hrs:, continued and Flights covered 8 miles in two hours and 7 miles in 1 ¾ hours.
A SHILLONG HILL Party, F/O. REDINGTON i/c., left with 18 men only as the allotment was reduced to this figure. Applications for remustering to Aircrew and for Commissions, CPL: HOWTING and WATTS were interviewed and action taken.
Training in bussing and debussing was carried out by Fights with good results. This training will continue until efficiency is obtained.
Bussing and debussing training continued. A Hill Party of 23 men returned. Weather turned wet again and interfered with training.
F/O. EVANS reported sick and was admitted to Hospital. This Officer had been unfit for some time. An incidence of Malaria was evident,

several men being admitted to Hospital. The usual Church Parade was held, also the Squadron Parade.

Information was received that Flights in rotation would be attached to an Army Unit and proceed to the IMPHAL forward area for a three week training period. This news was well received as at last the back-area training, which had continued for 6 months with men of the of old "Special" Squadron and for 3 months with men of the new 2941 (R) Squadron, had some significance.

F/LT. MACGREGOR left for CALCUTTA to collect the allotment of 12 BREN Guns. Another rainy period set in.

No.3 Flight were selected to be the first Flight to move forward and F/O. REDINGTON, now at SHILLONG and Officer i/c No.3 Flight, was warned to return to Base. Fitting out of No.3 Flight commenced and this Flight was brought up to strength by drawing upon the Support Flight for men to replace those in hospital.
Reclassification of A.C.I's to L.A.C's took place before a board sitting for two days, as outside work was greatly impeded by continuous and heavy rain for three days.

F/LT. MACGREGOR returned from CALCUTTA with 12 BREN guns and these were allotted to Flights. Weather improved and the Flights went for a 18 miles Route March which was completed within 5 ½ hours:, with few falling out. This march was done in P.T. kit, Rifles, L.M.G's and side arms only as a first instance. No water was permitted.

F/O. REDINGTON returned from SHILLONG and re-organisation of Flights was completed today. The Support Flight was used as a pool for non-effectives and 2 Rifle Flights maintained at full strength. The Training combined with climate condition, had found out weak spots in physical ability of certain personnel and until the Depot could replace unfit men, these were drafted to the Support Flight and this Flight was non-effective. Flat feet, Appendicitis, ears, nose, chest and enlarged veins, were the main troubles of unfit men, whilst malaria, skin troubles and boils, sprains and stomach troubles were the main causes for temporary unfitness.
The training was so arranged and conducted that any unfitness would become evident during the training period, as passengers were not to be carried when operational work commnenced. The trying climate

was responsible for some of the ailments, but this was discounted and recongised as unavoidable under the circumstances prevailing. The usual Church and Squadron Parades took place.

No.2 and No.3 Flights did a competitive march of 8 miles and a tie was the result – after agreements. A full marching order Squadron Parade was held during the afternoon, to check equipment and adjustment of equipment.

A field range of 100yds: 200yds was sited and construction commenced.

The Hill Party returned minus 3 men left at SHILONG in Hospital.

Thursday is the usual 'free day' of the week – which allows for Squadron Office work to proceed uninterrupted.

The C.O. proceeded to Group to obtain tents and other requirements for Flights moving forward.

A Route March of 18 miles in light marching order took place and results were an improvement on the previous march of the same distance in P.T. kit – Time 5 ½ hors. Only 3 men dropped out but they rejoined before the Flights reached Base.

Camouflage nets were prepared for use of M.T. proceeding to IMPHAL. Bren Gun instruction was intensified. Church Parade was held.

C.O. returned with tents and necessities including a wireless set. No.3 Flight took over tents and were instructed in tent pitching and striking as drill. Fitting out of the Flight continued.

No.3 Flight's Rifles were Zeroed on the newly constructed ranged, two targets only being in use at this date.

C.O. proceeded to CALCUTTA to fix about Transport and transportation. It was arranged to collect 2 x 15 cwts: from CALCUTTA and take them direct to the forward area – whilst the Flight proceeded by rail from AKHAURA. The Squadron Jeep was at last found and taken over – being left in CALCUTTA to proceed to IMPHAL.

Day Off.

Range firing and other training continued.

C.O. returned from CALCUTTA.

2942 Field Squadron – Operational at Comilla Aerodrome

S/Ldr. Gordon, (G.D.O. 224 Group) arrived from Chittagong on a visit of inspection. He leaves for Agartala tomorrow.
F/O. Jordon left for Shillong with the third Hill Parties.
F/O. Hunter Arundel proceeded to R.A.F. Regt. Depot Secunderabad. Whilst on Calcutta to make arrangements re Collection of Transport. 1. N.C.O. and 5 men also sent as escort party to bring back vehicles.
Uneventful nothing to report, No.6 Hill Party returned from Shillong.
Owing to heavy rains, Gun Posts on 'drome flooded which necessitated standing down Gun crews. Range Party fired despite torrential rains.
Nothing to report. Brims of Teria hats turned down as per 24 Group H.Q. instr.
S/Ldr. Hoskings admitted to Hospital, F/Lt. Cattell assumed temporary Command. Major Tiffin A.D.C. commenced 14 days leave.
Field Training Programme unable to be carried out owing to roads to training grounds impossible.
Arrangements made to issue a Monthly Magazine "Stand Easy" by Airmen of the Squadron
16 B.O.R's sent on Signal Course to 221 Group Calcutta.
All water supplies in Camp contaminated, strict observance in boiling all water essential
Cycle Patrols started on Aerodrome at 18-00 Hours today.
First Squadron Concert held giving entirely by Airmen of 2942. A very good show. Morale and Espri de Corps very high.
Training of Indian troops undertaken by 2942. Rifle, Unarmed Combat etc. (2 weeks)
Owing to 9 Gunners having to be Replaced by Secunderabad, as unfit for Regt duties. Whole Squadron to be Medically examined by M.O. today.
F/O. Pelly Fry left for Shillong with the 4th Jill Party.
F/O. Jordan arrived back from Hill Party from Shillong.
F/O. Chaffin sent by Air to Calcutta to investigate delay in obtaining transport by escort party.
Rifle shooting on the range has proved very satisfactory this week and a great improvement on previous practices.

Convert Party working hard on show very fine esprit de corp.
Response for requests for articles for Squadron Magazine most encouraging. 1st copy due Aug.7th.
All available personnel went out on 9 Mile route march combined with tactical exercises, owing to heavy rains transport could not be sent to collect party, who had to return on foot.
Radio and Football equipment received from Comforts, despite heavy rains outdoor training continues rigorously. 4414 A.A. Flight arrived today at 10-30 hrs. F/Lt. Kelly Officer i/c.
Squadron Concert Party presented its first Show, repeat performance 29th -30th. Open to all R.A.F. personnel and the Nursing Staff of 921 GM.
S/Ldr. Hoskings returned to Unit from Hospital, and assumed Command of 2942 Squadron vice FL/LT. Cattell.
5th Hill Party left for Shillong F/O Pelly Fey detained at Hill Station on Medical grounds.
4 15 cwt. vehicles belonging to 4402 A.A. Flight brought back from 224 Group on loan to this Unit, were driven from Chittagong.

2945 Field Squadron – In transit at R.A.F. Chharra

Advance party arrived at No.1 Camp, R.A.F. Station, CHHARRA. This camp was in an appalling state, as
   (i)   All huts leaked, and had been used as cow-houses.
   (ii)   There was no sanitation and no water supply.
   (iii)   There were no cooking utensils, and no information about the number of followers who might be taken on.
   (iv)   Furniture had been left unattended for a long time, and was destroyed or damaged.

Main party arrived.
Arms drill for Sten gunners introduced. When riflemen slope arms, Sten gunners change arms, so that on the march all right arms can be swung. The following appointments were made :- Welfare and Sports Officer - F/Lt. Garnett. Messing Officer   - F/O. Ottoy.

| M.T. and Armament Officers - F/O. Wilnot. |
| Works Officer   - F/O. Ashton. |
| Training continued: particular efforts were made to give airmen range practice, and opportunities to handle live grenades and EY rifles. |

4402 A.A. Flight – Moved from Dohazari now operational at Chiranga

| A fatigue party completed the construction of an oven for the Cookhouse this morning, while a further fatigue took down and brought in to camp a tent, formerly used by a gun post crew, but now untenanted owing to the complete flooding of the adjacent gunpit. LAC's Harrison, Radcliffe, Sparks, and Sumner each received sentences of C.C. for failing to immobilise firearms before leaving this station. |
| A party of men this morning visited the cemetery and tidied up the area. Weeds and thick creepers made the path almost impassable which heavy rain had caused subsidence of the ground in places. Three hours work saw the place quite presentable, while a further party should finish the task. Finishing touches were also put to the cookhouse oven. The remainder of the men were engaged on armoury work. |
| A fatigue party this morning constructed a pit on some waste land for use when throwing grenades, a practice we intend to have very shortly. With our stock of live grenades (1 gross) we can easily afford to give practice of one live thrown per man. The rest of the men repaired the drainage tunnel in one of our gunpits. Our former Cook No.1059351 AC1. Jones left this station for Chittagong this morning. |
| An inspection of firearms and billets was this morning made by F/Lt. Cory. Afterwards the respirators of all available men were tested and kept them on for 15 mins. The parade was then taken on practice throwing of the null s Grenade, in preparation for their live Grenade practice, which will take place shortly. |
| Three men of this Unit namely 1046686 LAC. Eland J. 994499 LAC. Harrison G and 132277 LAC. Stockley L.W. have now been posted non |

effective sick, in accordance with BPO letter reference BPO/6601/D1 dated 10/6043 to BHQ Calcutta. Despite heavy rain, which fell throughout yesterday afternoon and all night a party was taken on grenade lectures and later had practice throwing. The respirators of all men at present on this station have now been tested and found satisfactory.

A party this morning brought in the tripods from our two U/S gun posts, another party cleaned & oiled our spare tripods in the armoury. The morning duty was completed by two NCO's and a man cleaning the Cemetery in preparation for the burial of an Army Lance Corporal who died yesterday from Cholera, they also erected a cross on 1234366 LAC Chapman's grave. The Group Padre held a service in the Canteen at 11.30hrs this morning.

F/Lt. Cory visited Chiranga today to ascertain what billeting arrangements had been made for the Flight posting. He took with him Sgt. Birtless. Owing to rain, the morning work consisted entirely of cleaning in the armoury.

The entire parade this morning were taken to a large stretch of waste land, where a grenade throwing bay had previously been constructed. Every man threw alive grenade, and no difficulties were experienced. Ten men and two NCO's, beside men in hospital; and the present Hill Party's now remain to throw. LAC. Richards 1436254 was admitted to Dohazari hospital yesterday.

The remainder of the men who had not already thrown a live grenade were taken to the range and threw one each this morning. Men who had already thrown were told off for duty in the armoury. 1436254 LAC Richards was discharged from hospital today.

A fatigue party cleansed and packed armoury equipment not at present in use, in preparation for our probable move. Equipment for men who have been posted non effective sick (as per BPO instruction reference BPO/6601/D1. Dated 10/6/43) was crated and is now awaiting the roads to become serviceable, so that it may be dispatched by rail to RAF. Regt. Depot Secunderabad. The remainder of the parade carried on cleaning up work at the Cemetery.

A party of men this morning went to the aerodrome to ascertain whether or not the local natives had ploughed any part of the strip and to check damage to huts etc. They reported when they returned that all was in order. 1529206 LAC. Lipsall was discharged from hospital.

The Parade was divided into two equal parties. One party patrolled the aerodrome and generally kept the natives in order, while the other carried on with the daily cleaning in the armoury.

The whole Parade was this morning taken on to the range and given sten gun practice. Each man fired 40 rounds,20 from the shoulder and twenty from the hip. Practice was completed without a hitch. On returning to the camp all guns were cleaned, and oiled, and magazines checked and cleaned.

This Flight received instructions from Group HQ to move as soon as possible to Charinga. Heavy rain again fell this morning and the entire Flight carried on with preparations for the move. The roads, however, are as yet impassable, and at present no exact date for the change over can be fixed.

The two corporals who departed for Calcutta on duty a week ago, this morning returned. Dry rations for three weeks were drawn from the Rations Store, Dohazari, in preparation for the Flights move. The men spent the morning packing away all kit not wanted for the next few days. 1507071 Lac. Herman was today admitted to Hospital. The Hill Party returned minus three men namely Lac's Clark, Parker and Aspen, all in Hospital.

The advance from No.261 Squadron, on its way to Chiringa, arrived here also, and at present is staying on at this station until the roads are passable. F/Lt. Corby visited Group H.Q. Chittagong, to discuss matters concerning our move to Chiringa.

Reports from Chiringa were today unfavourable, and a letter informing Group of the situation was despatched. The men, however, spent the morning , clearing up the camp and loading the Armoury lorry, as the news from Chiringa did not reach us until the afternoon. Tripods from our remaining Gunpits were also dugout cleaned.

F/Lt. Cory, together with the officer i/c No.261 Squadron advance party, today visited Chiringa. It was decided that the advance party should depart this afternoon with this Flight following on tomorrow.

653726 Lac. Darbyshire was admitted to Hospital. Final packing of stores was again the chief task today.

The Flight today moved from Dohazari to Chiringa. The roads between the camp and Dohazari were in terrible condition, but with the aid of planks, matting, and a Studebaker winch lorry, the loads were pulled through. The remainder of the journey was uneventful, and the Flight quickly settled down in their new quarters.

The entire Flight today completed sorting out of stores (Canteen, Cookhouse and Armoury), and also erected a cover for the cookhouse fires. In addition several "Slit Trenches" were started.

The C.O. and N.C.O's of the Flight this morning made a complete round of the aerodrome, inspecting each gun post. Of the 18 posts on the drome, 4 were U/S, but the rest were in condition. The men were busy today constructing slit trenches and latrines. At present only one set of latrines containing only two buckets is available.

Tripods were sunk in six gunposts today, (Nos. 1, 4, 7, 8, and 18). These pits command a complete field of fire over the whole strip and likely approaches, and are the maximum number that can be manned at the Flight's present strength. A further two men reported sick this morning. 1000443 Lac. Watson was admitted to hospital.

With another man in hospital, and twelve men on gun post duty, we are now in a rather disturbing position. The Flight stands as follows:-
Total No. of men 29, Hospital 8, Sick 2, Other Duty 2, Available 17, Gun Post Duty 12. It will be seen, therefore that only Five men remain to relieve twelve. Even working two days on and one off, there are still insufficient men. In addition there is a night patrol to be conducted, comprising of six men. Six of the guns crews, therefore, have to do both duties. Should any further men report sick and be excused or light duty, the manning of six posts will be impossible.

Usual Gunpost duty was carried out today. There was nothing to report. 1507071 Lac. Herman was discharged from Hospital today. The Group Staff Medical Officer visited the camp and departed at 13.00hrs.

There was nothing to report today, except that Lac. Spencer was admitted to Hospital.
Gun posts were manned as usual and there was nothing further to report.
Heavy rain throughout the day, nothing to report.
Lac. Spencer was discharged from Hospital today. The following airmen were posted as non effective sick to B.H.Q. Calcutta, 1487428 Lac. Wetherall. G. w.e.f. 14/7/43. 1357906 Lac. White. K.C. w.e.f. 23/7/43.
F/Lt. Cory and Sgt. Birtles spent the entire afternoon inspecting all the gunposts.
Two replacements namely 15150924 Ac.2. Mackenzie. F.R. and 1469085 Ac.1. Cripps. M. arrived here today, in place of Lac. Stockley, and Lac. Hendrerson, who have been posted as non-effective sick to B.H.Q., R.A.F., Calcutta. (As per 5/7/43. Two airmen namely 1002997 Lac. Clark. A.W. and 1357906 Lac. White. K.C., returned from B.H.Q. Shillong today. Lac. White, who is now posted to B.H.Q., Calcutta, as non-effective sick, will proceed to Calcutta in due course. An N.C.O. with a party of men erected three bridges leading to four of our gunposts today. The Group Padre (S/Ldr. Bellingham) held a Church service in the Canteen at 13.30hrs. today.
Bridges across the drainage channels to gunposts were completed today. The C.O. No.261 Squadron visited the drome and spoke to F/Lt. Cory.
A slit trench in our camp was this morning completed. Owing to water logged earth and subsidence, a slit trench is difficult to dig satisfactory. The only way was to dig down some three feet until water began to show, and then sandbag the inside of the trench and erect a parapet to give extra protection. Another replacement arrived today namely 1305937 Lac. Wright. A. from R.A.F. Regt. Depot, Secunderabad. 1357906 Lac. White. K.C. departed for Calcutta this morning.

4403 A.A. Flight – Operational at Cox's Bazaar

Very fine weather to date. No trouble at all in using roads

Non effective sick postings of airmen not working to plan. After posting airmen non effective sick three of them turned up at this unit for duty.
Very heavy rain for two days.   Took over new operations from on road Rumu - Cox's Bazaar found it occupied by enemy troops.
S/L Gordon. 224 Group defence officer visited the unit, he found everything satisfactory.
Discussed defence plan for R.A.F. in Cox's Bazaar with Administrative Commandant. The main point arising was that the strip would be run integral part of Major defence of the Cox's Bazaar and would therefore be incorporated in 26 Division defence scheme for the area.
Very dull weather for the last three days.
Defence plan for R.A.F. installations showing our responsibilities submitted to Administrative Commandant for incorporation in the main scheme. The plan was approved.
Authorisation given for collection of transport which we are in urgent need of. Sent off one Cpl. And six airmen to collect and escort the vehicles here. They were instructed to report to 224 Group for further instructions.
Granted powers of a detachment Commander. One B.D.R. cook added to the establishment. India 664/1. Refers a clerk G.D. is justified by the amount of orderly room work to be done.
166 Wing Defence Officer visited here to compile a close defence scheme for the R.A.F. Units in this area.
Bengal Command defence officer visited the unit discussed dispositions and defence measure.
Weather fairly bad intermittent rain.
Defence scheme finished discussed with unit Commanders.

4404 A.A. Flight – Operational at Feni

S/Ld Gordon (224 Group) visited Feni. It was arranged that the C.P.W.D. should build 6 gun pots in brick, that the balance should be built with U/S petrol tins under the supervision of the Flight

Commander. It was however found that sufficient tins were available for only 2 gun pits and consequently the C.P.W.D. were authorised to build 12 pits.
Extra accommodation, ablutions, kitchen range etc., were completed to the Flight's domestic camp.
W/Co Fowke (Bengal Command) & S/Ld Gordon visited FENI. The new camps for the R.A.F.R. Squadron & No.4415 A.A. Flight, were inspected & found satisfactory in all respects.
No.4415 A.A. (F/LT EDWARDS) arrived at FENI.
11 Squadron Gunners V proceeded on attachment to Base Headquarters, Calcutta.
General Flight Establishment was amended by list No.56 dated 14/7/43 to include 1 A.C. Cook in Flight Headquarters.

4405 A.A. Flight – Operational at Chittagong

One .303 Browning pit completed. This makes a total of 3 .5 Pits and 2 .303 Gun Pits completed and manned.
On authority od 224 Group the guard at 224 Group H.Q. of 1 N.C.O and 6 A.C's ceased to be carried out by the unit wef today.
Shelter trenches dug around domestic camp area. Visit by 224 Group Defence Officer in the afternoon.
Work Progressing.
No.5 Wing detachment of 3 N.C.O's and 13 A.C's left for No.1 R.A.F. Regt. Depot SECUNDERABAD. Flight took on Charge the .5 Browning Guns and tools left by the above detachment, on authority of 224 Group H.Q.
All available Gunners ordered by O.C. 166 Wing to form a search party in an effort to trace some items of equipment stolen during the night of 5th – 6th – 7th -7-43 from 45 Sqd Dispersal Area. Search of Native huts continued until night fall without success. L.D.C. visited North Camp.
Search continued for missing items – nothing found.
Search continuing O.C. Flt. led a party across the KARMAFULI RIVER and searched the area of COOMBES PILLAR. Two Natives were apprehended

and handed over to the R.A.F. Police for being in possession of items of R.A.F. Stores. These search parties are greatly interfering with construction of Gun Pits.

Search continuing. Leave started - 4 men at a time for a period of fourteen days.

Nil.

Church service held in Canteen. Greatly appreciated by Airmen. It is hoped to hold these every Sunday evening.

Work proceeding on the third .303 Browning Pit. This should be completed within a week.

Three men on sick leave - Two men on a Camouflage Course, 28 men of 166 Wing and 615 Sqd. Left for Regt. Depot.

Nil.

Backers up course (166 Wing Personnel) starts at 08.00hrs tomorrow. Two Cpls. From R.A.F. Regt. Depot have been provided as instructors. The course will last 5 days and will be attended by 20 Backers up. 166 Wing Defence Officer proceeded to Cox Bazaar leaving O.C. Flt. i/c Backers up.

Nil.

The Command Defence Officer accompanied by 224 Group Defence Officer visited the aerodrome and inspected Gun Posts and domestic sites. The Cookhouse and water supply are still out of order, having been condemned by the M.O. as long ago as March of this year. Plans for a new Cookhouse have been drawn up but approval for the work to be in hand is still awaited for, from 224 Group.

Two Airmen of 4411 A.A. Flight were drowned while bathing in the sea.

Nil.

Second Backers up course started. In an aerodrome where units are greatly dispersed the ideal for backers up would be to have a training camp in the area, to which personnel would be attached while undergoing the course. This would ensure that everyone starts on time and would cut out the long break at Tiffin time which under the present system is necessary in order to allow personnel to return to their respective units for a meal. It would also enable instructors to have their own stores of training equipment on the

spot. It is hoped in the near future to obtain the use of South Camp for the above purpose.
Nil.

4407 A.A. Flight – Operational at Chittagong

3-ton Chevrolet allotted to Unit on Transfer from Air H.Q. (Bengal) Signals. RAF letter written to No.224 Group, pointing out the lack of armouries at A.M.E. Stations, and emphasising the consequence difficulties of storage of ammunition and weapons, both for the Units themselves and R.A.F. Regiment detachments stationed there. (Ref.4407/S.202/Arm 3/7/43)
No.3 Section completed construction of No.1 Gun-Post at No.879 A.M.E.S.
No.3 Section manned No.1 Gun-Post at No,879 A.M.E.S. with quadruple Browning Guns MK.II. No.2 Post sited and work began.
Conference at H.Q. No.224 Group, with Group Defence Officer, Major Brodie, Area Defence Commander, Patenga Peninsula revealed the necessity for an elementary defence scheme for the non-Regiment personnel of the coastal A.M.E. Stations. No's 378, 879 and 864 A.M.E.S.
F/Lt. L.R.H. Portlock detached to No.3 Hill Depot, R.A.F. for investigation. 1163325 Sgt. Burdett, J.L. assumed command ofUnit.
R.A.F. Regiment Instructions, Series B, No's 1-6 received. These were instructions issued in U.K. and re-issued in India, where they were largely applicable.
Delivery taken of 4 5/15 cwt. Chevrolet trucks, implementing transport establishment (Allotment Air H.Q.(1)158M.T. HQB/MT/639). The trucks were sent from Calcutta (No.329 M.U.) by No.54 Embarkation Unit. On arrival they were in poor condition, but a suggestion that they should be put in to M.T.M.U. for servicing was not acted upon and steps were taken to carry out servicing at the Unit. Difficulty was experienced owing to the lack of D.M.T's and gunners with authority to drive. Arrangements were made with a view to getting likely gunners tested by Group prior to issue of requisite authority.

Addition to Unit establishment of one A.C. Cook (Amendment No. India 664/1 dated 18th June 1943). Powers of a Detachment Commander, under K.R. and A.C. 1 para, 1139, granted to F/Lt. L.R.H. Portlock, as O.C. Unit (Authority: HQ 224 Group letter 224G/S.2024/P-1-dated 14th. July 1943). This was rendered necessary by the fact that Regiment Units were administered directly by Group and not by Wings.
F/Lt. L.R.H. Portlock detained at No.68 I.G.H. (c). Sgt. Burdett assumed command of Unit during absence.
One LAC detached to Base H.Q. Calcutta for Air H.Q. (Bengal) No.3 Cookery Course. Received general policy letter on "Ground Defence" of Airfields and Establishments of the Air Forces in India" indicating policy for both Regiment and non-Regiment Units Air H.Q.(India) 342/Air/G.D. dated 1st July 1943.
F/Lt. L.R.H. Portlock proceeded to No.3 Hill Depot Shillong on Hill Party attachment. Sgt. Burdett J.L. took over command of Unit.
Service Documents were received in respect of 26 airmen of the Unit during the month. Hill Party allotments were made by Headquarters No.224 Group. As the result of which 1 Cpl. And 11 BOR's were attached to No.3 Hill Depot Shillong, at varying times during the month for the normal two weeks rest period.

4410 A.A. Flight – Operational at Cox's Bazaar

'A' - NIL - 'B' - Sight and Range selected and sanction given by Senior Admin Commander Cox's Bazaar.
ORG. Visit by S/LDR. GORDON, 224 Group, Defence Officer R.A.F. Regt. First visit by B.E.S.A. to Cox's Bazaar which was very much appreciated.
Visit by F/LT. YATES, Wing Defence Officer - Re. Defence Scheme of Cox's Bazaar - Recce made of Signal Hill and surroundings.
Visit by A.H.Q. Bengal Defence Officer, W/Cmd. Foulkes - Inspection of strip and gun posts, and Signal Hill.
EQUIP. 4 V.G.O. Machine Guns and 40 Mags. Returned to Kankinara. Auth. S/Ldr. Gordon, 224. Group Defence Officer. R.A.F. Regt.

EST. India/664 (E.C.) Amendments - Add 1 A.C. Cook - Delete 1- Grade I.

ORG. Officer Commanding. 4410 A/A Flight R.A.F. Regt. Detailed to supervise 4401 A/A Flight R.A.F. Regt. During absence of F/Lt. Page. Visit by P/O. Howlett from H.Q. 224 Group, Re. 'P' Staff and other queries.

Arrangements made with F/Lt. YATES and F/Lt. MEREDITH to supervise 4403 A/A Flight R.A.F. Regt. During leave of F/Lt. MEREDITH.

'D' Training:- Lewis Gun, Rifle, Sten Gun.

Bayonet Fighting, A/C Rec. (Japanese and Allied)

Map Reading, Sighting (Ring and Aperture)

Field Work,

P.T.

Anti Gas - N.C.O. from H.Q. 224 Group.

'E' - NIL -

'F' - NIL -

'G' - NIL -

August
2941 Field Squadron – Operational and Training at Agartala Aerodrome

The fourth month of training at AGARTALA. The usual Squadron and Church Service were held.

Very wet weather. No training undertaken. Roads in vicinity of Camp were flooded. Warning Order - Change of Location for Training issued by C.O.

No.3 Flight commenced second series of Range Practices at 100 & 200 yds. - grouping, application and snap shooting. Results were satisfactory taking into account the little practice done in the last six months. All Airmen of No.3 Flight fired the BREN Gun.

Route March. No information regarding movement of No.3 Flight to IMPHAL. Training in use of BREN Tripod for grounds and A.A. carried out.

Free day for the Squadron (5th) F/O F.W. EVANS proceeded to DARJEELINE on fortnights Sick Leave. No.3 Flight continued Range Practices.

Other Flights instructed in tent pitching and striking. S/LDR. H.J. FORBES taken ill (fever).

Tactical training continued. BREN Gun revision for all Flights. F/O. EVANS posted 4414 A.A. Flight to fill F/LT vacancy.

S/LDR FORBES confined to his quarters with fever. F/O. LITTLEFAIR attached to Wing as Defence Officer. Available Officers F/LT. MACGREGOR, F/O. REDINGTON and F/O. SUTTON, (Adjutant). The usual Church Parade and Squadron Parade held. Signal received instructing F/O. SUTTON (Adjutant) to attend Admin Course, POONA. Advice received of despatch to BONGAIGON of one Jeep and two 15 cwts. Four Airmen, including drivers sent to take charge of vehicles.

Preparations made to move Squadron to No.8 Camp. Training of all Flights continued. No.3 Flight fired STEN Gun.

Squadron move commenced. Very heavy rain- roads extremely muddy necessitating loan of four wheel drive trucks to move heavy equipment. F/O. SUTTON left by Air for POONA to attend Admin Course. No.3 Flight provided advance and fatigue parties.

Squadron move completed. Approximately 50% personnel moved in the forenoon in full marching order, and remainder in the afternoon. C.O's health normal.

Squadron free day, opportunity taken to settle-in.

No.1, 2 and available strength of Support Flight continued training. Sports Grounds marked out and prepared by No.3 Flight at 19.00 hrs approx:

No.3 Flight prepared to move. S/LDR. FORBES left for Calcutta by Air at approx: 13.00 hrs. F/LT. F.G. MACGREGOR assumed Command. No.3 Flight moved out at approx: 23.00 hrs and entrained at AKHAURA at 01.28 hrs on 15th.

Squadron and Church Parades.

Bayonet Course developed. Grenade training. Lectures on Aircraft Recognition continued.

General training continued. Route March on 18th - marches easily accomplished with little casualties.

Squadron free day. F/LT. EVANS returns from DARJEELING. No.2 Flight Rifles zeroed.

F/LT. EVANS proceeded to COMILLA to take over No.4414 A.A. Flight. General training continued. Embussing and debussing in Light Marching Order satisfactorily carried out.

Church Parade. N.C.O's conferences instituted. Useful discussions matters concerning welfare and training.

Kit Inspection of Nos.1, 2 & Support Flights.

Advanced Handling of L.M.G's, taught, also setting of Tripods on Fixed Lines. Bayonet training intensified.No.2 Flight on the Range the whole of this day firing practices with Rifle and BREN's. Results were satisfactory.

Usual Route March.

Squadron Free Day.

Group Defence Officer, 244 Group, S/LDR. G. ANDREWS M.C., visited the Squadron - saw an inter flight football match - inspected camp and visited the airmen at dinner. Squadron parade on 28th in Light Marching Order and were inspected by S/LDR. ANDREWS. Group Defence Officer, after inspecting some L.M.G. A.A. Posts on Pukka Strip, left by air at approx: 13.30 hrs.

Padre was away and no service was held. Airmen appreciate the Church Services.

Training programme altered to include P.T. & Bayonet training before breakfast. P.T. commenced at 05.45 hrs terminating at 06.15 hrs. First parade was altered to 07.00 hrs to 09.00 hrs and the second parade from 09.30 to 11.30 hrs.

A series of interesting lectures arranged by the Officers of 169 Wing commenced on this date, making a welcome change for the airmen. S/LDR COTTON D.F.C. gave the opening talk.

Training in Rifle Bomber drill commenced. Early morning period from 07.00 to 09.00 hrs taken up in Flight in attack, for No.2 & Support Flight. Recce of country between camp and Aerodrome carried out by No.1 Flight. From the 15th to 31st F/LT MACGREGOR was the only Officer available for Squadron work and training.

2942 Field Squadron – Operational at Comilla Aerodrome

First Party of 607 Gunners went to Shillong for 7 days res. Second party to proceed on the 4th, prior to their return to R.A.F. Depot, Secunderabad.
S/Ldr. Hosking proceeded on 26 days Sick Leave, F/Lt. Gattell assumed Command. Two B.O.R's detailed to proceed to Calcutta to bring back Squadron Vehicles which have been there since 22-6-43. A short Night Operation was carried out by the Training Flight, this consisted mainly of movements by night.
A marked improvement in the Transport position was noticeable to-day when Training was resumed on the Training Ground.
S/Ldr. Forbes O.C. No.2941 Squadron to-gether with several officers and N.C.O's of that Squadron visited this Unit when going through to the O.F.D. They had the pleasure of watching the Squadron Football beat the Police, afterwards the officers were entertained and dined in the Mess.
O.C. 2941 Squadron and Party left for their Unit after the first parade. 1 Sgt., and a party of 11 Gunners were returned to the Depot as Medically unfit, replacements are now needed.
A Practice "Stand To" was held, the first of its kind for this Unit. It was generally good as most personnel was caught unawares during the rest period. Everyone was on parade and ready to move off in Battle Order in 7 minutes.
All personnel were inoculated against Cholera and other inoculations were brought up to date. F/Lt. Kelly proceeded to Calcutta on temporary Duty. 4414 A.A. Flight placed in charge of O.C. 2942 during his absence.
S/Ldr. Gordon arrived with S/Ldr. Andrews the latter paying his first visit on taking over 224 Group.
S/LDr. Gordon and S/Ldr. Andrews left for Agartala.
S/Ldr. Kelly returned from Calcutta on Posting to 2944 Squadron as O.C.
S/Ldr. Kelly left for Banshi and 2944 Squadron, having handed over to F/Lt. Evans.
W/C. Fowke Command Defence Officer visited this Unit.
W/C. Fowke left for Calcutta and Command.

S/Ldr. Hosking returned from Sick Leave having been detained in Calcutta.
S/Ldr. Hosking Medically Boarded and has to proceed to Calcutta B.M.H. for observation under S.M.O Base H.Q.
During the whole of this Month this Squadron has operated with 2 Officers short as F/O. Polly-Fry, is still detained in Shillong, application has been made to 224 Group for a replacement for this Officer and Posting instructions are awaited.

2945 Field Squadron – Arrival and settling in at Feni Aerodrome

S/Ldr. Garner returned from CALCUTTA, where he had been to consult A.H.Q. BENGAL on various matters, and immediately went to hospital, having reported that the Squadron would be moving to FENI within 10 days. F/LT. GARNETT assumed command of the Squadron in his absence. The following difficulties were encountered at CHHARRA:- (i)   The C.O. found himself also C.O. of R.A.F. Station, CHHARRA. This meant such extra work and responsibility, when the organisation of the new Unit of itself provided much. A great deal of time had to be wasted in forwarding, and often replying to, correspondence addressed to units which had long ago left the station: and a great deal on getting the camp habitable. (ii) There was no doctor nearer than ASANSOL, 60 miles away, and no accountant officer even there. (iii) The surrounding country consisted largely of paddy fields, and was quite unsuitable for training. (iv) Central Registry, 221 Group, had us located at RANCHI.
Signal from A.H.Q. BENGAL that Squadron was to move to FENI as soon as possible.
3 deaths from cholera immediately adjacent to the camp. All ranks confined to camp.
1511987 LAC JOHNSON.R., summoned on compassionate grounds to U.K. by signal, to reach BOMBAY by August 19th, 1943. Airman despatched from ASANSOL by train, and ALLAHBAD signalled to provide air transport.

Signal from R.A.F. Movement that movement of Squadron was postponed 2 hours till 0830 hrs. on August 18th, 1943.
F/O. OTTOY and 30 B.O.Rs. left PURULIA for FENI.
F/O. STUART HART and 45 B.O.Rs. left PURULIA for FENI. S/Ldr GARNER returned from C.M.H. ASANSOL.
S/Ldr. GARNER, F/Lt. GARNETT and 49 B.O.Rs. left PURULIA for FENI, S/Ldr. GARNER taking 7 days leave en route. F/O. WILMOT and 2 B.O.R's left by road to CALCUTTA to deliver a truck to 221 Group and collect 12 Bren Guns. In connection with this move 17 signals were received in all. They arrived out of order and corrupt, and few of the arrangements mentioned in them were implemented. A report was submitted to No.224 Group, a copy of which is attached as an appendix.
Advanced party arrived at FENI. First part of main party arrived.
F/O. WILMOT and F/O. ASHTON arrived.
Second part of main party arrived.
8 15 cwt. trucks arrived at FENI for the Unit.

Training began by reconnaissance of the surrounding country. Flights marched out as a whole and came back in small parties. The Squadron undertook an M.T. patrol covering the dispersal area, Wing Headquarters, Wireless Points, roads through domestic camps, and Noakhali Rd. as far as 376 A.M.E.S.: each patrol to consist of one section and last for 3 hours.
 	
Appointments :- Savings Officer   F/O. OTTOY.
               Security and Equipment Officer F/O. ASHTON.
               P.A.D. Officer   F/L.GARNETT.

S/Ldr. GARNER reassumed command of the Squadron.

4402 A.A. Flight – Operational at Chiranga

Gun Posts were manned as usual.
Another two replacements arrived today namely 1419661 Lac. Davies, and 541703 AC1. Bennett, from R.A.F. Regiment Depot, Secunderabad. Directly on arrival Lac. Davies was returned to B.M.H. Chittagong. This is the second airman arriving at this Unit, as a replacement, who has had to be admitted to Hospital on arrival. Another man namely

1422976 Lac. Sparks. L.G. reported sick this morning and was admitted to Hospital. A few more trees which were in the line of fire of one of our gunpits, were removed.

An inspection was carried out this morning by F/Lt. Cory, of all personal arms and ammunition. Sten guns rounds were taken out of the magazines, oiled and replaced. The inspection was satisfactory.

653726 Lac. Darbyshire. J. returned to this Unit, from 68 I.G.H. Chittagong.

The office equipment was moved up to our new camp today. The Armoury, and Canteen stores were put in a hut half way between the camp and our new site.

The move was completed today. 1305937 Lac. Wright. A. was admitted to Hospital.

The first eight planes, of No.261 Squadron arrived and were dispersed along the strips as taxi-tracks were not completed. Numbers 1, 4, 8, 9 and 14 gunposts were manned.

Owing to heavy rain and flooding No.14 gunpost was not manned this morning. The crew were taken off No.8 gun post during the morning as the flood water had surrounded the post and was entering it. The remaining planes, of No.261 Squadron, were due in today but, owing to the bad weather they did not arrive.

Yesterday evening 1014748 Lac. Aspden. R.B. returned, to this Unit, from B.M.H. Shillong.

1422976 Lac. Spark. L.G. was discharged from Hospital.

Acting on instruction this unit today posted 1353276 Cpl. Atkinson as "u/t pilot" he proceeded to port of Embarkation this morning.

541703 AC1 Bennett. F. was admitted to hospital yesterday evening.

1305937 Lac. Wright. A.T. was discharged from hospital today.

No.261 Squadron left this station today, with the exception of their M.T. vehicles and M.T.L.R.D. personnel. The Commanding Officer of No.4402 A.A. Flight R.A.F. Regt. took over complete charge of all R.A.F. interests on the station.

1305937 Lac. Wright has been remustered to ACH/GD authority BPO/2006/1/A2 w.e.f. 2nd April, 1943. Furthermore the same airman is posted to H.Q. No.224 Group Unit w.e.f. 4th August 1943, authority BPO/D 11094.

1510924 AC1. Mackenzie. F.R. and 1469085 AC1. Cripps. M. have been posted to this Unit from R.A.F. Regiment Depot Secunderabad, authority BPO/D 10966 sated 3rd August 1943. 541703 AC1. Bennett. F. and 1419661 Lac. Davies. F.G. have been posted to this Unit from the Depot, authority BPO/D/ 11261 dated 6th August 1943.

1354106 Lac. Cooke. J. and 1237593 AC1. Edwards. R.W. are attached to this Unit, from R.A.F. Regiment Depot, w.e.f. 18th August 1943.

Four airmen namely 1459593 Lac. Bunn, 653726 Lac. Darbyshire, 1515580 Lac. Naven, and 1414850 Lac. Nicholas, proceeded on 14 days leave to Calcutta today.

Two airmen namely 1430896 Lac. Beattie. R. and 1539129 Lac. Chambers. J, were admitted to hospital this morning.

A temporary operational ground order incorporating all the various units connected with this station, has been drawn up by the officer commanding this unit. These orders are only temporary for the reason that when 261 Sqdn. Arrive they will be responsible for manning the L.M.G. posts ad also the Defence Localities. This will release 4402 A.A. Flight to carry out its task of a mobile unit. Further operational ground orders will be drawn up as and when the officer commanding 261 Squadron arrives and takes over the command of the station (See appendix No.1 attached).

Two airmen namely 1237593 AC1. Edwards. R.W. and 1419661 Lac. Davies. F.G. were admitted to hospital this morning.

1420896 Lac. Beattie. R. was discharged from hospital this morning.

4403 A.A. Flight – Operational at Cox's Bazaar

Intermittent rain.

Suppressive for Malaria started. Percentage of Malaria cases on this unit are actually lower than any others in the area, due probably to the fact that the camp is situated away from the native bazaars, and strict measures are taken to keep away undesirable natives.

Further two gun posts constructed making a total of seven for this unit. All gun posts have stood up to the monsoons remarkably well.

Very fine weather,

One Cpl. Posted non-effective sick.

The other A.A. Flight defending the 'drome i.e. 136 Sqdn. Detachment flight under orders to move back to R.A.F. Regt. Depot Secunderabad. No other flight having been sent to replace them means this unit is the only one left to defend the strip. We are practically up to strength and able to man gun posts continually and a further two on an alert being sounded. Four of the posts are quadruple Brownings so that a heavy volume fire can be directed against any hostile aircraft.

Suppressive treatment for malaria proving very effective, since its inception, not one case of malaria has been reported on the unit. The largest percentage of sickness on this unit is caused by airmen proceeding on rest leave to Shillong. Practically 50% of personnel report sick on arrival there, caused doubtless by change of climate and temperature.

The new 224 Group Defence Officer, S/L Andrews visited the unit today. He seemed quite satisfied with the work being done. Training policy and general organisation were discussed with him.

A policy of training R.A.F. Regt. personnel on maintenance of M.T. vehicles has been adopted by 224 Group. This should prove of invaluable help to small units in maintaining transport in a reasonable state of efficiency without and from M.T. mechanics.

Two replacements arrived at this unit under the non-effective sick policy. One of these replacements is for an airman who has returned and been posted back to this unit bringing us one over establishment.

Visited by Group M.T. Officer who informed me that four vehicles allotted to us were in Chittagong, but instructions had been issued to the effect that they were not to be sent here until after the monsoons have ceased. He undertook to try and have two sent down to achieve our immediate needs.

4404 A.A. Flight – Operational at Feni

Fine weather with heavy showers. Strong wind blew almost continuously. Enemy activity considered improbable. An average of 4 or 5 gun posts manned daily. In addition 2 posts can be manned in a few minutes. During this period the flight was 12 men below full strength.

Sgt Campbell & 5 airmen proceeded to No.3 Hill Depot. Cpl. BELL appointed to act as N.C.O. i/c Flt.
Sq/Ldr. GORDON & Sq/Ldr. ANDREWS from 244 Group visited FENI. A thorough tour of the aerodrome was made including 877 A.M.E. Station, DANDRA.
Owing to the possibility of a re-occurrence of CONGRESS activities light patrols were doubled.
Two airmen completed the 3 Cookery Course in CALCUTTA. The course was described as disappointing. 3 TWIN LEWIS gun accessories originally held at 167 Wing Defence Section & taken over temporarily by this unit, were handed over to 4415 A.A. Flt, to complete their establishment of A.A. weapons.
Information received that 4 X 15cwt trucks allocated to this unit were awaiting collection at Chittagong. The FENI - CHITTAGONG road was reported as being impassable at the time.
A mock raid by a squadron of Hurricanes simulating bombers was carried out on FENI aerodrome, with the objective of testing the defences. The raid acted as a useful practice in the quick manning of gun posts for this unit and several lessons were learnt. However it could not be a true surprise test, as the time had been too widely advertised.
A surprise air raid warning was sounded in this area only, to correct the mistakes of the previous day.
Large practice was carried out. Every man in the flight was an opportunity of firing a rifle, a sten gun and throwing a live grenade.
The advance party of No.2945 Squadron R.A.F.R. arrived.
The main body of No.2945 Squadron R.A.F.R. arrived.
F/LT Mackwood proceeded on 2 weeks leave. F/LT.EDWARDS acted as OC Flight during his absence.

4405 A.A. Flight – Operational at Chittagong

NIL
Concert held in the canteen - a great success.
NIL

Collected M.T. from 224 Group today. The establishment allows 4 15 cwt vehicles - this would be ideal of the roads in this area were good, but under the present conditions four wheeled drive vehicles are the only ones on which you can rely. The allocation would have been a great deal better had it been something like the following:- 2 30 cwt 4 wheeled drive and one jeep. As it stands we cannot get the 15 cwt's anywhere the camp site & consequently we have to place a guard over them on the aerodrome as night.
NIL
166 Wing Defence Officer posted to RAF. Regt Depot Secunderabad.
244 Group Defence Officer accompanied by S/Ldr. Andrews R.A.F.R. visited the aerodrome and inspected the new Squadron camp.
Heavy rain.
Three Cpls. And thirty two airmen of 615 Sqdn R.A.F.R. detachment proceeded to the Depot.
South Camp closed down - all remaining gunners transferred to 166 Wing.
30 cwt 4 wheeled drivers loaned from 166 Wing M.T. Section advised. This necessitates a "gun room and armoury" being maintained on the aerodrome itself and it is impossible to bring guns to North Camp for maintenance and cleaning, due to the roads being impassable for 2 wheeled drive vehicles. It cannot be stressed too strongly that four wheeled drive vehicles are the only type which are of use in this district during monsoon weather.
All guns and ammunition are now kept on the aerodrome and a guard is maintained for 24 hrs.
It is suggested that some provision should be made for garage accommodation of the Flight M.T. At present they remain in the open in all weather.
NIL
New cookhouse approved by Group - work to start approximately 22nd August.
Anti-malarial squad started cleaning area of camp.
NIL

Defence Officer from A.H.Q. Bengal visited the aerodrome accompanied by 224 Group Defence Officer. Exchanged all new belted ammunition for belted.
Work proceeding on two gun posts.
Telephone laid to crew-room.
Work held up on the gun posts through lack of bricks. One MT. vehicle U/S/ through carelessness or lack of knowledge on the part of the gunner – driver.
One Cook (Group III) posted to the Flight. This raises the question of personal arms for tradesmen, other than gunners, posted to RAF Regt Unit letter ref 4406/S/10/DIR dated 28/843 to 224 Group Defence Officer refers

4407 A.A. Flight – Operational at Chittagong

Air H.Q. (INDIA) Signal Staff Instructions No.28 dealing with Secret and Confidential Publications received.
F/Lt. L.R.H. Portlock re-assumed command on return from detachment at No.3 Hill Depot. 1 Cpl., 2 gunners tested by H.Q. No.224 Group for driving ability. Application subsequently made to Group for appropriate driving authority for these personnel on F.637.
Flight Headquarters set up at Headquarters, No.182 Wing. Revised scale of weapons and accessories for R.A.F. Regiment units, received (HQB/S/2324/4/E5 date 2nd August, 1943).
Unit allotted identification letters for M.T.-------"RI".
1163325 Sgt. Burdett, J.L. proceeded on 14 days privilege leave.
S/Ldr. G. Andrews, recently appointed Group Defence Officer, No.224 Group, toured Flight posts and billets. Official report contained in H.Q. No.224 Group letter 224G/S.7419/Def. dated 23rd August 1943.
Firing carried out No.879 A.M.E.S. with quadruple Brownings from No's 2 & 3 Sections (one each). Considerable difficulty experienced with trigger mechanism resulting in non-synchronisation of firing between inner and outer guns.
New scales of ammunition for ground defence issued by Air. H.Q. Bengal (HQB/S/2318/6/E4 dated 17th August 1943), issued.

Particulars of scheme for redistribution of machine guns and mountings for A/A and ground to ground use forwarded by Air H.Q. Bengal, this Flight allotted 18 Browning Guns for use mounted as twins on Motley Stalk mountings. Ancillary equipment for this purpose also allotted.

1053216 LAC Langan, P. posted to Base H.Q. Calcutta n/e sick. Flight football team played its first match, beating a Filter Room team by 4-2.

1163325 T/Cpl. (A/S/U) Burdett, J.L. appointed to paid Acting Rank of Sergeant wef 6.5.43. (Auth. Air H.Q.(I) phonogram P3/634 dated 21.5.43). Driving permits received for one Sgt. And two AC's from No.224 Group.

Two LAC's detached to M.T. L.R.D. Chittagong, for M.T. Maintenance Course for R.A.F. Regiment personnel. 1053216 LAC Langan P. attached to Unit supernumerary on discharge from Hospital pending disposal following posting to Base H.Q. n/e sick.

September
2941 Field Squadron – Operational at Agartala Aerodrome

The fifth month of training at AGARTALA. The Month's training opened with a Route Marching in Light Marching Order. Lecture on "fighting with Air Support" given by S/Ldr. MARSLAND of 169 Wing.

Training continued. Lecture by F/Lt. BEE on "Accounts - Service and Civil" No information to hand regarding movement of No.2 Flight to forward location.

No.1 Flight fired the Bren. Results were fair. More practice necessary. Field Training was carried out by No.2 and Support Flight. Instructions received from S/Ldr. FORBES to move No.2 Flight forward to arrive MANIPUR on September 14th.

No Church Parade held owing to absence of Padre. Squadron Meeting was held to discuss Welfare.

Kit Inspection of No.2 Flight carried out. Flight short of certain items of Kit - socks being the main difficulty.

No.1 Flight carried out Rifle Practices on Range. Results were fair. F/O. REDINGTON returned from forward areas and proceeded to Headquarters, No.224 Group the same day. Position regarding lack of

Officers submitted to Group in letter (appendix 'B'). F/O LITTLEFAIR recommended for static employment of Officer in Medical Charge, 169 Wing.

F/O. LITTLEFAIRS's application forwarded to Group. Flight training continued. Signal received from No.224 Group withdrawing No.3 Flight from it's forward location and ordering cessation of Flight movements to IMPHAL. F/O. LITTLEFAIR instructed by Group to hand over his Wing Defence duties to O.C. Ack-Ack Flight, due to arrive in a few days. F/O. REDINGTON returned.

No.2 Flight's preparation to move forward were cancelled. Training resumed. Forced March from 07.00 to 09.49 hrs. Distance covered approximately 13 miles. Considerable interest was taken in the lectures given by the Officers of 169 Wing.

Squadron free day. Information received of the posting of 123728 F/O. CAMERON to the Squadron to fill vacancy created by the posting of F/LT. EVANS to 4414 Ack-Ack Flight.

All Flights engaged in siting guns for Ack-Ack Defence of Camp Area and ground protection. Marked increase of personnel reporting sick Weather extremely humid. F/O. LITTLEFAIR resumed duties with Squadron. F/LT. MACGREGOR completes 26 days with Squadron with no Officer assistance.

Squadron Route March for the first three hours. No casualties. After some reorganisation and allocation of tasks the general maintenance of M.T. vehicles show improvement.

Squadron Parade. No Church Service held. Padre away from Station. F/O. REDINGTON proceeded to 2942 (R) Squadron on attachment.

Support Flight Rifles and Brens zeroed. Several Rifles most inaccurate but no equipment or Armourer Sergeant at Wing to effect necessary adjustments. F/O. CAMERON reported this day.

Support Flight fired Brens on Range. Other Flights carried out training. Rehearsal of Wing Parade in commemoration of the "Battle of Britain" at 18.00hrs.

The Squadron was represented by Nos.1, 2 & Support Flights commanded by F/LT.MACGREGOR. Excellent turnout at the Parade and general bearing and drill of the men produced considerable comment and appreciation.

Squadron moved out of Camp at 19.45 hrs on a night march in Light Marching Order to AKHAURA via AGARTALA. Roads very broken in sections. Rain fell for a short period. Distance covered eighteen miles. Squadron returned 01.30 hrs on 16/9.
Squadron free day. Re-organisation of Flights and allocation of weapons commenced.
Drill for Section in Attack carried out, based on new organisation. Squadron practiced in rapid turn-out in Battle Order.
Forced March for all Flights. Few casualties. General fitness of men excellent. Airmen of No.1, 2 & Support Flight were checked for T.A.B., Cholera injections and vaccinations.
Squadron Parade and Church Parade. General inspection of billets. F/O. G.M. SUTTON (Adjutant) returned to Unit from SCHOOL OF ADMINISTRATION, R.A.F. POONA. Signal received appointing S/LDR. J.P. PUGH to the command of 2941 (R) Sqdn. Vice S/LDR. H.J. FORBES M.M. posted to No.2946 (R) Squadron, DUM-DUM. Squadron establishment - Officer 5, O.R. 152.
Morning Period utilised for re-organisation of Squadron. Signal received from S/LDR. FORBES of return of No.3 Flight from forward areas. Trucks sent to Rail head at 23-30 hours with F/O: CAMERON.
No.3 Flight arrived Rail head at 01.00 hours. S/LDR. FORBES proceeded to Headquarters, 224 Group by air at 13-15 hours. No.1 & 2 Flights practiced Embussing in Light Marching Order. Support Flight trained in Bren and Grenade Rifle.
Squadron Route March at 07-00 - 11-30 hours. No.3 Flight re-organised in conformity with other Flights. Loss of Bren breach block reported.
Squadron free day. Practice Air Raid alert 17-30 hours. Practice satisfactorily carried out. Grave shortage of Anti-Gas clothing for sentries and Decontamination Squads.
Battle Drill for all Flights during early morning period. No.1 Flight personnel fired Sten Gun - practices being 5 single shots from shoulder and hip, and three bursts of 2 rounds fired from shoulder and hip. Automatic fire results generally poor.
Fieldcraft training for all Flights. No.2 Flight fired Sten Gun - similar practices as for No.1 Flight. No.1 & Support Flights - Grenade practice. Two 15 cwts and Jeep returned from IMPHAL. Two

L.M.G. tripods reported to be mislaid at SHENAM. High incidence of Malaria in No.3 Flight recently returned from IMPHAL. Ten cases admitted to hospital to this date.
Squadron and Church Parades. Squadron paraded with Wing personnel for "Battle of Britain Sunday". Afternoon free. S/LDR. H.J. FORBES M.M. returned, and departed by plane, to Calcutta.
Annual training Programme commenced on this day, commencing with individual training. First period 06-00 to 06-20 hours set aside for Drill. Training periods for the whole day organised into 9 - 40 min. periods. S/LDR. PUGH and F/O. BAXTER arrived AKHAURA Station at 21-00 hours and were accompanied to the Camp by F/O. LITTLEFAIR. F/O. CAMERON proceeded to Calcutta for treatment of Conjunctivitis of the left eye.
Training according to programme. Airmen requiring T.A.B., Cholera injections and vaccination proceeded to Sick Quarters on 28th Sept/43.
169 Wing Football League Cup was won by the Squadron team. Cup Final played on 10th Sept/43. The team winning the league by one point.

2942 Field Squadron – Operational at Comilla Aerodrome

A farewell Parade was held on the occasion of the departures of S/Ldr. J. E. Hosking to Calcutta on Medical Grounds. On the same day No.4421 A.A. Flight, under the Command of F/Lt. Rogerson, arrived from R.A.F. Regiment Depot.
Air Vice Marshall T.M. Williams, A.O.C. Bengal Command attend a performance of the Squadron Concert Party.
A "Stand To" was carried out at 02-45 hours and the subsequent exercise finished at 07-00 hours at "B" Troop Heavy A.A.
No.4414 and 4421 A.A. Flights removed to another Camp.
1038773. L.A.C. Newman died in 92 I.G.H. at 13-00 hours on the same date, postings Signals for F/O. Chaffin, Jordon and Budgen, to 4436, 4435 and 4438 A.A. Flights respectively, came through.
1039773. L.A.C. Newman was buried at Comilla with full Military honours, bearers, Escort and Firing Party being provided by the Unit.

F/O's Chaffin and Jordan left on posting to the Depot. Sgt Marron left for Calcutta where he was instructed to carry out some P.S.I. Welfare business.
F/O. H.G. Redington arrived on attachment from 2941 Squadron.
F/O. J.C. Danckwerts and F/O. A.I. Mitchell arrived from R.A.F. Regiment Depot by Air, on Posting.
A Colour Hoisting Parade was held as Wing H.Q. to celebrate the 3rd. anniversary of the "Battle of Britain". F/Lt. Budgen, F/O's Kitchell and Redington and a Flight of armed Gunners from this Unit, attended.
This Unit provided a Firing Party, consisting of 1 Cpl. and 10 Airmen, for the funeral of an Observer from Agartala at Comilla.
F/O. Polly-Fry returned from Shillong.
Posting Signal for S/Ldr. E.M. John to the O.C. vacancy of this Squadron was received the same day F/O. Polly-Fry became Sick in Quarters, with Lumbago.
S/Ldr. E.M. John arrived on Posting from 4410 A.A. Flight.
F/Lt. Budgen, F/O's Mitchel and Redington and a Flight of armed Gunners from this Unit, attended a Church Parade at Wing H.Q., in celebration of the "Battle of Britain" anniversary.
F/LT. G.R. Cattell handed over Command of the Squadron to S/Ldr. E.M. John, at a special parade ordered for that purpose. The same day, F/O. Polly-Fry left for Calcutta to attend a Medical Board, and F/Lt. Budgen left for Chittagong on posting to 4438 A.A. Flight.
The Squadron Football Team won the "BENODE SHIELD" in the Comilla League.

2945 Field Squadron – Operational at Feni Aerodrome

No Record

4402 A.A. Flight – Operational at Chiranga

In accordance with revised establishment (224G/S.620 0/6 1/Org, dated 14.7.43) a B.O.R. Cook, namely 1419750 LAC. JEFFS. H. arrived today from 78 R & R Party.
The Defence Officer, from Headquarters, No.224 Group (S/Ldr. G. Andrews) arrived for the day. He carried out an inspection of all

billets, dining hall, canteen etc. which form the camp of this Flight. After lunch he inspected various gun posts and spoke to a number of the men. The inspection was completed by 16.00hrs. The Group Defence Officer expressed satisfaction on all he saw: He hoped it would be possible to grant more leave very shortly as a number of the men had not had any for over twelve months.

An airmen namely 1449567 LAC. JOHNSON. J. was today appointed to the unpaid rank of A/CPL. The authority to be quoted is 224G/C.2 401/3/203/P3. Dated 8th. September, 1942 and para 496 pf K.R. & A.C.I.

1469085 AC1.CRIPPS. M. and 1510924 AC2. MACKENZIE. F.R., have today, satisfactorily passed a Trade Test Board for the reclassification to LAC.

A full parade of all personnel on this station (made up of personnel from 261 Squadron, R & S.U., Wireless and Cypher as well as this Flight) was held this morning at 09.00hrs to commemorate the "BATTLE OF BRITAIN". A short address was given by F/Lt. CORY and followed by the reading of the message from the A.O.C. in C. India. A copy of this message is attached, as per appendix No.1.

No.4432 A.A Flight, under the command of F/Lt. Marson. Arrived at this station to assist this Flight in the duties of providing ground to air coverage and defence in general.

4403 A.A. Flight –Operational at Chittagong Aerodrome

Weather – Very Hot
Alert sounded 11.00hrs confirmed that a Japanese Reconnaissance Plane was over CHITTAGONG.

News received of Allied invasion of Italy. Morale up tremendously.

Weather – Very Dry & Hot
Visit by 224 Group S.M.O. W/C BAKER. He gave the Unit a commendation in his report for initiative & cleanliness.

Took two suspicious looking natives into custody for questioning & found they were in possession of nominal rolls of Bofor Gun personnel handed them over to Security Police.

Paraded the Flight to watch the killing & skinning of sheep with the object of

a) Accustoming them to the sight of blood
b) If ever we have to live off the country they will have an idea of how to kill & skin.
Alert sounded 14.00hrs.
Apprehended two natives taking bamboo from a dispersal pen issued instructions for a sharp watch to be kept against such offenders.
Weather – Fine & Dry Lively interest aroused by the appearance of a Lockheed 12A two members of the Flight identified it.
Notified by 224 Group that Japanese are moving aircraft to their forward dromes -black out enforced. Addressed the Flight on the Anniversary of the Battle of Britain.

4404 A.A. Flight – Operational at Feni

Four 15 cwt trucks received from 224 Group. All trucks were received in bad condition and a thorough overhaul was necessary to make them serviceable for the road. Very few tools were handed over and it appears that they were stolen en route, it also appears likely that some of the batteries had been changed.
A twin engine enemy recce plane flew over the aerodrome in a North Easterly direction at approximately 20,00ft. No general alarm was sounded but the Civil Sirens in FENI were heard. Eight gun crews stood to.
F/Lt. MACKWOOD returned from leave.
Six airmen were charged before the Station Commander (GROUP CAPTAIN OMMANNEY) at their own request for failing to be in possession of small arms whilst on Gun Post duties.
Owing to the lack of discipline in the Flight and various other factors, application was made to 224 GROUP Headquarters to post two NCO's and two airmen from the Unit.
Normal training carried out, including range practice.
Two airmen proceeded to CHITTAGONG to attend an M.T. course.
Special programme of training for AC1's was carried out prior to taking LAC Trade Test.

LAC Trade Test held. Five airmen out of ten were recommended for LACs.
Two airmen proceeded to CALCUTTA for camouflage course.
Two airmen proceeded to School of Technical Training AMBALA, for armament course.
Heavy showers were experienced every day. Probably the tail end of the monsoon.

4405 A.A. Flight – Operational at Chittagong

Work progressing on building Gun Posts.
F/Lt. Worth assumes command vice F/Lt. Sutton.
New site planned for building .303 Browning Gun Post.
Bamboo building caught fire, approx. 23.00hrs. Guard turned out. No casualties.
Work progressing on Gun Pits.
All arrangements made for the movement of Flight. Four .5 Brownings.
Handed (temp) over to relieving Flight.

4407 A.A. Flight – Operational at Chittagong

Firing practice carried out at No.378 AMES with quadruple Brownings by No.1 Section. Trigger mechanism again shown to be defective.
Unit Standing Order No.2 (reporting of Enemy Aircraft) issued.
Aircraft Log Books introduced for all Gun Posts, recording date, time, type, number direction and estimated height of all aircraft observed.
Firing practice at No.879 AMES with quadruple Brownings of No.2 Section. Perfect result except for usual trigger mechanism difficulties.
Norton M/C, previously removed from No.5029 AMES returned to No.182 Wing, to provide transport for Chittagong Filter Room.
Unit Standing Order No.3 (Orders for Post Duty) issued, cancelling Standing Order No.1.
Unit obtained 1st and 3rd places at No.1 RAFR M.T. Maintenance Course held at M.T.L.R.D. Chittagong. (LAC Brooks R - 80%. LAC Pugh V.V. - 71%)

Movement Order No.2 issued.
No.1 Section moved from No.378 AMES, FINDLI to No.5029 AMES, PAHARTAN changing localities with No.2 Section. This movement was effected (1) to practice mobility (2) to assist M.T. position at H.Q. (3) to afford a change for the Gunners of each Section and enable them to get experience of new conditions. 224 Group called for assessments of NCOs and promising LACs for forthcoming review of RAFR NCOs in India. This letter also suggested possibility of paid F/Sgt rank for Senior NCOs while commanding Flights. LAC Standley C. V. and LAC Brooks, R., this Unit recommended for promotion.
Comprehensive scheme of annual training for RAF Regiment Squadrons and Flights, India, issued by 224 Group. This provided for total training of 216 periods of 40 minutes each. Manpower difficulties, however, rendered Section and Flight training impossible for this Unit under existing conditions.
224 Group ordered Unit to move to Agartala Airfield to man L.A.A. defences in conjunction with No.4401 A.A. Flight, the move to be completed by 16.00hrs 2 October 1943. This Unit to be relieved by No.4405 A.A. Flight.
Unit Movement Order No.3 issued.

October
2941 Field Squadron – Operational at Agartala Aerodrome

The sixth month of training at Agartala started with the annual training programme.
The alarm for Ground attack and the procedure to be adopted was detailed. The annual training programme was carried on with Weapon Training.
Church Parade was held. Training was continued a special guard wad asked for by Wing to defend the HF/OF Station where a known saboteur had been seen. S/Ldr. Pugh & three men provided guard. Nothing was seen of the saboteur.
A practice day Ground attack alarm was held. The results proved very satisfactory. The HF/OF Guard was provided again and consisted of F/Lt. MacGregor and three men. No unusual occurrence. A guard of 1

N.C.O. and six airmen were posted at the HF/OF Station, and it was decided to provide that number all night.

F/O. Cameron returns from hospital.

A Recce of the airfield was made by S/Ldr. Pugh & F/Lt. MacGregor. The Camp was inspected by the Garrison Engineer and repairs & alteration required where reported by him. A night practice alarm was held with satisfactory results. The A.D.C. was present and was well satisfied.

A Recce of the airfield was made by S/Ldr. Pugh and the A.D.C. Day Off.

Sten Gun firing. The A.D.C. goes on leave and his duties were taken over by S/Ldr. Pugh.

F/O. Redington returns from attachment to 2942 Sqdn.
F/LT. MacGregor left for dental treatment in Calcutta.
F/O Sutton (Adjutant) admitted to hospital for observation.
F/O Baxter takes over the duties of Adjutant. A night practice alarm was held.

The "A" Team win Station Football Cup.

Section training in accordance with annual training programme commenced.

Four native apprehended by HF/OF guard and taken to Wing for interrogation. A practice night alarm was held and a Squadron exercise was carried out.

Section Training continued.

Visit from F/Lt. Tidmarsh (Group Education Officer) & form Wing Catering Officer (F/O. Cummings). S/Ldr. Andrews Group Defence Officer arrived to inspect the Squadron. F/Lt MacGregor returned from Calcutta. Day Off.

The A.D.C. returned from leave.

S/Ldr. Andrews left for Chittagong. F/O. Sutton returns from Hospital and resumes duties of Adjutant.

Church parade - afternoon off owing to bad weather.

Classification range sited by S/Ldr. Pugh and F/Lt. MacGregor with Wing Armament Officer. F/O. Baxter posted to 211 Group H.Q.

Flight in defence scheme in Camp area. Recce of airfield by S/Ldr. Pugh & the A.D.C.

The A.D.C. goes on leave & his duties taken over by the C.O. Yellow Air Raid warning in the afternoon.
Squadron provides a guard of Honour, commanded by F/Lt. Mac Gregor, for the Supreme Commander. Visit postponed with 22nd Oct. Training was carried on in the afternoon.
Guard of Honour mounted at Watch Office again but visit of the Supreme Commander cancelled. Pay Parade.
Group Captain commanding R.A.F. Station Agartala congratulated the Guard of Honour on their smart turnout.
Recce of Airfield by Station Commander, C.O. of Squadron and C.O's of 4401 & 4407 A.A. Flights. Night Ops Satellite area one flight in defence and two flights in attack.
Day-off. Recce of Rendevous area by C.O. & F/O Cameron.
Approach march of complete Sqdn to Rendevous area. Intercommunications made with Battle H.Q. by signallers. Selection of defended localities by Flight Commanders.
Practice approach by transport and foot to Rendevous. Visit by M.T. Officers to inspect transport.
Yellow air raid warning at 08-20 hrs necessitated cancellation of Sqdn exercise. All clear at 09-30 hrs. No hostile action. A practice night alarm was held at 2400hrs.
Day Off.
Work on the new Classification range carried out. Exercise held at R.V. 3 & 4 Flights defending Rendevous area. Against 1 & 2 Flights attacking. Good results. The new Padre visited the camp.
Training continued with Bren Gun & anti-tank rifle instruction. Range instruction continued. Lecture by SMO. On First Aid & a meeting of the P.S.I.
Church Parade. Demonstration of erecting bivouacs by F/Lt. MacGregor & followed by practice.

2942 Field Squadron – Operational at Comilla Aerodrome

A new syllabus of Training, based on 224 Group instructions, was put into force and carried out throughout October.

F/O. Polly-Fry leaves for Base H.Q., Calcutta (Posted Non-effective Sick) after returning from Medical Board. F/Lt. G.H. Cattell (2nd i/c) proceeds on 14 days leave.
F/O. A.I. Mitchell is admitted to 165 Wing Sick Quarters and transferred to No.3 Hill Depot, Shillong for treatment. Posting Non-Effective Sick recommended.
F/O. M.G. Redington ceases attachment to this Unit and returns to his parent Unit, 2941 Squadron.
S/Ldr. G. Andrews, Group Defence Officer 224 Group, arrives at Comilla on official visit, and is accommodated in Squadron Officers' Mess.
Air Raid Warning "Yellow" passed by 'phone at 15-45 hours. "All Clear" at 16-05 Hrs. No incident.
2942 Squadron Football Team wins the Final of the Benode Shield beating Y.M.S.A.
The Commanding Officer (S/Ldr. E.M. John) and the Adjutant (F/O. J. C. Danekwerts) and the whole Squadron except the Duty Flight, attend a Mass Parade of 165 Wing at Wing H.Qtr. On the occasion of the visit of Lord Louis Mountbatten, C-in-C. S.E. Asia Command.
2942 Sqdn. Football Team wins the Final of the Roy Cup, by beating the R.A.F. "Nomads".
f/O. A.I. Mitchell returns to this Unit from Shillong, fit for duty.
F/O. J.W. Phipps and F/O. Polly-Fry arrive at this Unit from R.A.F. Regiment Depot, on posting.

2945 Field Squadron – Operational at Feni Aerodrome

No Record

4402 A.A. Flight – Operational at Chiranga

The Group Defence Officer (S/Ldr. G. Andrews), today, visited the Camp, He inspected the camp in general and the gun posts and crew.
No.261 Squadron arrived at this station today.

4403 A.A. Flight – Operational at Chittagong

Visited target area little damage to military personnel or installations, some loss of life amongst the civilian population. Probable target seemed to be the Detties. R'ccied Air Force Property for delayed action or unexploded bombs found four UXB's around MT yard. Erected barricades, detailed a guard & notified R.E's.
S/L ANDREWS 224 Group Defence Officer visited the Unit. Flight tasks and general administration policy discussed. He appeared satisfied with the work of the Unit. Alert sounded 19.15hrs. Later identified as a friendly Wellington.
Sir Harold Howitt member of the Air Council arrived by plane CinC General Auchimliek arrived by Anson at approx. 15.00hrs.
CinC Left.

4404 A.A. Flight – Operational at Feni

No Record

4405 A.A. Flight – Operational at Chittagong

Took over from 4407 A.A. Flight at 182 Wing. Flight divided into 3 Sections. Each Section providing A/A Defence for A.M.E.S. Stations.
C.O. made a tour of Inspection of A.M.E.S. Stations. Checking equipment and enquiring into accommodation and welfare.
Remainder of Flights equipment transferred from North Camp, Chittagong Airfield, to 182 Wing. Armament tools, ammunition etc. dispersed amongst the A.M.E.S. Stations. Four .5 Brownings were handed over to 4438 A.A. Flt complete with ammunition and tools.
Training Programme continued.
Personal firing Quad Browings, Sten Carbines and small arms.
Range Party cancelled owing to bad weather.
Continuing firing Brownings, Stens and small arms.
Air Raid. No casualties in Flight.
Range Party continued.
6 Brownings to be transferred to 4402 A/A/ Flt. Auth 224 Group. 4 Brownings took from 5029 A.M.E.S. One twin Lewis mounted in place.
2 Airmen detached to 2946 (R) Sqd for an aircraft recognition course.

Firing on Range continued. Fire Sten Carbines and small arms.
The Section detached to 5029 A.M.E.S. moved from South Camp 182 Wing to Observation Hill, w.e.f. from today they are fully accommodated etc. by 5029 A.M.E.S.
C.O. made tour of inspection of various stations.

4407 A.A. Flight – Moved to and operational at Agartala Aerodrome

Unit relieved at Chittagong A.M.E. Stations by No.4405 A.A. Flight, Sections with equipment assembled at Muslim High School, Chittagong by 16.00hrs. All according to plan!
Movement from Chittagong to Agartala completed by road in Unit Transport, the whole Unit being moved at once. This was the first movement by road made in India by an R.A.F. Regiment Unit. All was completed without incident, all vehicles running perfectly under heavy load. Main lesson was that personal kit occupied a disproportionate amount of room, although it was obvious that with full scale of equipment it would be impossible to obtain complete mobility due to total weight involved. The convoy left Chittagong at 03.00hrs and arrived at Agartala at 20.30hrs. This period included an adventurous 3-hour delay in crossing bamboo raft ferry at FAZILPUR and a similar delay at the ferry just north of COMILLA. Amendment to establishment No. 664/4 authorised 3$^{d.}$ additional pay for 2 Gunners employed on armament maintenance duties, in accordance with A.F.I. (I) No.131 of 1943.
In agreement with No.4401 A.A. Flight, this Unit took over LAA Defence of the area around the main strip, Agartala airfield, manning Twin Lewis guns on loan from H.Q. No.169 Wing, pending supply of mountings for Browning Guns. In view of poor construction and siting of existing posts arrangements were made for construction of new posts in new locations. 224 Group Administration Instruction No.23 authorised issue of authority to drive M.T. to R.A.F.R. Flights on the basis of one airman for each Prime Mover "A" held. As all M.T. was listed as Prime Movers "B" this meant NO drivers were allowed.
EY Rifles and Discharge Caps introduced for RAF Regiment Flights.

224 Group agreed authority for two drivers for RAFR A.A. Flights on the basis of suggested amendment to establishment transferring 2 Prime Movers "B" to Prime Movers "A".
Amendment No.664/3 to Establishment adding "Note 1. 20 unnumbered Flights (Numbers will be notified later)".
Joint Canteen formed with No.4401 A.A. Flight, each Unit supplying three representatives to Committee. Any profits to be allocated on basis of 50% for each Flight.
224 Group ordered transfer of Qty 8 Guns Browning to 4401 A.A. Flight.
Urgent signal request to Bengal Command for Motley Stork Conversion Sets as existing armament of Lewis Guns was wholly inadequate.
Visit of F/Lt. A.S. Tringham, Group M.T. Officer. Unit highly complimented on excellent state of M.T.
Amendment No.664/5 to Establishment, adding one AC Fitter M.T.

November
2941 Field Squadron – Operational at Agartala Aerodrome

The seventh month of training at AGARTALA commenced with Flight fire & movement exercise. Bivouac demonstration and practice in the afternoon.
Bren Gun firing carried out at the Stop Butts. Six M.T. drivers returned from Maintenance Course, results very satisfactory. Average marks obtained were 70%. An attempt to break into the Armoury, by persons unknown, was foiled by Guards (Cpl WATTS i/c Guard).
Observation & intercommunication exercise was carried out in the morning. F/O. LITTLEFAIR on bridge construction over stream on way to Rendevous. The bridge had been constructed form bamboo and proved very satisfactory. Bivouac practice was carried out again in the afternoon.
Day-off HF/DF guard report unauthorised native approached the hut and when challenged, ran away. Several Sten Gun shots were fired by the Guard Commander (Cpl. CASON) but the native escaped. Matter reported to Wing Intelligence Officer. Two natives were later

apprehended by F/O. LITTLEFAIR and handed over to the Wing Guard Room and were released after being with questioned.

Twenty Four hour exercise carried out. F/O. CAMERON i/c BLUE, F/O. REDINGTON i/c RED. Padre out during the night with the troops.

Exercise ended at 1000 hrs. Troops fit & keen. F/Lt. MacGREGOR posted the to the Depot, SECUNDERABAD to fill D.T.O. vacancy.

Memorial Service was held at the Cemetery for the three pilots who lost their lives over Burma. A Guard of Honour was provided by this Squadron. Station Commander inspected the range and passed it for immediate use. Squadron 'B' team win the Station Sports Competition.

Bren Gun firing was carried out on the new Range. F/Lt. STEWART posted to this Squadron vice F/Lt. MacGREGOR. Cups and prizes presented at the cinema by the Station Commander.

Bren Gun firing again on the Range. S/Ldr. PUGH had an interview with S/Ldr. MARSLAND re Special Night Operation. At 2130 hrs. a sweep was made of the whole area in the vicinity of the runway for any civilians, as there have been several cases of Sabotage lately. 133 civilians were rounded up and brought into Camp.

Prisoners were handed over to the Wing S.P's at 1900 hrs. Rifle firing on range, rapid and snap, was carried out and a mild form of Battle Innoculation given. Instruction were received that R.A.F. Regiment personnel were to be trained in Re-arming and Re-fuelling of aircraft.

Rifle firing continued. C.O. has an interview with Wing Engineer Officer and Armament Officer re R&R.

A forced march was carried out between 0745 and 0930 hrs distance about 5 miles. Lecture in the afternoon by F/Lt. MacEACHON (Engineer Officer) on Re-arming and Re-fuelling. Station Commander attended a concert given by members of the Squadron.

Day-off. W/Cmdr. FOWKE arrived to inspect the Squadron.

W/Cmdr. FOWKE left at 0700 hrs. Church Parade at 0900 hrs. Major PHILIPS returned and reassumed the duties of A.D.C., which had been performed by S/Ldr. PUGH in his absence. Arrangements made for on Flight at a time to be instructed in R&R duties by 27 Squadron.

No.1 Flight start R&R duties which will be carried on for the week. Men very keen and interested. No.2 Flight fired Bren Guns at the stop butts. The Range which had been constructed near the Kutcha Strip was put out of bounds, as personnel were being quartered in the vicinity. A recce was made for another site without success.

No.2 Flight force march to Rendevous area. 3 & 4 Flights fired Bren Guns on the

No.1 Flight carried in with R & R. The other Flights carried out intercommunications practice. C.O., taken ill with malaria.

F/Lt. STEWART arrived. S/Ldr. PUGH. Guard of Honour provided for Deputy A.O.C. in C, and A.O.C., Bengal Command. Very smart turn out.

Nos. 2, 3 & 4 Flights carried out Recce patrols exercise.

No.1 Flight carried on with R & R. Brown Gun instruction given to Nos.3 & 4 Flights on Bren.

Squadron Parade followed by Church Parade.

No.2 Flight takes over R & R instruction. No.1 Flight firing on 30 yard range. Nos.3 & 4 Flights practice grenade throwing. Lecture in afternoon on Theory of S.A. fire.

A.A. Posts dug around the camp area. Bren Gun training was continued.

Rifle firing on 30 yards range and more grenade throwing practice. No.2 Flight continued with R & R.

Day-off.

24 hour exercise was carried out by Nos.1 & 3 Flights. Flights moved off at 1430 hrs., Scheme was reasonably successful. No.3 Flight administration very good.

24 hour Scheme ended at 1230 hrs with forced march on return to camp. Instructions received from W/Cmdr. FOWKE that F/Lt. STEWART was to proceed immediately on attachment to 2943 Squadron. F/O. SUTTON (Adjutant) appointed to takeover command as S/Ldr. PUGH still in hospital.

Squadron Parade at 0830 hrs. Church Parade at 0900 hrs. New 3-tonner arrived.

Nos. 3 & 4 Flights take over R & R duties. No.1 Flight on the range. No.2 Flight on Field Engineering. Air Raid in the afternoon; A.A. posts manned but did not open fire as E/A came over at about 16,000ft. No bombs were dropped in the vicinity of the Camp. A report received that parachutists had been seen descending. Patrols were sent out but nothing was seen of any parachutists. The matter was reported to the A.D.C. The barber (un-erolled follower) was taken into custody and handed over to the Police, as he had told an airman (L.A.C. GOLDSWORTHY) about ten minutes before the warning was given, that there was going to be an Air Raid at 4 o'clock.

Flights carried out the same duties as yesterday. Guard Commander of the Aerodrome and Dispersal Guard reported that one of his patrols (L.A.C. COMMONS) had opened fire at 2030 hrs., on a person (or persons) who had been heard moving about near an aircraft and who, when challenged, ran away. A search was made but nothing was seen. Report of incident sent to 169 Wing Headquarters. Pall bearers and a firing party were provided for the burial service of an airman of the A.M.E.S. who had been shot during guard duties the previous night.

2942 Field Squadron – Move to "Hay" runway near Ramu

F/O. Mitchell goes to Chittagong and Dohazari (4402 A.A. Flight) on investigation concerning M.T. Transport. Returns to Unit 7-11-43.

F/O. Danckwerts (Adjt.) goes to Calcutta on Temporary Duty for Opthalmic consultation. Returns 9-11-43.

S/Ldr. John (Officer Commanding) goes to 224 Group for interview with Group Defence Officer and siting of new camp at "HAY". Returns to Unit 9-11-43.

F/Lt. Cattell returns from leave, and remains at Comilla under Medical observation, pending posting. He is Medically Boarded and proceeds to Shillong on Sick Leave; meanwhile posting note for this Officer to 4433 A.A. Flight received.

S/Ldr. John, F/O. Polly-Fry and Advance Party of Squadron leave by road for No.1 Camp "HAY".

F/O. Danckwerts, F/O. Phipps and Main Party proceed by rail and road to "HAY".

F/O. Mitchell and Rear Party leave Comilla for "HAY" by rail and road.

Squadron football team win the final of the "Benarjie" Cup, beating the Wiltshire Regt., 2-0.

4443 A.A. Flight (i/c SGT. Weeds) arrives on attachment to this Unit for Rations, Accommodation and Discipline.

Completion of Unit move, with arrival of Rear Party, signalled to all concerned Squadron football team beats representative R.A.F. team at Cox's Bazaar,

F/O. Danckwarts (Adjt.) admitted 72 L.G.H., with Malaria; returns to Unit 1-12-43.

Visit of W/Cmdr. Elsden, new Commanding Officer, 165 Wing and S/L. Crethers S.A.O., 165 Wing.

Visit of S/Ldr. Peek, S.M.O., 165 Wing.

Recce of new Camp site made. Visit of S/Ldr. Waterman.

Visit of S/Ldr. Andrews, Group Defence Officer and F/Lt. Smith R.A.F.R.

2945 Field Squadron – Operational at Feni Aerodrome

Revision of Appointments.

Adjutant   - 123710 F/O. ASHTON.   J.E.

No.1 Flight Commander   - 118315 F/O. STUART-HART. K.

No.3 Flight Commander   - 540749 F/Sgt. MORRICE. W.J.

Other appointments unchanged.

An interesting exercise was carried out by the whole Squadron in which two flights were started at a point MR 79 M/8 527464 to proceed through dense scrub jungle with high grass to a point MR 79 M/8 592478, whilst the other two flights traversed the jungle in the opposite direction, the object being to observe the opposing flights without being seen. The two flights moving from W.to E. observed one section of the opposition only but were themselves completely ambushed. The jungle was so dense that it was quite remarkable that any contact was made, it being very difficult for those proceeding in the same direction to keep contact.

Range Firing.

Night patrol by No.4 Flight, who carried out a reconnaissance of the area by the Little FENNY RIVER from a point MR 79 M/8526385, reporting on roads and bridges.

Normal Training Programme.

Night patrol by No.1 Flight, who made their H.Q. at LENUA R.L.G. (MR.79 N/5 626332) patrolled the area down to the A.M.E.S. at a point in the vicinity of 665275, and W. to 616323 round to 589358.

Normal Training Programme.

Night Patrol by No.2 Flight, who proceeded to a point MR 79 N/5 577257, where a H.Q. was established and patrols sent out in a westerly direction to the LITTLE FENI RIVER. It was reported that the roads in the area patrolled contained many more and acute turns than are indicated on the map.

Range Firing in the morning followed by Pay Parade and a General P.S.I. meeting when details were given by F/LT. GARNETT on how the Canteen profits were being utilised for the improved welfare of the men.

Commanding Officer's Parade and Conference of Officers and N.C.O's. The C.O. read out a signal which had just been received, giving warning that Japanese aircraft, including a new dive bomber, had been moved up within range if this airfield and that an attack might be expected at any time. N.C.O's were instructed to see that everybody was fully conversant with P.A.D. orders, that they knew where to go and that all BREN gunners had drawn their reserve ammunition.

At the end of the Conference the Senior N.C.O's were asked to stay behind and were given a 'pep' talk in which responsibilities were pointed out to them as there had been one or two occurrences recently, such as bad 'turn-out' and discipline on Pay Parade, which would not have occurred had the senior N.C.O's been up to their job (this does not apply to all senior N.C.O's in the Squadron).

As we are still without a Padre, no Church Service was held again this week. It was considered that we might hold our own, but the idea was abandoned owing to the absence of hymn books.

Night patrol by No.3 Flight, who established a H.Q. at MR 70 M/3 495444, and carried out a 'recce' of the area of the LITTLE FENNY RIVER N. of that covered by No.4 Flight on the night of November 2nd 1943.

Range Firing. The programme of training has been specially arranged this week to carry out tests of Elementary Training of the whole Squadron, in order to sort out the backward men for special training, and the AC1s. suitable for reclassification to LAC. Tests are to be carried out in the following subjects:

(i)	Rifle (Trigger pressing, snap shooting, care and maintenance, sight setting, range firing, laying an aim).
(ii)	Sten (Range Fire).
(iii)	Bren (Holding, aiming and sight setting, magazine filling and barrel changing).
(iv)	Target recognition.
(v)	Distance Judging.
(vi)	Map Reading.
(vii)	Signalling.
(viii)	Aircraft recognition.
(ix)	Drill.
(x)	General knowledge.

Duty flights took over the inside patrols by night from the 2nd Baroda Dett.

T.O.E.T.

T.O.E.T.

Heats were run off for the Squadron Sports to be held on Saturday next.

T.O.E.T.

Squadron Sports Day. The following events were held:- 100 yds (open), 100 yds handicap (over 30), 220 yds, 440, 880, 1 mile, 1 mile walk, high jump, long jump, throwing the cricket ball, inter-flight relay race, and inter-flight tug-of-war. Silver cups were presented by officers to the individual winners and flight points were also awarded. The inter-flight tournament was won by No.1 Flight, No.4 Flight second, No.2 Flight third, H.Q. Flight fourth and No.3 Flight fifth. A Squadron Concert was held in the evening when the C.O. presented the prizes, and the concert party was entirely composed of Squadron personnel. Much credit is due to F/O. K. STUART-HART who organised both Sports and Concert.

F/O. F.C.P. WILMOT appointed to the acting rank of F/LT. on posting to No.4440 A.A. Flight. This officer has worked extremely well with the Squadron since its formation, especially in the capacity of M.T. Officer, and will be much missed.

This makes the Squadron two officers below strength, although a sergeant (potential F/Sgt) has been posted by A.H.Q. India to fill the officer Flight Commander vacancy occasioned by the posting of F/O. OTTOY, but has not yet reported for duty. (since understand this posting will be cancelled).

T.O.E.T. completed by all available personnel, the average results by flights being interesting as follows:-

No.4 Flight - 56.2%.

No.2 Flight - 52.3%.

No.1 Flight - 51.0%.

No.3 Flight -46.1%.

Appointments.

F/O. K. STUART-HART temporarily i/c No.2 Flight on the departure of F/LT. F.C.P. WILMOT.

F/O. K. STUART-HART also retains command of No.1 Flight.

F/O. J.E. ASHTON - Sports Officer in place of F/LT. T.R. GARNETT.

Volunteers were called for to make a Composite Flight under the command of F/Lt. T.R. GARNETT to go into the jungle on a four day expedition. Many more than the required number volunteered and a selection was made. The flight set out at 1400 hours, taking with them rations for four days and chlorinating tablet sufficient for 100 gallons of water. A camp will be set up at MR 79 N/5 815300 and a reconnaissance of the surrounding country will be made.

Message received from 'Fighter Ops' that a Japanese aircraft had been shot down approx. 3 miles S.W. of 877 A.M.E.S. A patrol was sent out immediately and the wreckage of an Army '100' T/E 'Recce' aircraft was located at 1730 hours at a point MR 79 M/8475324 (approx.). The crew of two had already been removed (dead) and the aircraft was being guarded by the A.R.P. This guard was taken over by the Squadron and will be maintained as long as required.

Contact was made with the Composite Flight at MR N/5 815800 where a very good camp had been made. The whole flight were very happy and enjoying the experience.

An exercise was carried out by the personnel not out with F/Lt. GARNETT'S Special Flight, taking the form of a night attack on the Special Flight's camp.

The attacking force left Squadron H.Q. at 1400 hours and proceeded by transport to KARER HAT (MR N/9 745293) and from here proceeded on foot to 776293, were camp was made. It was not expected that they would be successful but by making them the larger party it was hoped that the defenders would the attack was over when they had annihilated them, as they should do, there being only one possible route for an attacking party to take. The attacking party, consisting of the Flight Commander and one section, then hoped to take the defenders by surprise by stalking the Camp four hours later. As it turned out, both parties were successful due to reasons stated in F/Lt. GARNETT'S report.

F/LT. GARNETT returned to H.Q. with two sections of this Special Flight but the third section failed to put in an appearance at the point were it was arranged they should be put up. (F/SGT. MORRICE was in charge of this section).

F/SGT. MORRICE and his section arrived approx. 22 hours late, just as a search party was starting out to look for them. The Flight Commander of the Special Flight (F/LT. T.R. GARNETT) rendered a most interesting report of the operation, pointing out the various lessons learnt, and extracts are attached hereto as an appendix. All the men who took part in the expedition were very thrilled with their experiences and if nothing else it had a very good effect on morale generally.

Message received from 'Fighter Ops' that a 'Hurricane' had crashed landed on the bend of the FENI River beyond FAZILPUR. This was located at 640265 and a guard was placed on it.

A new Padre has arrived and Morning Prayer and Holy Communion were held in the Canteen.

Commanding Officer's Parade and Conference of Officers and N.C.O's. A discussion of last week's exercise showed much enthusiasm for further exercises of this nature.

Range firing and general training. 'Red Warning' received at 0905 hours, lasting for nearly two hours but no enemy aircraft reached this area.

Report from 'Fighter Ops' of a further crash. This was located at NOAKHALI and a guard placed on it.

Normal Training routine.

Flight in defence and attack.

Normal Training routine.
Normal Training routine.
Airfield attacked by a small force (approximately ten bombers with fighter escort) of Japanese aircraft. Emergency gun-posts were manned but the enemy aircraft dropped their bombs from approx. 20,00 feet, well out of range of our L.M.G's. No bombs fell in the Squadron Camp, those on the airfields being W. of the strip and very little damage was done although the telephone exchange sustained damage. Morning Prayer and Holy Communion held in the Canteen.
Commanding Officer's Parade and inspection of the Camp, followed by normal training. New systems of weekly Duty Flights instituted whereby Camp Guard, Ex Crash Guards, and a section for training by 177 Squadron in the Elementary Handling of Aircraft, will all be supplied by the one flight, enabling the rest of the Squadron to be at full strength for training. Air raid message 'Red' but no incidents were reported.
No.1 and 2 Flights, under the command of F/O. K. STUAT-HART set out on a 3-4 day jungle reconnaissance. No.4 Flight om training. No.3 Flight - Duty Flight.

4402 A.A. Flight – Operational at Chiranga

No Record

4403 A.A. Flight – Operational at Chittagong

Weather - Clear One Gunner employed in armoury after completing armourer course at AMBALA.
Alert no plane visible but machine gun fire heard.
Alert sounded. No hostile aircraft sighted.
One other 15cwt Chevrolet collected for this Unit bringing our total to two
Alert sounded one reconnaissance plane reported.
Weather - Fine Supreme Commanders "Order of the Day" read out to all ranks.

Orders received to fully man all Gun Posts at night during the waning of the moon. Sqd/L BARNES assumed command of Cox's Bazaar.
Received three Alerts during morning.
News received of the attack on Chittagong all posts warned to be extremely vigilant during the next week.
Ninety five (95) friendly aircraft sighted moving south. Visited George L.G. to make a reconnaissance with a view to taking over there. Report on GEORGE submitted to 224 Group.
Notification received that four R/T sets are awaiting collection at 313 MU, Calcutta. Escort despatched to take them over.
Sqn/L ANDREWS 224 Group Defence Officer visited the Unit. We were informed that our move to GEORGE had been cancelled. Expressed satisfaction of the Units activities.

4404 A.A. Flight – Moved to and settling in at Dohazari Aerodrome

Normal gun post duties and training were carried out.
Movement order received from H.Q.224 GROUP with instructions of this Flight to move to DOHAZARI at 13.00hrs on the same day. Two sections with service & personal equipment left FENI in three 15 cwt trucks at 13.00hrs.
Advanced Party left CHITTAGONG.
Advanced Party arrived at DOHAZARI.
Pear Party (2 sections) left FENI with service & personal equipment in three 15 cwt trucks. Two trucks were loaned from No.4415 A.A. Flight for the move.
Arrived at Chittagong and stayed the night in the TRANSIT CAMP.
Rear Party left Chittagong in convoy.
Rear party arrived at DOHAZARI.
Move of Unit was completed 48hrs after receipt of movement order.
Slit trenches round domestic camp were dug.
Domestic camp was tidied up. Owing to the cookhouse not being ready and the lack of water facilities the airmen fed with 167 Wing.
No.4442 Flight arrived at DOHAZARI. Strength 1 Sgt. 34 A/C. Officer Commanding No.4404 A.A. Flight appointed by 224 Group to command

No.4442 A.A. Flight. Until such a time as an Officer becomes available.
Three sets of quadruple Brownings received from 224 Group on loan, until the new sets of twin-Brownings recently taken over from 39 E.P. were complete with Motley Stock mountings & conversion sets.
Digging commenced on gun pits.
Digging continued on gun pits.
Three gun pits were completed and quadruple Brownings were mounted and manned.
Work continued on the gun pits.
A further three gun pits were completed. Two Corporals admitted to hospital,
Sergeant CAMPBELL admitted to hospital.
Work continued on gun pits.
Air Raid Warning. All guns manned (3 sets quadruple Brownings). No enemy aircraft were seen. Two A/C replacements attached to Flight from HQ 224 GROUP.
Further three gun pits were completed, making a total of six.
Practice shoot with Brownings. Two sets found correct, slight defects in third set.
Air Raid Warning. No enemy aircraft were sighted.
All gun pits completed.

4405 A.A. Flight – Operational at the A.M.E.S. near Chittagong

Inspection of gun posts by C.O. at 5029 A.M.E.S.
Gun Post build in aerodrome with instructions from Group Defence Officer.
2 Airmen proceeded to CALCUTTA on escort duty. C.O. inspected 378 A.M.E.S.
Kit inspection held for personnel at 378 A.M.E.S. and 879 A.M.E.S.
Kit inspection held for personnel at H.Q. 182 Wing and 5029 A.M.E.S.
.303 Browning stores collected from 224 Group. C.O. inspected 879 A.M.E.S. 2 airmen returned to Unit on cessation of Aircraft Recognition Course.
2 Airmen detailed to attend Aircraft Recognition Course.

Personnel of 378 and 879 A.M.E.S. firing rifles. 2 men from each Section to report to Dental Centre 224 Group.
1 Airmen sent to Rauchi for Aircraft Recognition Course. 2 men from each section to report to Dental Centre 224 Group.
2 men from each section to report to Dental Centre 224 Group.
Lectures on .303 Browning given to personnel of 5029 and 879 A.M.E.S.
C.O. inspected 378 and 879 A.M.E.S.
F/Lt. Smith from 224 Group inspected gun post.
C.O. inspected various Sections.
Air raid warning 10.00hrs and 11.05hrs. No action or casualties.
Nil.
Air raid warning. No action. No casualties.
Nil.

4407 A.A. Flight – Operational at Agartala Aerodrome

Standing Orders No.4 (Orders for Gun Post Duty) and No.5 (Orders for Corporal i/c Watch) issued.
224 Group rules, in reply to this Unit's enquiry, that non-Gunner personnel on Unit strength were not to be regarded as embodied in the R.A.F. Regiment, but were to be trained sufficiently to take their place in battle when called upon.
224 Group called for fresh assessment of N.C.O.s for India Command review of all Regt. NCOs.
Bengal Command Operational Directive No.18, giving disposition of all RAF Regiment Units to be complete by 1 JAN 44 indicated note 1 A.A. Flights and Squadrons. "No change" shown in this Unit's location.
Following suspected sabotage in theft/service papers, this Unit in conjunction with No.4401 AA Flight, carried out search of villages at South end of Airfield. No information obtained, but exercise gave useful training in jungle movement, including unorthodox methods of river crossing!
Visit of W/Cdr. J.C. Fowke, Bengal Command Defence Officer.

F/Lt. L.R.H. Portlock, O.C. Unit proceeded on temporary duty to C.V.A.R.I.S, RANCHI, for Aircraft Recognition Course. F/Lt. R.S. TAYLOR, O.C. 4401 Flight assumed command of this Unit.
Unit formed part of newly introduced South East Asia Command.
224 Group ordered that during monthly waning moon period, all AA Posts to be fully manned for "Stand To" from ½ hr before dawn.
224 Group ordered reconnaissance of PARASHURAM Landing Ground for purpose of siting Gun Posts and with view to move at 48 hrs notice.
224 Group authorised issue of temporary driving licences to non-licenced personnel for specific journeys in emergency only.
F/Lt. R.S. TAYLOR, Acting Flight Commander, accompanied Cpl. GREEN,. C.C., reconnoitred the landing ground. Unit left in charge of Sgt. Burdett, J.L. under general supervision of F/Lt. J. Stewart, No.2941 Squadron.
Report on above reconnaissance submitted to H.Q. 224 Group. Approx. 12 Type 99 2EB LILY escorted by small number of TYPE 01 F OSCAR bombed airfield from about 20,000 ft, destroying Flight Office, and several huts. Some bombs on runway, which was quickly made serviceable. No action taken by this Unit owing to high altitude of attack. Total damage to Unit equipment was one small whole in windscreen of a 5/15 cwt truck caused by bomb splinters!
224 Group ordered Unit to move to PARASHURAM on 15 December 1943.

4422 A.A. Flight – Operational at Cox's Bazaar

No.2 Section – 210 AMES, third twin Browning AA Post completed and tested.
Warning received from 224 Group (Signals AD90.A158.4NOV). of further increase JAP aircraft probably including new dive bombers in BURMA. Attacks anticipated. All sections warned to be particularly alert.
AIR RAID ALERT – NOTHING to report.
1 15 cwt. truck received from 224 Group M.T. Pool (No tools or spares).
165 WING take over Local Administration of Unit (224G/S6201/103/2Org 9/11/43).

Lt.Col LYNCH, R.E., 456 Fwd. Airfield Engineers visited Flight H.Q. requesting Operations Room & Domestic Site.
S.E. Asia Command formed, under Admiral Lord LOUIS MOUNTBATTEN, Supreme Allied Commander S.E. Asia. 'ORDER OF THE DAY' read to all sections by Flight Commander.
Leave allocations for four airmen arranged at Racecourse Hostel, CALCUTTA.
Signal received from 224 Group (AD97 18.NOV). During the period of the Waning moon every A.A. Post is to be fully manned, from half an hour before dawn until full light.
Two airmen detached for Aircraft Recognition Course, CHITTAGONG.
Orders received from 224 Group to reconnoitre new location of unit. Contacted 165 WING re. new location- REINDEER I strip.
Sited domestic camps and A.A. gun post areas. REINDEER I. 6 Airmen detached for first of a series of 3 day courses "re-arming & Re-fuelling" arranged with 85 R&R PARTY.
Further reconnaissance of REINDEER I.
607 SQUADRON aircraft arrived REINDEER I - contacted 165 WING for information. S/L. ANDREWS 224 GROUP DEFENCE OFFICER and S/L. JOHN O/C 2942 Sqdn. R.A.F. Regt. visited H.Q. section and discussed details of Unit move to REINDEER I strip.

December
2941 Field Squadron – Operational at Agartala Aerodrome

Nos. 3 & 4 Flights Refuelling and Re-arming with 27 Squadron. No.1 & 2 Flights practising boat building.
3 & 4 flights R & R. Stand Down for 1 & 2 Flights. Inter Flight Cricket.
S/Ldr. J. P. PUGH returns from Hospital and re-assumes Command of Squadron. He reported to the Station Commander and to the A.D.C.
Nos.1 & 2 Flights Weapon Training and Boat Building. Nos.3 & 4 Flights R & R. Satellite Recce'd for Gun Post Sites with A.D.C. Flight Commanders conference on next weeks training.

3 & 4 Flights R & R. Remainder of Squadron Parade and Flight Commanders Training. C.O's inspection of Camp.
No.1 Flight R & R. 2, 3 & 4 Tactical Training. Fieldwork and Map Reading. C.O., A.D.C., and F/Lt. TAYLOR (4401 A.A. Flight) siting Gun Posts on Satellite.
Bayonet Training by all Flights followed by Tactical Training. Inspection of the Squadron by G/CPT. J.H. HARRIS (C.D.O.) and W/CDR. FOWKES (C.D.O. BENGAL). Full Squadron Parade and one Officer and 13 other ranks interviewed by C.D.O. Visit of F/LT. TAYLOR (A.H.Q.) re Equipment.
No.1 Flight - R & R. No.2 Flight Compass March and instruction in direction finding. Nos.3 & 4 Flights - Sten Gun instruction and firing.
No.1 Flight - R & R. Remainder Stand Down and Sport. Surprise practice Air Raid Alarm on moonlight night - Results very satisfactory and no confusion.
No.1 Flight - R & R. No.2 Flight - Sten firing. 3 & 4 Flights Range Practice (Rifle) Bomb Recce Lecture at W.H.Q. attended by 7 N.C.O's. Instructions received from 224 Group to detach a Flight for Ground Defence of Satellite, pending A.A. Flight being sent from Depot.
No.1 Flight detached to No.1 F.R.D. as instructed. Exercise on boat building and River Crossing by 2, 3 & 4 Flights on Tank. Extreme care and forethought is required for this operation and more practice is needed. Five Mk.108 R/T Sets tested by Wing Signals with make up batteries. Reception only possible for ¾ miles, but it is hoped that proper batteries, when available will strengthen this. Signallers of Squadron instructed by Wing Signallers N.C.O's in operation, care and maintenance of sets.
Squadron Parade (2, 3 and Support Flights) Church Parade. Camp Inspection. Anti-Gas Training. 3 Drivers and 3 Gunners to COMILLA for A.F.V. convoy. F/LT. J.M. STEWART returned from attachment to 2943 (R) Squadron. Visit from R.C. Padre (COMILLA).
Tent Pitching. Instruction in Browning and Grenades. F/O. G.M. SUTTON proceeds to FENI to act as O.C. A.F.V. Convoy. F/O. W.H. LITTLEFAIR assumes duties of Adjutant.

No.2 Flight - Rifle Range. No.3 and Support Flight Battle Drill and Field Engineering. Signaller receiving instruction in 108 R/T/Sets with batteries borrowed form Wing Signals. Night Ops. Searching Ground R.V. Area during hours of darkness. Three out of four "enemy" rounded up. Movement and discipline good.
Stand Down- Sports.
No.2 Flight - Compass March. 3 & Support Flights - Devises for Water Crossing. Pay Parade.
No.2 Flight -Boat Building. 3 & Support Flights - Compass March incorporating water crossing. Flight Inter-Comm. Training.
Squadron Parade. Church Parade. Air Raid Warning 10.30 hrs - 11.15 hrs. No bombs dropped nor enemy aircraft seen. Visit from S/Ldr. SULLIVAN Group Equipment Officer.
No.2 Flight - Rifle Range, 3 and Support Flights A.A. Post Digging Practice. Visit from F/O. NELSON - Group Explosives Officer who passed suspect Grenades as O.K.
3 and Support Flights Rifle Range. No.2 Flight Digging and Field Engineering 3 Bren Gunners return from A.F.V. Convoy - no accommodation en-route. F/O. H.G. REDINGTON detached to 2944 Squadron on orders from A.H.Q. BENGALL.
All Flights on Range for Knock out competition won by No.1 Flight. Driving instruction given by Senior N.C.O's.
2, 3 & Support Flights on Exercise (Vs. Paratroops) Exercise not altogether a success owing to lack of aggressive Spirit on behalf of "Paratroops", but defensive positions and patrols of "Mobile Reserve" good.
2, 3 and Support Flights - Grenade throwing, one Blind demolished. 2 Flight Boat Building. 3 and Support Flights - A.A. Post Construction.
Christmas Day; Stand - Down. Organised Games. First Squadron Magazine combined in Christmas Dinner Menu and Xmas Card (appendix 'E'). Camp inspected by O.C., R.A.F. Station, Agartala and 169 Wing Adjutant.
Squadron Parade. Church Parade. Anti-Gas and Internal Economy.

Organised Games.
No.2 Flight – Control and Inter-Comm. 3 and Support Flights –Range. Afternoon – Clothing Parade. Sgt. (A/F/Sgt) PASQUALL. Left Unit for Depot.
No.2 Flight – Range. Nos.3 and Support Flights – Control and Inter-Comm. Movements in M.T. Convoy. Air Raid 'RED' Warning 13.10 – 13.50 hrs. No Bombs dropped nor E/A seen. Sgt. QUIGLEY arrived from 2942 Squadron to act as F/Sgt.   1 A.F.V. arrived from Calcutta.
Movement in M.T. Convoy; Road Blocks and Ambush. Camouflaging of A.A. Posts and Weapon Pits. A.F.V. preliminary trials. Clutch slipping on High Ratio and rear axle could not be disengaged; otherwise satisfactory.
No.2 Flight –Wing Clothing Parade.   3 and Support Flights and Squadron H.Q. on Range.   Tactical Lecture –M.T. Convoy.
No.2 Flight – Sand Table construction.   No.3 and Support Flights – Wing Clothing Parade.   Pay Parade. No.1 A.F.V. Crew detailed and practicing.   2, 3 and Support Flights –Sand Table Exercise (Flight in Attack).

2942 Field Squadron – Operational at Comilla Aerodrome

Squadron Adjutant (F/O. Danekwerts) returns to Unit, on discharge from 68 L.G.H.
Group Defence Officer (S/Ldr. Andrews) and F/Lt. Smith R.A.F.R., leave on conclusion of visit.   W.E.F. 22-11-43 detachment of this Squadron are assisting in the refuelling and rearming of aircraft of the R.A.F. and U.S.A.A.F., on the Ramu airfields, thus fulfilling the new R.A.F. Regiment policy.
F/Lt. Harvey arrives to take over Command of 4443 A.A. Flight.
Visit of Group Equipment Officer (S/Ldr. Sullivan) and Wing Equipment Officer (F/Lt. Clarke).
First visit of Chief Defence Officer (G/Capt. Harris) to this Unit; accompanied by S/Ldr. Andrews (Group Defence Officer).   4443 A.A. Flight moves over to Reindeer 1.

09-40 hours. Air Raid Warning "Red" 09-50 hours. All Clear. No incidents. 16-20 hours. Air Raid Warning "Red" 16-40 hours. All Clear. No incidents.
Squadron football team beats 136 Squadron at Cox's Bazaar, 7-0.
F/Lt. Noble arrived from 4433 A.A. Flight on posting as 2nd i/c Squadron.
W.E.F. 7-12-43 this Unit provided night patrols on Reindeer 1 and Lyons airfields, and 165 Wing Domestic Area.
W/Cdr. Eladon, O.C. 165 Wing and S/Ldr. John, O.C. 2942 Squadron select new camp site near "HAY" strip, M.R: Burma & India sheet No.84./3 and 79./15 (1" to 1 Mile) 026107. Work on roads, bridges etc., commenced.
Squadron football ream beats 165 Wing H.Q., at Cox's Bazaar (8-1).
Visit of Group Accountant Officer, F/Lt. Sharpe, Bengal Command Accts., and F/Lt. Mathews, 165 Wing Accts.
Christmas arrangements for Squadron. Games, Competitions, Tombola. Xmas dinner menu attached.
Officers & Senior N.C.O's versus Airmen football match at Cox's Bazaar - result 4-4. Air Raid Warning "Red" - 12-30 hours. All Clear. 13-00 hours. No incidents.
Squadron moves under canvas - to No.2 Camp, Hay (see entry above for 14-12-43). Move signalled to 224 Group (R) A.H.Q. Bengal (R) B.P.O. (R) 165 Wing.

2945 Field Squadron – Operational at Feni Aerodrome

Commanding Officer visited camp made by flights out on recce, at MR 79 M/12 761433. Patrols are to be carried out to MANU BAZAR 851471 and the various spot points within the surrounding area with the object of discovering if a look-out could be established which would be able to see across FENI. An excellent camp had been established and there were no complaints, in fact, many men expressed the wish that they could be out for a longer period than four days.
Normal training by No.4 Flight by day. No.3 Flight made a night attack on the camp occupied by Nos.1 and 2 Flights but the defence

was too good for them, having had twenty-five minutes warning of their approach by a system of listening posts.

Nos. 1 and 2 Flights returned to H.Q. at 1800 hours, all fit and well.

Normal training programme and discussion on exercise.

Morning Service and Holy Communion.
No.4 Flight took over from No.3 Flight as Duty Flight for the week.

Commanding Officer's Parade, Inspection of Camp and Conference of Officers and N.C.O's. Nos.1, 2 and 3 Flights on training. Current Affairs - Discussion on the Beveridge Report.

Field Firing - flight fire and movement.
Bren guns and rifle bombers on range.

Firing round cover and Battle Drill with live ammunition.

All Sten guns tested on the range and seven found to be completely unserviceable, together with six magazines. These being returned to 302 M.U. for exchange as per instructions.

Squadron inspected by the Chief Defence Officer, accompanied by Defence Officers from Bengal Command and 224 Group. The Chief Defence Officer expressed his satisfaction with the Squadron.

Normal training programme. Night exercise - 'Firing on fixed lines'.

Morning Service and Holy Communion in the Canteen.

F/Lt. T.R. GARNETT proceeded on a Junior Commander Course (3 weeks) at JHANSI. Commanding Officer's Parade, Inspection Weapons, Inspection of the Camp and Conference of Officers and N.C.O's. Discussion on Current Affairs - "The Bombing Offensive in Europe" following a talk giving facts and figures by the Commanding Officer.
No.1 Flight - Duty Flight.
No.2 Flight - Training.
Nos.3 and 4 Flights -Preparation for fur day jungle exercise.

Nos.3 and 4 Flights under the command of F/O. J.E.S. ASHTON went out to a point MR 79 M/12 782386 to establish a camp and carry out patrols from this point to MAMUNBHAGNA, TRIG POINT 542 and S.W. to the FENI RIVER. The objects:- to find out if it is possible to overlook the airfield from the trig and spot points marked on the map in this area, and also to carry sufficient rations for the four days without relying on any extra rations being brought out from Squadron H.Q.

The Commanding Officer visited the jungle camp at MR 79 M/12 770388, it having been found impossible to get to the original point owing to the range of hills being so steep and covered with dense undergrowth, and the path shown on the map being completely overgrown. The site chosen was however excellent, with a spring supplying good water, and the Camp surrounded on three sides by high and thickly covered hills.

Patrols were sent out to explore the high points, and reports received stated that it was possible to observe the airfield, where aircraft could be plainly seen, the distance being approximately fourteen miles.

The Camp was attacked at night by No.2 Flight commanded by F/O. K. STUART-HART. Despite every precaution being taken, the attackers managed to get right into the Camp without being seen or heard, the entire flight passing within five yards of one sentry on the darkness just before the moon rose. This taught the lesson on how difficult it is to protect a Camp at night in thick country if the enemy are prepared to crawl very slowly, making use of such aids as the occasional rustling of trees by the wind, and the dripping of dew to cover their movement.

The Flights returned to H.Q., one man only complained of being sick and fever was suspected. This, however, did not develop and no one was any the worse for the experience, many stating that they wished they could have stayed out longer. The rations taken were found to be in excess of requirements, and in future tinned meat can be reduced. For the four days approx. 2lbs. per man was taken and this can be cut down to 4ozs. Per man.

Discussion on Exercise and normal training.

Morning Service and Holy Communion.

Commanding Officer's Inspection and Conference of Officers and N.C.O's.

Squadron personnel inoculated against Cholera, the Medical Officer having reported that 97 people died of Cholera in FENI last week.

Anti-Cholera precautions were published in Squadron D.R.O's last week.

Range firing.

Normal training routine.

Normal training routine. Message received at 2100 hours that an aircraft had crashed in the vicinity of MIRSARAIMR 79 N/9(767110), and a patrol was sent out to locate it. They went to the Police Station at MIRSARAI and were directed to a tank approx. five miles West on which the wreckage of a 'Mosquito'.

The Engineering Officer from 243 Wing arrived at about the same time and undertook to take all necessary action, whilst we mounted a guard which will be maintained until the wreckage is taken over by the Salvage Unit.

Squadron Sports Day. Practically everybody entered for something and great keenness was displayed. The Inter-Flight Competition was again won by No.1 Flight, No.2 Flight second, No.4 third and No.3 fourth.

The Padre held a special Christmas Day Service in the Canteen.

The airmen sat down to an excellent meal at 1300 hours, consisting of tomato soup, fish, duck, sausage, bacon, ham, Christmas pudding and fruit salad. Each man had a bottle of beer, tot of rum, cigarettes and a cigar. The Officers and Senior N.C.O's served in the customary style and there were "no complaints"! In the evening it was arranged with the Canteen Contractor that each airman should receive a free supper, and this was taken advantage of despite the sumptuous feed at mid-day.

The guard on the crashed aircraft was relieved by No.3 Flight who took over as Duty Flight at 1000 hours, thus enabling the previous guard to return for their belated Christmas dinner.

A football match was played in the afternoon v A R.P., who had imported several players from CHITTAGONG, and a very even match resulted in a draw 1 - 1.

At night the Concert Party organised by F/O. K. STUART-HART entertained the Squadron and the visiting A.A. Flight (4441) who were the winners of our R.A.F. Regiment Inter-Flight Football League. The Commanding Officer presented the cups for this and the individual winners of the Squadron Sports.

It was decided that Nos.1 and 2 Flights who were due to go on jungle exercise this week, should make camp at MIRSARAI and take over guarding the wrecked aircraft sending out patrols from there.
Delivery was completed of the first of the Armoured Fighting Vehicles allotted to this Squadron

No.3 Flight guard on crashed aircraft returned having been relieved by No.2 Flight. No.4 Flight in the range.
Message received form F/O. K. STUART-HART, i/c Nos.1 and 2 Flights, that patrols had been sent out from MIRSARAI and transport would be required to meet them at the places and times stated.

(a) Sgt. CLEARY and 30 men at MR 79 M/12 713412 (Tank). 1600 hrs. 30.12.43.
(b) Cpl. LORIMER and 7 men at MR 79 N/9 745294 (CHATTARUA). 1400 hrs. 29.12.43.
(c) Cpl. NEWEY and 9 men at MR 79 N/9 745294 (CHATTARUA). 1400 hrs. 30.12.43.
(d) Cpl. CARTWRIGHT and 6 men at MR 79 N/9 721105 (guard on crash aircraft) to be relieved on 30.12.43.
(e) F/O. K. STUART-HART and balance at LENUA R.L.G. MR 79 N/5 625325

Patrol (b) picked up at the appointed hour.

All other patrols returned safely with the exception of patrol (a) who had failed to arrive by sundown and it was arranged that transport should go out again at dawn. Crash guard (d) returned with the relief guard who were no longer required. Funeral party supplied for the burial of the crew of the crashed aircraft.

Patrol (a) returned safely all fit and well. They failed to make their reference point by nightfall so made camp and carried on at dawn.

4402 A.A. Flight – Operational at Chiringa

The S.D.O. (G/Capt. Harris) accompanied with the Group D.O. (S/Ldr. Andrews), to-day, visited and inspected this Flight. He expressed satisfaction on all he saw and had no suggestions or adverse critism to make.

1414850 LAC. NICHOLS. J.A. was today posted, from this Unit non-effective sick, to B.H.Q., R.A.F., Calcutta, in accordance with B.P.O's letter reference BPO/6601/D.1., dated 10th June, 1943.

No.4432 A.A. Flight left this station with a result that this Unit is the only R.A.F. Regiment Flight on this Station.

1351199 CPL. BIRTLES. F. (A/Pd/Sgt.) has been promoted to T/Sgt. w.e.f. 19th October, 1943, authority is B.P.O's letter reference BPO/2001/2/A2., dated 11th December 1943, and H.Q.S.E.A.A.C. letter GD/2424, dated 1st December, 1943. Also 1449567 LAC. JOHNSTON. J. (A/U/Cpl.) was promoted to T/Cpl. w.e.f. the 15th November, 1943, authority BPO/2001/2/A2., dated 11th December 1943, and H.Q.S.E.A.A.C. letter GD/2424, dated 1st December, 1943. In accordance with amendment to Establishment, (authority G og I 3106/424/1/Org./AF., dated 15th October, 1943), 1634629 LAC. JACKSON. A.H. - F.M.T. reported on posting, to this Unit today, ex U.K.

Two Gunners, namely 1306164 LAC. FOWLER. H.W. and 1497128 LAC. WILDSMITH.J.R. arrived on posting to this Unit, to-day, as replacement for LAC.STOCKLEY and LAC. HENDERSON., who were posted non-effective sick on the 13th December, 1943.

4403 A.A. Flight – Operational at Cox's Bazaar

Weather Clear: Motley Stork Mountings and ancillary equipment received making this Unit completely equipped with arms and equipment, except for Bren Guns.

Clear: Air Raid Warning - No hostile A/C sighted here out to sea. Later reported that 100 H/A were 50 miles out at sea.

Clear: A.O.C. visited station. Air Raid Warning - No H/A sighted.

Clear: 4 R/T sets received batteries not available

Clear: Warned of possibility of Japanese Commando Raids during next week. Defence meeting called by Admin. Comm. To co-ordinate all defensive measures. Doubled patrols at night time.

Clear: C.D.O. G/Capt. HARRIS visited the Unit and discussed various aspects of the general organisation and administration.

Clear: Supreme Commander Lord Louis Mountbatten visited the station. Introduced to all officers and gave an informal talk to the men.

Cloudy: Bren Guns received.

Clear: "Blanket Treatment" commenced on the Unit anti-malarial precautions.
Beaufighter landed. Two wounded crew on board.
Clear: Xmas Day festivities commenced at 14.00hrs, skeleton crews left on Fun posts.
Clear: Alert 11.30 – 12.30 90+ H/A raided Chittagong, reported 6 destroyed – no H/A sighted here.
Clear:
Clear: Air Raid Warning 10.30. No H/A sighted.

4404 A.A. Flight – Operational at Dohazari

Normal duties and training carried out. Air raid warning at 11.00hrs. No enemy aircraft seen.
Classification range completed.
WING COMMANDER FOWKE, Defence Officer Air Headquarters, Bengal and FLIGHT LIEUTENANT TAYLOR, Air Command South East Asia, visited DOHAZARI on tour of inspection.
Normal duties.
Air raid warning. No enemy action and no enemy aircraft seen.
Fitter M.T. posted to Unit.
Normal duties and training carried out.
LORD LOUIS MOUNTBATTEN, Supreme Commander, South East Asia, visited the aerodrome and addressed all Officers and Airmen on the Station.
Work on revetting gun pits commenced.
LIBERATOR aircraft from No.159 and No.335 Squadron landed at DOHAZARI, prior to taking off on first large-scale raid on BANGCOCK.
At 03.00hrs. LIBERATORS returned. Air raid warning sounded owing to one or two enemy aircraft returning with the LIBERATORS. No enemy action.
Normal duties and training carried out.
No.4442 A.A. Flight's guns manned in addition to our own. Air raid warning at 11.30hrs. Formations of unidentified aircraft could be seen flying at a very great height in a North Westerly direction. A heavy raid was carried out on the CHITTAGONG area and 6 enemy

aircraft were destroyed for certain. Four enemy shot down were seen from this aerodrome.
Air Raid warning at 13.30hrs. Two unidentified aircraft were within 10 miles of the aerodrome and approaching it. The aircraft turned out to be MOSQUITOES.
Changed over from QUADRUPLE BROWNINGS to TWIN BROWNINGS on Motley Stork Mountings. Six pits manned.
Normal duties.
Siting Board, including SQAUDRON LEADER ANDREWS, visited DOHAZARI for the purpose of siting the domestic camp for an R.A.F. REGIMENT SQUADRON.
Normal duties. Air raid warning at 15.30hrs. Unidentified aircraft were heading for the aerodrome from the South West. Height approximately 25,000ft. Single engine planes were seen very high over the aerodrome. N enemy action. Our fighters damaged one plane.

4405 A.A. Flight – Operational at A.M.E.S. near Chittagong

378 A.M.E.S. inspected by C.O.
879 A.M.E.S. inspected by C.O.
5029 A.M.E.S. inspected by the C.O.
2 Airmen granted 14 days leave.
2 Airmen detached for Aircraft Recognition Course. 378 A.M.E.S. inspected by the C.O.
Nil.
1 N.C.O. sent to 39 E.P. to collect Browning Conversion Sets. C.O. inspected 879 A.M.E.S.
Conversion sets arrived from 39 E.P.
Assembled Motly Stork mountings with Twin Conversion Sets.
Lectures given to N.C.O's regarding new mountings.
Nil.
Gunners at 378 A.M.E.S. were given lectures and fired the twin conversion sets. One new gun post was also sited.
Work commenced on new gun post at 378 A.M.E.S.
Gunners at 879 A.M.E.S. were given lectures and fired the Twin Conversion Sets. One new gun was also sited.

Work commenced on new gun post at 879 A.M.E.S.
Flight notified of move, preparing for same.
Flight moved from 182 Wing to Double Mooring's. Move completed by 18.00hrs.
Complete day devoted to camp organisation.
3 Gun Posts sited and commenced building.
3 Gun Posts completed and another 3 sited.
3 Gun Posts manned, work continued on remainder.
Work continued on gun posts, latrines etc.
Slit trenches built in area of camp. Field Kitchen sited and commenced building.
Airmen had Christmas dinner at No.8 I.A.F. Sqd. 3 Gun Posts completed.
3 more gun pits manned making a total of 6
Work continued on building slit trenches and filed kitchen.
Field Kitchen completed. Arrangements have been made for the Flight to start its own messing W.E.F. from tomorrow.

4407 A.A. Flight – Move to Parashuram Landing Ground

One Motor Cycle (Indian) collected from 224 Group M.T. Pool.
Unit Movement Order No.4 issued.
Motley Stork Conversion Sets collected from 39 E.P.
Advance Party of 1 Cpl. and 5 B.O.R.s. proceeded to PARASHURAM Landing Ground to prepare sites, operational and domestic.
Frequency allocated for use with Units T/R Sets 108, delivery still awaited.
F/Lt. L.R.H. Portlock returned from temporary duty on Aircraft Recognition Course and re-assumed command of Unit.
Movement of Unit from AGARTALA to PARASHURAM by road in Unit Transport via Comilla and Fenny, convoy leaving AGARTALA at 07.30hrs and arriving without incident at new location at 16.45hrs. For the second occasion all M.T. vehicles ran faultlessly. Accommodation occupied in basha huts in No.124 Squadron camp, no accommodation being available near the strip, and tentage being insufficient.

Recce landing ground by O.C. Unit. Gun positions sited and digging began by Flight personnel in absence of native labour.
No.243 Wing appointed to undertake Cash and Pay Accounting for this Unit in place of No.169 Wing.
T/Cpl.(Acting Sgt. Pd.) BURDETT. L.J. promoted T/Sgt.
Unit forms part of 3rd Tactical Air Force in new Eastern Air Command. New course of training began with 8 B.O.R.s. shielded from all other duties for six days. Other personnel of Unit to undergo similar training in rota.
Christmas Day celebrated in traditional manner. A good time had by all. Soccer match with No.134 Squadron resulted in a win for Squadron by one goal to nil.
1325905 LAC BROOKS, R. appointed A/Cpl./Paid.
931778 CPL. GREEN, C.C. posted to No.4436 A.A. Flight.

4422 A.A. Flight – Move to "Reindeer I" airstrip

G/CAPT. HARRIS, Chief Defence Officer, India visited H.Q. Section, accompanied by S/Ldr. Andrews, 224 Group Defence Officer. Immediate move of H.Q. Section to REINDEER I airfield authorised.
2 M.T. Drivers and escorts detailed to collect 2 15 cwt. Trucks, CHITTAGONG.
H.Q. Section moved into Basha accommodation E. side REINDEER I.
S/LDR. PEEK, 165 WING, M.O. visited camp.
2 15 cwt. Trucks arrived from CHITTAGONG.
1 AC. FMT reported for duty. Gunpost at H.Q. site completed and manned.
990191 SGT. FERGUSSON detached to R.A.F. Regt. Depot, pending posting.
224 Group Movement Instruction No.28 received. 224 G/S6201/194/1/ORG 14/12/43. S/LDR. CROTHERS, SAO. 165 WING agreed to accommodate & ration two sections pending provision of tentage.
No.2 Section moved into 165 WING quarters from 210 AMES. No.1 Section moved into 165 WING quarters from 884 AMES.
Conference with O.C's 2942 Squadron and 4448 A/A Flight re. Defence Scheme.

2 A.A. gunposts No.1 Section are manned and operational N. end of strip
3 A.A. gunposts No.2 Section are manned and operational S. end of strip
832588 CPL. WATSON reported for duty (posted)
224 Group Operational Standing Orders A.A. Flights R.A.F. Regt received. Ref 284G/89404/19/DEF.
4 180lb. tents drawn from 30 SALVAGE UNIT.
Xmas Day, Normal Routine. Good Xmas fare. 2 bottles beer free per man.
Warning received from 165 WING of concentrations of JAP aircraft, Sections warned to be alert for low flying attacks.
S/L. PEEK 165 WING M.O. visited camp - expressed satisfaction.
1 15cwt. Truck & 4 R.T. sets Type 108 received from H.Q. 224 Group.
No.1 and 4 Sections moved into Tented accommodation at N and S ends of airfield respectively.

No. 4402 A.A. Flight – Establishment Letter

From: O.C. No. 4402 A.A. Flight, R.A.F. Dohazari.

To: Headquarters, No. 224 Group. R.A.F.

Date: 10th June 1943.

R.A.F. REGIMENT "A.A" FLIGHTS - ESTABLISHMENT.

A copy of a letter 224G/8.6201/194/ORG. dated 7/6/43 regarding and under the heading "R.A.F. Regt. Sqdns. and Flights Administration and Equipment Accounting." has been duly received from your Headquarters. The letter in question calls for no reply and it is requested that this communication should not be considered as one, on the contrary, is hoped that any remarks or observations made, will be considered as expressing experience gained by an A.A. Flight, whilst complying with instructions, set out in the said letter, and which had previously been received verbally by this unit.

Needless to say, the instructions have been and will be carried out by this unit, but not without difficulty, as it is hoped to show by the following remarks.

The establishment of an A.A. Flight is :-

> a) 1 Officer
> b) 1 Sgt.
> c) 4 Cpls.
> d) 27 Gunners or Spare Gunners.
> e) 4 Signallers.

N.B. As there is no apparatus for Signallers, it will be considered, for the purpose of this letter, that they are extra Gunners, making 31 Gunners in all.

On paper, 31 Gunners would appear to be enough to man six Gun Posts, on this Station, but when one takes into account that this is a self contained unit, it does not prove to be the case. Starting off with 31 Gunners (including spare gunners and signallers) the following have to be deducted.

a) Less 5 being the average hospital over the last four weeks.
b) Less 2 being the average on light duty accorded by M.O.
c) Less 1 Clerk in Orderly Room, full time, as everything has to be written in long hand, NO TYPEWRITER.
d) Less 2 Cooks, have duty from 05.30. to 19.30. full day.
e) Less 1 M.T. Driver, 6 miles round Gun Posts 4 times a day, drawing rations, drawing water, etc.
f) Less 1 Working Bowser, cleaning latrines, oiling pondset. In fact doing medical orderly work.

This leaves 19 men to man the six Gun Posts and the above deductions do not take into account part time work, such as work in armoury, collection, sorting, and delivery of Mail, also many other small but quite necessary day to day duties.

There are on the average only 19 men to man six posts. Each Gun Post must have two men, making a total of 12 per day. These 12 do Gun Post duty by day and patrols or guards at night and are therefore on duty 24hrs. Following the 24hrs on duty they should be given the same amount of rest but this is impossible, if all six Gun Posts are to be manned. It would mean that this unit would require 24 Gunners instead of the 19 available. Even then, it means that they are on Gun Post duty every other day, with no time for Field Training etc. which is so important.

It will be seen from the above remarks that there is already a serious shortage of Gunners in an A.A. Flight and yet no allowance has been made for days off or the question of Leave.

Taking into account that men are working seven days a week, it seems reasonable that they should be given one day off, to themselves, for shopping of other private purposes, each two weeks at least.

This is not at present possible as it would mean two further men off and thereby reducing available Gunners to 17 instead of 19. How comes the question of leave or rather Hill Parties. The allotment to this Flight was 5 men, for the period 1st. June to 14th. June, but it was impossible to take advantage of this allotment for, it would mean that the available Gunners would be reduced to 14 of, if one day off in two weeks was allowed a further reduction to 12. In other words these 12 men would be permanently on gun post, guards or patrols.

To carry out the duties of an A.A. Flight and to comply with various instructions regarding training etc. This Flight has had to take the following steps, since it became the only A.A. Flight on this station.

1) Reduce the Gun Posts, which are manned to four (The aerodrome in not operational).
2) Allow no days off except when detailed to Chittagong or elsewhere on duty.
3) Allow no leave or Hill Parties.
4) Engage a local native cook at their own expense.

On this basis the Flight can manage for the time being but when one takes into account the long hours of duty, carried out, by the men, it soon becomes apparent that some time off must be arranged for shortly. This is even more apparent when one takes into consideration the conditions men work under – either excessive heat, whilst on Gun Post, or alternatively excessive rain and mud.

Officers and N.C.O.'s.

Having gone somewhat fully into the position regarding the Gun Crew personnel, it might well be asked, what of the officer and N.C.O.'s do, and could they not help with some of the duties allotted to other men? It would be an easy question to answer, should it be asked, for it is a full time job for them. Training men, inspecting gun posts by day and by night, issuing rations and doing their best to run a Canteen so that men, when not on actual duty, have somewhere to go. This is nothing to say of the ordinary everyday administration work, of which there is plenty. In addition, at this Station the R.A.F. Regt. personnel have to keep an ever watchful eye on the following:-

(a)   One gang of 25 native workmen doing repairs to bombed buildings.
(b)   One gang of 25 native carpenters repairing windows, doors, beds.
(c)   Two gangs, 25 each, filling in bomb holes, mending roads etc.

It was stated in Headquarters letter, referred to in the opening paragraph of this, that "Squadrons and Flights of the R.A.F. Regt. should not be allowed to become an added burden to the domestic staffs of other units." As this Flight is entirely on its own perhaps it could be said that other units should not place extra work on the already shortly manned R.A.F. Regt. Flight.

As already stated, this letter is not one of complaint but rather an endeavour to place on record how difficult it is for a Flight of this size, to work as a complete Independent Unit, without, on occasions, calling for assistance from other personnel.

With goodwill and cooperation between R.A.F. Regt. personnel and other various units on a station, these difficulties solve themselves.

Officer Commanding,

No.4402 A.A. Flight R.A.F. Regt.

No.4402 A.A. Flight – Temporary Operational Ground Order

SECRET   R.A.F. CHIRINGA.   Copy No. 5

1. INFORMATION.

1. The enemy is known to be in some considerable strength approx. 60 miles South to South East of this Station. It is not expected that the enemy can attack this station, in any strength by using soley ground forces, without giving ample warning of his intention. The enemy can, however, attack this station in the following ways for which little or no warning need be given.

    i) Parachute landing on the airfield.
    ii) Airborne landing on the airfield.
    iii) Ground attack by patrols or small parties of troops.
    iv) Sabotage.

2. Own Troops. Considerable forces of our own and allied troops bar the way to a direct ground attack in force. In addition we have considerable air superiority over the whole of Bengal and Burma. Army and Air Force Personnel, for the Defence of this station, comprise of the following:-

a) "B" Troop, H.A.A. (8th Belfast).
b) Battery of L.A.A. (26th L.A.A. Bty. I.A.)
c) Flight of R.A.F. Regt. (No.4402 A/A FLt.).
d) Company of Field Royal Engineers.
e) Detachment of R.A.F. Personnel. (No.261 Sqdn.)

2. INTENTION.
    a. To deny the use of Chiringa Airfield to the enemy.
    b. Prevent the loss or destruction of R.A.F. and Military stores or equipment.
    c. Annihilate the enemy attempting anything mentioned in a or b above.

3. METHOD.
    a. "B" Troop H.A.A.

The Officer Commanding the 8th Belfast H.A.A. Troop will issue the necessary orders for the defence of his guns and position to the last man.

The A.A. role will be maintained as along as possible, but should the A.A. position become untenable, all weapons, including 3.7" guns, will be used for Ground Defence. The Officer Commanding this Troop will be prepared to put down a round barrage, when called upon to do so by the Officer in charge of the Defence of this Station.

The Fuze, Bearing Q.E. will be worked out, in advance, for all important ground targets such as Aerodrome strips, roads, rivers etc. When the enemy has been destroyed of driven off the A.A. role will immediately resume.

b. <u>Battery of L.A.A.</u>

The Officer Commanding the 26th (Sikh) L.A.A. Battery, I.A., will issue the necessary orders for the defence of all his guns and positions. These positions, to-gether with Battery H.Q. and "A" and "B" Troop Headquarters will be considered as strong points and defended to the last man. During the hours of darkness Battery H.Q. (L.A.A.) will have at its disposal two mobile sections with the primary roll of reinforcing those L.A.A. gun sites numbered 4, 7, 8, and 10, on the attached plan. The remaining L.A.A. gun sites, will if necessary, be reinforced from Battle H.Q.

c. <u>Flight R.A.F. Regiment.</u>

The Officer Commanding No.4402 A.A. Flight will issue the necessary orders for the manning and defence of L.M.G. gun positions numbered 1, 4, 8, 9, 14, and 18 on the attached plan. The positions will be considered as strong points and defended to the last man. In addition the R.A.F. Regt. will have the additional task of patrolling the area adjacent to their camp.

d. <u>Company of Field R.E's.</u>

The Officer Commanding Field Coy. R.E's will issue the necessary orders for all his personnel, with the exception of three sections (8 men each) to withdraw from their camp and to deploy by sections in the area surrounding Battle H.Q., they will be retained there for use as mobile sections. The three sections remaining in the "R.E's" camp will be responsible for patrolling that area, including No.2 Camp, R.A.F.

e. <u>Detachment of R.A.F. Personnel (261 Sqdn).</u>

The Officer Commanding R.A.F. will issue for all R.A.F. personnel to vacate the domestic areas of the camp, including No.2Camp. All such R.A.F. personnel with the exception of M.T. drivers, M.T.M's, Signal and Cypher will proceed to and form the defence of Battle H.Q. R.A.F. M.T. drivers and M.T.M's, will stand by their vehicles and have them ready for instant use. Signal and Cypher personnel will proceed to their respective buildings and "Stand By".

4. <u>ADMINISTRATION.</u>
Officers Commanding the various Units will issue the necessary orders, to their personnel, under the following:-

i) Equipment and Dress.
ii) Medical, there being First Aid Posts at, H.A.A. Coy H.Q., L.A.A. Battery H.Q., and adjacent to Battle H.Q.
iii) M.T. Transport.

iv)   Food and Water
v) Destruction of Secret Documents when necessary.
vi)   Reserve Ammunition.
vii) All unnecessary lights to be extinguished.

5. INTER COMMUNICATIONS.
    a. Combined Battle H.Q. will be at Station H.Q., (R.A.F.)
    b. Communication between strong points, H.A.A., and
       Battle H.Q. will be by:-
           a. Vary Signals
              i. Red, Action Stations ALL
               personnel.
             ii. White, Reinforcements required.
             iii. Green, situation under control.
        And/or
           b. Telephone.
           c. Runner.

27.8.43.

Distribution :-

O.C. Chiringa.

O.C. 26th Light A.A. Bty. I.A.

O.C. R.A.F. Chiringa.

O.C. 23/8 Belfast H.A.A.'B' Troop

Form 540.

File.

Signed

Defence Officer,

R.A.F. Chiringa.

Copy No. 1.
"   "   2.
"   "   3.
"   "   4.
"   "   5.
"   "   6.

No.4402 A.A. Flight – Gun Post Sketch Map

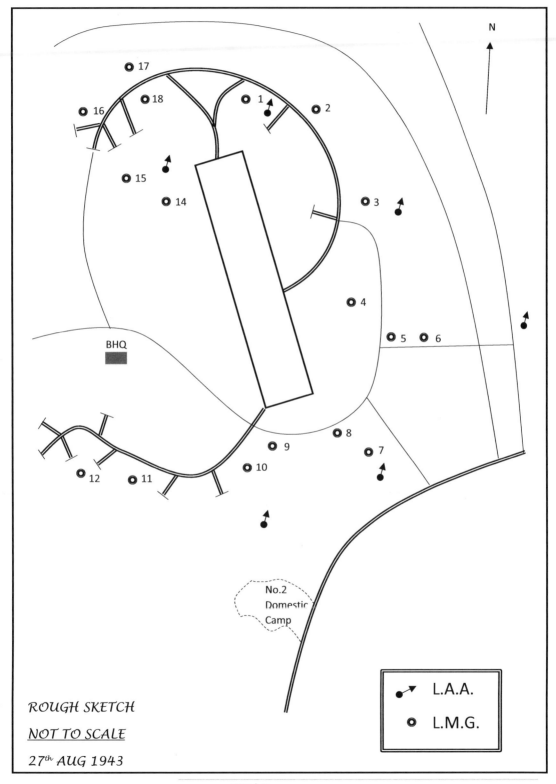

N

17
18
16
1
2
15
14
3
BHQ
4
5 6
8
9
7
10
12 11

No.2
Domestic
Camp

L.A.A.

L.M.G.

ROUGH SKETCH

NOT TO SCALE

27th AUG 1943

No.4407 A.A. Flight – Duties of Officer i/c R.A.F.R. Flight – A.M.E.S.

```
                                          Appendix "D" to Form 540
COPY.                                     No. 4407 A.A. Flight, R.A.F.R.

                                          May, 1943.
```

```
                DUTIES OF OFFICER I/C R.A.F.R. FLIGHT

             PROTECTING A.M.E. STATIONS IN CHITTAGONG.
```

1. He will be responsible for all A/A L.M.G.s protecting A.M.E. Stations in vicinity of Chittagong whether these weapons are manned by members of his own Flight or by other airmen, unless these other airmen come under the command of another R.A.F.R. officer, in which case he will be so informed.

2. He will assure himself that no airman who has not a thorough working knowledge of the gun is allowed to be a member of the gun team.

3. He will be attached to 5029 H.A.M.E.S. for rations, discipline and accommodation.

4. He will not be employed on any duties other than those normally obtaining to R.A.F. Regiment.

5. Nominal roll (number, name, initials and rank) to be fwd this H.Q. please.

```
                                     (Signed) M. GORDON, S/Ldr.
                                          Group Defence Officer.

     22/IG/S.7400/2/Def.                         22nd May, 1943.
```

No.4407 A.A. Flight -Storage and Care of Ammunition memo

COPY.

      APPENDIX "A" TO FORM 540 (Page 1) for JULY, 1943 - No. 4407

                   A.A. FLIGHT, R.A.F.R.

From: Officer Commanding, No.4407 A.A. Flight, R.A.F. Regiment.

To: Headquarters, No.224 Group, R.A.F.

Date: 3rd July, 1943.

Ref: 4407/S.202/ARM.

              STORAGE AND CARE OF AMMUNITION.

Reference your 224G/S.7405/DEF dated 27th June, 1943, the following comments are made for your information and necessary action.

Para. 5. It will be realised that at A.M.E. Stations in this area no provision whatever has been made for an armoury. In view of this, the shortage of personnel for guard duties and the kutcha nature of the bashas which constitute the only buildings, it is difficult to see how this paragraph can be put into effective operation.

An example of this is provided by the position at No.378 AMES, KATTALI, where No.1 Section of this Flight is manning one quadruple set of guns and has to store and maintain a second set, pending the completion of the second gun post now under construction. No other store is available for the guns than a basha in which the gunners are billeted and where at least one man is always available as a guard. Group Headquarters will not undertake the safe custody of the guns until they are required.

At the same time, the Section has to maintain the operational ammunition for both sets of guns and there is no alternative than to store it in the same place. Besides this, there are also the gunners personal weapons (rifles and Stens) in the billet.

It is recognised that this position is highly unsatisfactory, but there seems to be no way out unless adequate lock-up accommodation is provided at these Stations.

Even where R.A.F. Regiment personnel and weapons are not concerned, the A.M.E. Station proper requires storage room for the weapons and ammo. allocated to its own personnel. On two occasions recently in this area, the undersigned has found cases where both arms and ammo. were stored together, mainly due to lack of accommodation and the impossibility of arranging for adequate guard.

Your careful consideration and advices in this matter would be appreciated.

<u>Para. 8.</u> May this Unit please be advised what is the correct ammunition establishment applicable.

Before leaving the R.A.F. Regiment Depot, the undersigned was handed what was suggested as being the pucca establishment (attached as Appendix "A"), but when asked for the authority, the Depot were unable to produce it. In any case, there has been no indication since arrival here that this establishment will be adhered to (cf. Grenades H.E. No.36, now allotted on a basis of 96 per A.A. Flight).

(Signed) L.R.H. PORTLOCK,

F/LT., Commanding,

No.4407 A.A. Flight,

<u>R.A.F. Regiment.</u>

No.4407 A.A. Flight - Group Defence Officer visit memo

APPENDIX "A" TO FORM 540 for AUG. 1943   SECRET.

No.4407 A.A. FLIGHT R.A.F.R.

From. Headquarters, No.224 Group. R.A.F.

To. Officer Commanding, No.4407 - A.A. Flight. R.A.F.R.

Date. 23rd August 1943.

Ref. 224G/S.7419/Def.

Following on the visit by the Group Defence Officer on 21st Aug. 1943, the following points are brought to your notice.

1. Findli. Work is to proceed on the gun posts and completion effected as soon as possible.

   Kattali. A third site is to be selected and a gun post built instead of the one known to be badly sited.

   Chittagong. The gun posts are to be made good and the undergrowth cleared consonant with good camouflage.

2. The question of the issue of drivers licenses had been taken up with the Group Transport Officer.

3. A scale of a 45 men set Cooking Utensils is attached. Demands for these are to made at once. It is considered that if this done through No.182 Wing the demand will be met expeditiously.

4. The general turn out and bearing of your flight was excellent being marred only by:-

   (a)   Cases being observed of men wearing their hats turned up at the left side. The brim of the hat is to be worn flat.

   (b)   Anklets were being worn. Boots and short puttees are to be worn. If however anklets are considered more serviceable locally, then let all be dressed alike.

5. As opportunity arises training is to be resumed and the mobility of your flight tested. Time is short and your Flight must be perfection itself by the 15th October 1943.

(George Andrews.)

For Air Commodore.

Air Officer Commanding,

No.224 Group, R.A.F.

Copy to:- Air Headquarters, Bengal.

(For the attention of the Defence Officer.)

No.4407 A.A. Flight – Explosives, Supply & Distribution memo

<u>COPY.</u>

APPENDIX "B" TO FORM 540 (page 1) for AUGUST, 1943 - No.4407

A.A. FLIGHT. R.A.F.R.

From:- Air Headquarters, Bengal.   Admin Ex.5 Thro' Bengal

To. A.A. Flights R.A.F. Regiment.

Date. 17th August, 1943.

Ref. HQB/S/2318/6/E. 4.

EXPLOSIVES- SUPPLIES & DISTRIBUTION - GROUND DEFENCE

SCALES OR AMMUNITION.

All Squadrons and Units are to be notified that the scales of issue of Ground Defence ammunition given in this Headquarters letter of even reference dated 8th April are cancelled and are superseded by the following.

<u>Weapons</u>

        (a)   Twin Brownings on Motley Stork Mountings
        (b)   Single Lewis guns on bipod Mountings
        (c)   Rifle.
        (d)   Sten Gun
        (e)   Revolver .38
        (f)   Revolver .455
        (g)   Pistol .455
        (h)   .45 T. Sub Machine Gun
        (i)   .50 machine gun

<u>ESTABLISHMENT</u>
<u>INITIAL ARMING.</u>   OPERATIONS

(a). 1000 rounds per gun (in links)   1000 rounds (1 box) per gun per month

(b). 2000 rounds per gun (bundle packed)   2496 rounds (2 boxes) per gun per month

(c). 100 rounds per rifle (Bandolier and   50 rounds/rifle charger packed)

                                           Per month

(d). 150 rounds per Sten Gun   -

(e). 12 rounds per revolver   -

(f). 12 rounds per revolver   -

(g). 12 rounds per pistol.   -

(h). 2500 rounds per gun   -

(j). 4000 rounds per gun   -

    4000 Links Belt per gun   -

TRAINING. The following may also be demanded for training:-

              (a)   50 rounds per man.)
              (b)   47 rounds per man.)
              (c)   25 rounds per man.)   Per Course.
              (d)   15 rounds per man.)
              (e)   NIL   )
              (f)   15 rounds per man.)
              (g)   15 rounds per man.)

Ammunition for (a) and (b) is to be demanded in the set proportions 85% ball 5% Armour Piercing and 10% Incendiary (all "Land Service") (c) Ball ammunition only.

2. Demands for ammunition to bring holdings up to stocks in accordance with the above scales are to be submitted to the nearest Ordnance Field Depot holding R.A.F. explosives. These are listed as follows:-

              (i)   No.55 O.F.D. Durgapur (Near Asansol)
              (ii)   No.56 O.F.D. Kanglatongbi (Nr. Imphal)
              (iii)   No.59 O.F.D. Comilla
              (iv)   No.60 O.F.D. Chittagong
              (v)   No.61 O.F.D. Silchar
              (vi)   No.212 A.A.D. Jamalpur Bihar
              (vii)   No.203 B.A.D. Manipur Road
              (viii)   No.217 A.A.D. Mymensingh

No.4407 A.A. Flight – Standing Order No.4 - 'Orders for Gun Post Duties'

APENDIX "A" to F540. November 1943

<u>NO.4407 A.A. FLIGHT, R.A.F.R.</u>

<u>STANIDNG ORDER NO.4.</u>

<u>'ORDERS FOR GUN POST'</u>

1. <u>Tour of Duty</u> To be as detailed in Routine Orders. All reliefs are to be promptly carried out. Details must not be permitted to leave their post except with the express permission of the Flight Commander. All posts are to 'Stand To' from 30-minutes before dawn until 30-minutes after dawn and from 30-minutes before sunset until 30-minutes after sunset.

2. <u>Personal Weapons</u> Gunners are to have their personal arms and ammunition with them at all times on duty.

3. <u>Dress</u> All gunners are to be shaved, hair well cut and properly dressed at all times. Webbing equipment with small haversack and filled water bottles are to taken on duty. Steel helmets and respirators are to be immediately available at all times.

4. <u>Equipment</u> On mounting the post and at every change of detail, the gunner taking over is to check all post equipment as crossed against the post inventory.

5. <u>Guns</u> <u>Lewis</u> To be kept uncocked with full magazines in position, safety catches to be left off. Immediately on an alert, guns are to be cocked ready for action.

    <u>Browning</u> To be kept uncocked with the Safe Unit as "Safe". Immediately on an alert, guns are to be cocked and pit on "Fire".

6. <u>Cleaning of Guns</u> Thorough cleaning of all guns is to take place at least once daily at times to be specified by the Corporal i/c Watch. These times are to be strictly adhered to. In no circumstances is more is more than one gun pit mounting to be stripped at any one time. The clean condition of the guns is the responsibility of the Gunners on duty. Inclement weather may necessitate additional cleaning.

7. <u>Cleaning of Ammunition</u> All ammunition to be cleaned at least once daily by the Gunners on Duty.

8. <u>Opening of Fire</u> Fire is to be opened on any aircraft recognised as hostile or committing an hostile act within a

range of 800 yards. Disciplinary action will be taken against any Gunner on duty failing to open fire at a reasonable target.

9. Aircraft Log Book A log is to be kept by the Gunners on duty of all aircraft sighted, both friendly and enemy, specifying, type, number, estimated height, and direction of flight. This log will not include aircraft od resident squadrons doing circuits and practice flights.

10.   Cleanliness of Posts All posts are to be kept clean and camouflage maintained at all times. Crews on duty will be held responsible for any untidiness.

YOUR OPPORTUNITY MAY COME ONCE ONLY - AND WITH THE
SPEED OF LGHTENING. YOU MUST SIEZE IT THEN WITH BOTH
HANDS AND ALL YOUR GUNS!! THERFORE -------
KEEP YOUR GUNS IN PERFECT TRIM
KNOW THEM PERFECTLY FROM A TO Z
ALWAYS KEEP ALERT AND EXPECT ACTION

11.   This order cancels Standing Order No.3 dated 12th September 1943.

Signed

F/LT L.R.H. PORTLOCK

1 October 1943   Commanding

No.4407 AA Flight RAFR

No.4407 A.A. Flight – Standing Order No.5 – 'Orders for Corporal i/c Watch'

APPENDIX "B" To Form 540 – November 1943.

<u>No.4407 A A FLIGHT RAF REGIMENT</u>

<u>STANDING ORDER NO.5</u>

1. This tour of duty will be as detailed in Routine Standing Orders from 21.00hrs to 21.00hrs.

2. He is to ensure that all Gun Post are as detailed in the Routine Order, parade for duty at the proper times as is to ensure that guns and equipment taken to each Post are in accordance with the inventory for that post.

3. He is to ensure that each Gunner is detailed for specific hours of duty and he is also to issue orders as to times for cleaning guns, care being taken to ensure that cleaning is not permitted at more than one post at any one time.

4. He is to be present at the mounting of each post and to ensure that all Gunners know and understand their orders.

5. He is to accompany all meal runs and supervise the issue of rations to personnel on duty. He is to report any shortage or complaints without delay to the Flight Commander.

6. He is to visit all posts at irregular intervals throughout his tour of duty. He is to check maintenance of guns, cleanliness of posts, alertness of Gunners, and camouflage. Any unusual occurrences is to be reported by him to the Flight Commander immediately.

7. He is to supervise the dismounting of each post at evening 'Stand Down' and is to check all equipment when returned to the Armoury.

Signed

F/LT L.R.H. PORTLOCK

Commanding

No.4407 A.A. Flight

<u>RAF Regiment</u>

1 October 1943

No.4407 A.A. Flight – A.A. Pit Sketch Plan

APPENDIX "A" TO FORM 540

No.4407 A.A. FLIGHT R.A.F. REGT

JUNE 1943

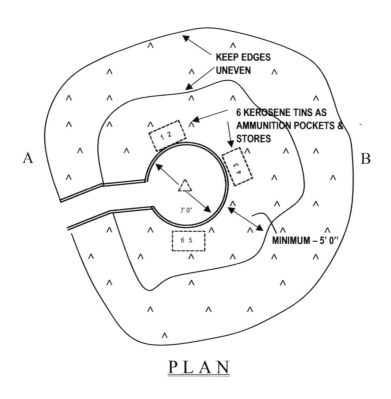

KEEP EDGES UNEVEN

6 KEROSENE TINS AS AMMUNITION POCKETS & STORES

A

B

7' 0"

MINIMUM – 5' 0"

PLAN

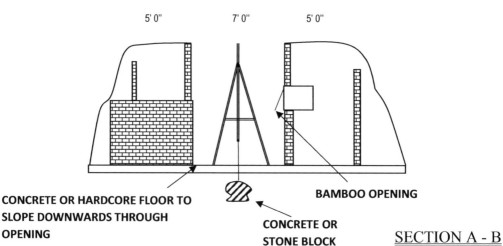

5' 0"   7' 0"   5' 0"

CONCRETE OR HARDCORE FLOOR TO SLOPE DOWNWARDS THROUGH OPENING

CONCRETE OR STONE BLOCK

BAMBOO OPENING

SECTION A - B

GENERAL DETAILS & DIMENSIONS OFF A.A. PITS

4407/252/DEF 10TH JUNE 1943

No.4407 A.A. Flight – Reconnaissance Report (Parashuram Landing Ground)

Appendix "C" to Form 540 – November 1943

MOST SECRET   29- 11 - 43

To. Officer Commanding. Headquarters 224G. RAF Ref 224G/57404/7/Det.

From. Officer Commanding. 4401 AA Flight RAF Regt Ref. 4407/251/Det.

Reconnaissance Report (Parashuram Landing Ground)

Ref. Map No.79 M. Comilla Co-ordinate 6362

The above landing strip is approached by crossing Feni Aerodrome from the west, and proceeding practically due north for a distance of approximately 14 to 15 miles, along a very far, dry weather road, running parallel to Feni- Belonia railway extension and capable of carrying under existing road bridge and calvert conditions, vehicles from 3 to 5 tons. There are no roads branching west from Feni to Parashuram in order to gain access to the main Comilla – Feni road. The runway runs due north and south 6,000ft x 600ft. The domestic quarter is situated approximately one mile away and adjoins the west side of the village of Parashuram. There are several points from to Parashuram where vehicles could be loaded up from railway trucks.

1. DOMESTIC CAMP
   Accommodation is available for 30 Officers, 50 Sergeants and 350 BORs (with beds & shelving for kit of bamboo construction) 60 followers, complete with cookhouses (Oven installed), Latrines (deep trench), Incinerators, 6 Wells with Pumps (all working), Ablutions (dated to be completed by Dec 1st, Dining Halls, with rows of tables (bamboo construction). A compact camp excellently equipped with good accommodation, non dispersed.

2. LANDING GROUND
   The runway is of levelled paddy field construction 6,000ft x 600ft running due North to South. 3,000ft completed and rolled another 1,000ft to be completed by Nov 30th and the remainder to be completed by Dec 5th. The undersigned considers that this will be carried out, and that in any case, even in its present state could be used in an emergency.

3. DISPERSAL
   All dispersal tracks have been levelled. The north-east dispersal pens are not yet started. The south-west dispersal pens have been started, as have the south-east dispersal pens. Squadron Officers, stores, crew rooms, bomb dumps and petrol dumps have been started, and the MES stated that they would be

completed by the Dec 1st and that all work as ordered should be completed by Dec 11th.

4. GUN POSITIONS
   The run posts have been sited and an NCO from 4407 AA Flight fully conversant with each position and its task and also understands the priority of construction and where necessary, due consideration has been given to the use of high ground to obtain fields of fire, ground to ground and to air, and mutual support. A certain amount of difficulty has been rendered on the west side of the Landing Ground in siting positions to give tactical cover for dead arcs of fire, both ground to air and ground to ground, owing to the woods and undergrowth in this locality, but all positions selected give a reasonable solution to this difficulty.

   A rough sketch (not to scale) is enclosed for your information and a copy has been placed in the file of 4407 AA Flight for future reference.

(Signed) R.S. TAYLOR F/LT.
Officer Commanding
4401 AA Flight
RAF Regiment

Copy held by O.C.
4401 A.A. Flight

No.2941 Squadron Warning Order

Appendix 'A' to Form 540   <u>SECRET.</u>

<u>For month of August 1943.</u>

<u>WARNING ORDER - CHANGE OF LOCATION FOR TRAINING</u>

<u>2 9 4 1   S Q U A D R O N,   R. A. F.   R E G I M E N T.</u>

BY

SQUADRON LEADER H.J. FORBES M.M.

<u>OFFIECR COMMANDING 2941 (R) SQUADRON.</u>

1) 2941 Squadron will be attached for forward troops of the 23rd Brigade 4th Corps for training and this attachment will be made in Flights in rotation in the order: No.3, No.2, No.1 Flights. No.2 Flight relieving No.3 Flight and no.1 Flight relieving No.2 Flight.

2) The first flight proceeding will be prepared to move early in August and be attached for training for a period of approximately three weeks, or until relieved by the incoming flight.

3) Movement will be by rail from AKHAURA to MANIPUR ROAD and movement forward from MANIPUR ROAD will be Army responsibility.

4) Flights will be self-contained for messing throughout the training period and provide their own cooks and cooking utensils.

5) Six days rations, tables 'B' (non-cooking) will be obtained from the forward supply depot, AKHAURA, for maintenance on the journey and until supplies are obtainable from the Army Sources.

6) Tentage, 0 X 100 lbs:, will be taken by the first flight and handed over to the relieving Flights in rotation.

7) Two 15 cwt Trucks will be allotted and moved from CALCUTTA to meet the first Flight forward location and these trucks will be handed over to relieving Flights in rotation, the last Flight withdrawing the vehicles with them on their return.

8) Armaments will be to scale. No. S.A.A. will be taken as reserve but 50 rnds: per Rifle, 200 rnds: Bren, and 400 rnds: 9 M.M. per Sten, will be taken from Base.

9) Flights will move to strength i.e. 1 Officer, 1 Sgt, 3 Cpls, and 34 AC's and in addition for the first Flight proceeding will have 1 Medical Orderly, 1 additional M.T. Driver,1 Cpl Messing and two Squadron Headquarters Signallers attached, who will remain in the forward area and be attached to each reliving Flight in rotation.

10)   Medical Orderly will be responsible for First Aid, water purification and general Medical requirements and will take with him one haversack Medical Stores pack-up.

11)   The Messing Cpl will be responsible for Rations under instructions of the Officer i/c Flight.

12)   Personnel of Flights will be paid two weeks in advance before leaving Base.

13)   Personnel will move equipped to full marching order, with one Blanket, Ground Sheet and Mosquito Curtain carried in their packs. No Baggage will be taken.

14)   A detachment of 2 Drivers and an escort party of 3 Airmen will proceed to CALCUTTA prior to the movement of the Flight, to take over the vehicles and proceed to MANIPUR ROAD as an independent party.

15)   Date of movement of first Flight from Base will be notified later.

AUGUST 2nd, 1943   S/LDR.

COMMANDING 2941 (R) SQUADRON,

R.A.F. STATION. . . . . .AGARTALA.

No.2941 Battle Diary No.1 Flight

Appendix 'D'

To Form 540 for month

of December, 1943.

2941 (R) Squadron.

BATTLE DIARY No.1 FLIGHT

1943.

December.

10th.	Flight Commander informed by Squadron Commander of impending detachment to Singerbeel and preparations began.
11th	Flight movement completed by 15.00hrs as arranged with O.C. F.R.D. Patrols and Guards supplied 1 Cpl. and 13 men.
12th	Half of Flight detailed for generally cleaning up the billet and surroundings, while the remainder collected charpoys and conveyed them to Guard Tent. Tents were erected in afternoon. Guard 1 Cpl. and 10 men.
13th	Air Raid protection insufficient so Flight commenced digging slit trenches. Afternoon – Organised Sports. Guard – 1 Cpl. and 10 men.
14th	Continued slit trenches and to familiarise Flights with Aerodrome defensive localities a general recce too place in the afternoon. Guard 1 Cpl. and 10 men.
15th	Slit trenches completed and camouflaged. Afternoon – Organised Sports. Guard 1 Cpl. and 10 men.
16th	Stand Down. Guard 1 Cpl. and 10 men.
17th	Gun positions for Bren A.A. sited and weapon slits for Bren Gunners began. Afternoon – Camouflage lecture and demonstration. Guards – 1 Cpl. and 10 men.
18th	Commanding Officer's Parade. Weapons check and internal economy. Afternoon – Organised Sports. Guards 1 Cpl. and 10 men.
19th	Weapon Slits completed. AIR RAID 10.30 hrs. Afternoon – Organised Sport. Guards – 1 Cpl. and 10 men.
20th	Two drains from the ablutions were constructed. Afternoon – Aircraft Recce. Guards – 1 Cpl. and 10 men.
21st	Clothing Parade. Foot inspection. Anti-Gas Training. Afternoon – Organised Sport defeated F.R.D. 9 -3 at hockey. Guards – 1 Cpl. and 10 men.

22nd   Practice alarm. Grenade Instruction and throwing dummies. Browning lecture. Afternoon - Aircraft Recce. Guards - 1 Cpl. and 10 men.

23rd   Rifle firing on range - inter Flight competition won by No.1 Flight. Afternoon - Organised Sport - defeated 147th Heavy A.A. at Soccer. Guards - 1 Cpl. and 10 men.

24th   Barbed wire fence erected at S - W corner of aerodrome. Afternoon - Bren A.A. Guards - 1Cpl. and 10 men.

25th   Stand down. Guards 1 Cpl. and 10 men.

26th   Organised Sports - Baseball, Hockey, Cricket and Football. Guards 1 Cpl. and 10 men.

27th   Constructing barbed wire fence around M.T. approaches. Afternoon - Browning instruction. Guards 1 Cpl and 10 men.

28th   Erecting double apron barbed wire fence between Sergeants' Quarters and Native Village. Afternoon - Organised Sport. Guards 1 Cpl and 10 men.

29th   Commenced wiring of Petrol dump. Afternoon - Aircraft recce. Defeated an F.R.D. team at soccer by five gaols to one. Guard - 1 Cpl. and 10 men.

30th   Re-wired South-West corner of Perimeter, constructed a thoroughfare between M.T. Section and landing strip for the use of natives. Afternoon - Organised Sport. Guard - 1 Cpl. and 10 men.

31st   Completed the work commenced on previous day. Afternoon - Map Reading revision. Guard - 1 Cpl and 10 men.

No.2942 Squadron Xmas Menu

CHRISTMAS DINNER 1943.

2942 (R) Squadron.

Chicken Soup or Tomato Soup.

*   *   *

Roast duck or Roast Chicken

And

Salted Beef.

Bacon Rolls of Savoury Stuffing.

Roast of Creamed Potatoes.

Vegetables.

*   *   *

Christmas Pudding & Rum Sauce.

Jelly, Fruit & Custard.

*   *   *

Biscuits & Cheese.

*   *   *

Coffee or Tea.

*   *   *

Cigars, Cigarettes.

No.2944 Hill Parties Chakrata

Admin. Ex. 7.

<u>Through Bengal.</u>

From: Air Headquarters, Bengal.

To: R.A.F. Movements Section.

      R.A.F. Base H.Q. Calcutta.

      A.H.Q. Bengal, (Radio),

      23 H.W.O.U.,

      313 Maintenance Unit,

      681 Squadron,

      R.A.F. Station, Kanchrapara,

      Bengal Maintenance Wing,

      2944 R.A.F.R. Squadron, Ranchi.

Date: 1st July 1943.

Ref: HQB/S.337/3/Org.

<u>HILL PARTIES CHAKRATA</u>

Further allocations of numbers for future Hill Parties are detailed below:

Train departs Howrah Station 2048 hours, all personnel are to report to Transit Camp Calcutta, on the day of departure, where five days railroad rations will be issued to-gether with 3 days emergency rations which will be carried in bulk.

The issue of hot water and ice will be arranged throughout the journey by R.A.F. Movements, Calcutta.

It is again stressed that all personnel <u>must</u> take full water bottles with them and all the warm clothing they possess together with greatcoat and mosquito nets. Mosquito cream will be carried for use on the journey.

Full details of personnel proceeding are to be supplied to Base H.Q. Calcutta, as much in advance of the day of departure as is possible, to enable arrangements to be completed. Any Unit desiring to exceed the allotment given may do so after notifying this Headquarters.

The following allocations of responsibility of supplying an Officer for these parties is given below:

    2944 R.A.F.R. Sqdn.   8/7, 9/7, 10/7, 11/7, 12/7.

    Base H.Q. Calcutta   14/7, 24/7, 26/7.

    A.H.Q. Bengal (Radio) 16/7, 22/7.

    23 H.W.O.U.   17/7, 21/7.

    313 M.U.   23/7.

    691 Sqdn.   13/7, 25/7.

    R.A.F. Kanchrapara   15/7.

Inability to fill an allotment should be notified to this Headquarters immediately.

R.A.F. Movements, Calcutta, will note that on "T" will not be required for parties under this H.Q. on the 18th, 19th, and 20th July.

                  (W.L. Kerr)

Copy to:-   AIR OFFICER i/c ADMIN.

H.Q. 221 Group.   Air Headquarters.

4 Hill Depot.   Bengal Command.

H.Q. 223 Group.

R.A.F. Transit Camp.

Dhra Dun.

	B.H.Q CAL.	AHQ (R)	23 HWOU	313 M.U.	681 SQDN	Kanchra- para.	B.M.W. Chandpur	2944 Ranchi
8/7	–	–	–	–	–	–	–	30
9/7	–	–	–	–	–	–	–	30
10/7	–	–	–	–	–	–	–	30
11/7	–	–	–	–	–	–	–	30
12/7	–	–	–	–	–	–	–	30
13/7	15	–	–	–	10	–	9	–
14/7	15	–	15	–	–	–	–	–
15/7	–	10	–	–	–	20	–	–
16/7	15	10	–	5	–	–	–	–
17/7	–	10	15	–	5	–	–	–
18/7	–	–	–	–	–	–	–	–
19/7	–	–	–	–	–	–	–	–
20/7	–	–	–	–	–	–	–	–
21/7	15	–	15	–	–	–	–	–
22/7	15	10	–	–	5	–	–	–
23/7	15	10	–	5	–	–	–	–
24/7	15	10	–	–	5	–	–	–
25/7	15	10	–	–	5	–	–	–
26/7	15	–	–	–	–	15	–	–

No.2944 Daily Syllabus of Training

DAILY SYLLABUS OF TRAINING

TRAINING HOURS 08.00 hours to 16.15 hours - 36 periods.

First week, Commencing 5th July 1943.

	No. of periods
Drill	2 ½ hours periods.
Bayonet Fighting & P.T.	4
Route march & Assault Course	6
Rifle	5
Bren Gun	4
Sten Gun	2
Judging Distance, searching ground, Indication of targets.	3
Fire Orders.	1
Organised Games.	4
Sighting.	2
Ammunition types.	1
Grenade	2
	36 periods.
Second week.	
Drill	2
Bayonet Fighting & P.T.	4
Route march & Assault Course	6
Rifle	5
Bren Gun	4
Sten Gun	2
Judging Distance Revision (practice)	3
Grenade	2
Range Drill	1
Sighting.	2
Fire Orders Revision (practice)	1

Organised Games.	<u>4</u>
	<u>36</u> periods.

<u>Third week.</u>

Drill	2
Bayonet Fighting & P.T.	3
Organised Games.	4
Route march & Assault Course	6
Range Drill	6
Bren Gun	4
Operational Orders.	1
Gas	2
Ammunition- Packing	1
Sighting, aiming practice with discs	2
Scouts, Patrols,	<u>5</u>
	<u>36</u> periods.

THREE MONTHS SYLLABUS OF TRAINING FOR No. 2944

SQUADRON, R.A.F. REGT.

WEAPONS TRAINING.   No. of periods

Rifle including Range Practice.	24
Bren Gun ditto	48
Sten Gun ditto	18
Grenade ditto	21
Ammunition - types - packing	2
Theory of Sighting including ring and aperture	6

FIELD TRAINING.

Battle Orders.	3
Uses, Ground & Covers. Fire Positions	12
Judging distance including indication of targets.	12
Fire Orders -	8
Attack and defence	18
Anti-tank Mines - with laying practice	2
Road blocks - defence and sighting	2
Scouts and patrols.	16
Field Engineering	3
Tank hunting	1
Aircraft recognition.	3
Anti Gas	3
Map reading	6
Drill - foot, arms, squadron.	24
Bayonet fighting, P.T. & Unarmed combat	53
Assault course, route marches.	72
Organised games.	48
Lost time	28
Total	432 Hours

Group 225 - General Reconnaissance

Overview

The move, at the beginning of September for No.4428 A.A. Flight, to the airfield at St Thomas Mount, proceeded without any difficulties. Following a short period of settling in, construction to upgrade the Gun Pits for the new Twin Browning Motley Stalk Mountings, was soon underway, and the flight took over its allocation of M.T. vehicles. The dual purpose of the flight was to provide low level air defence and to facilitate a programme of progressive fieldcraft and other training. This could be achieved as a single unit, however, a proposal had just been received which suggested the splitting up of the unit, dividing its time defending its primary site and new site at R.A.F. Cocanda, defending sea planes by manning mounted A.A. guns on Marine Craft.

The heavy Monsson rains in October resulted in widespread flooding of the local area and a number of the unit's Gun Posts, needed to be rebuilt. Although the units immediate focus was on salvage work and the rescue of stranded R.A.F. personnel, cut off by the floods. By the end of the month, the flight managed to complete and man 3 Gun Posts mounted with Twin Browning Guns.

At the beginning of November, No.4449 A.A. Flight received its orders to move to R.A.F. Cholavarum and on arrival, a few days later, sited a number of Gun Posts to cover the various dispersal areas. Work on the sites continued for the month, as conversion kits for the gun mountings had not been received. During the month No.4428 A.A. Flight completed the construction of the 6th Gun Post.

The 24-hour manning of the Gun Posts, took place during the "Moon" period of December and the men of No.4428 A.A. Flight took part in a practice "Stand Too", with the Army Bofor crews. A practice "strife" attack on the airfield by No.135 Squadron, allowed the siting of the guns to be tested, resulting in No.9 Gun Post being re-positioned.

At the airfield at Cholavarum, No.4449 A.A. Flight maintained its 24-hour manning, during the "Moon" period on 3 Gun Posts and undertook additional night patrols, during the hours of darkness. The flight though was soon ordered to head to the coastal base of Vizagapatam. On arrival, the unit sited and commenced constructing the Gun Posts, which due to the nature of the ground had to be dug deep and oblong in shape, to aid camouflage. For the time being, only 3 Gun Posts would be manned, so that the rest of the men could undertake construction work.

The map and table below show the locations of each of the newly formed units as at the 31st December 1943.

R.A.F. Regiment Units in 225 Group R.A.F. – December 1943

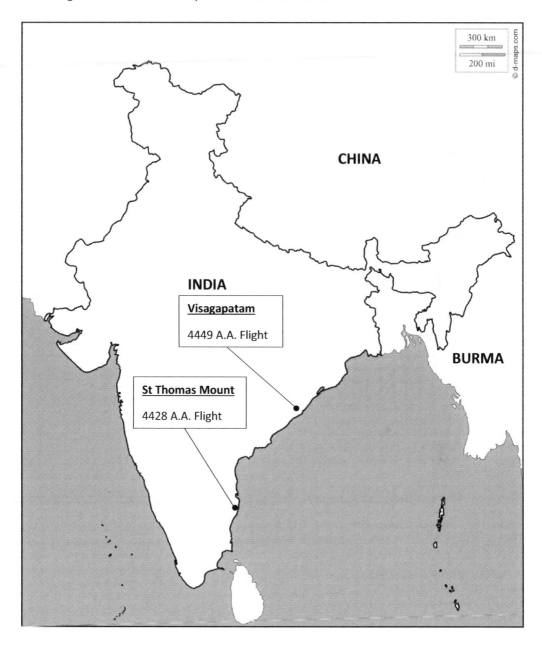

(Author Adapted - http://d-maps.com/carte.php?num_car=32142&lang=en)

R.A.F. Regiment Units in 225 Group R.A.F. – December 1943

Area	A.A. Flight	Field Squadron
Madras	**4428**	
Vizagapatam	**4449**	
Establishment Numbers	2 A.A. Flights = 4 Officers and 74 Airmen	Nil

Operational Diaries

September
4428 A.A. Flight – Embarked from Secunderabad to R.A.F. St. Thomas Mount, Madras

No.4428 Flight posted from R.A.F. Regiment Depot to R.A.F. Station, St. Thomas Mount, Madras. By this time it had become apparent that the main strength of the Flight consisted of gunners with a relatively low average age and of excellent initial morale. The majority had been in India some 18 months and had already undergone a prolonged spell of service in a Forward Area.

The movement to Madras was carried out entirely in accordance with pre-arrangements and the process of settling in at St. Thomas Mount was facilitated by the extreme co-operation and assistance of Headquarters, No.172 Wing, R.A.F. the controlling Unit on the Airfield. Billets, Messing and general living conditions were excellent, and office accommodation and general conditions of work highly satisfactory. One minor difficulty was created when a stationery "pack-up", issued as containing essential requirements for the formation of a new Unit was unpacked and found to contain little else but envelopes and sealing wax; a discovery which would have been of greater consequence had it not been for No.172 Wing. It was found that two partly constructed gun pits on the airfield were suitable for adaptation to the Motley Stalk Mounting and Twin Browning assembly with which the Flight is equipped. A programme of construction work was provisionally settled.

Work on gun post construction was started. The Flight took over M.T. Vehicles.

Officer Commanding Flight left St. Thomas Mount on Temporary Duty to Headquarters No.225 Group, Bangalore. Conversations with the Group Defence Officer took place on this day and the one following and general outlines of policy handed over. Broadly the role of No.4428 Flight at St. Thomas Mount was to be a dual purpose one of mounting and manning A.A. L.M.G's and the carrying out of a progressive course of field and other training.

Orders were given to the Officer Commanding Flight by Senior Administrative Staff Officer, No.225 Group, to detach a section of the Flight, to No.240 Squadron, at R.A.F. Station, Cocanada, for the purpose of manning A.A. L.M.G's mounted on Marine Craft, to patrol aircraft moored off the shore. The implications of splitting so small a unit so soon after its formation, and faced with a comprehensive programme of work at St. Thomas Mount were considered and it was suggested that a special section should be requested from R.A.F. Regiment Depot, Secunderabad. It was finally decided, however that the detachment would not be of sufficient duration to warrant this. The officer Commanding Flight was instructed to make contact with Officer Commanding 240 Squadron, at R.A.F. Red Hills, Madras on his return and to settle the practical details of this task.

October
4428 A.A. Flight – Settling in at St. Thomas Mount Airfield, Madras

Following instructions received from Headquarters, No.225 Group (detailed in September Section of this Unit's Operational Record Book, Events detailed on 29/9/43), a discussion took place between Officer Commanding No.4428 A.A. Flight and Officer Commanding No.240 Squadron Detachment, Cocanada. The details of this conversation were communicated to Headquarters No.225 Group vide this Unit's 4428/MS/3/Air dated 2/10/43 (Appendix A herewith).

Work commenced on the belting of ammunition, in the following recurring blocks of 5 (five):- VII -VII – G.II – W.I – B.VI.Z.

.303 Browning M.G's were received from No.312 M.U. These guns were unpacked and inspected, and found to be in excellent condition.

Headquarters No.225 Group Signal A.D.80 dated 5/10.43 was received, cancelling propositions regarding R.A.F. Cocanada (See previous entries).

Extremely heavy rainfall held up gunpost construction work and it was found that one of the two gunposts in existence when the Unit arrived at St. Thomas Mount airfield was completely flooded and surrounded by water. As a result of this and the fact that it had not been considered satisfactory in the first place from the point of view of design, a decision was made to rebuild these posts entirely.

The first Motley Stalk Mounting complete with conversion set and twin Browning M.G's was assembled. It was found that the bosses on the short ammunition chutes required redrilling.

The incessant and torrential rain of the previous week resulted in widespread flooding of the Area. All the resources of the Unit were directed towards salvage and rescue operations of R.A.F. Personnel cut off in the part of the camp affected.

Guards were posted as an emergency measure in the flooded area of the Airfield. This continued until evening of the following day. All Unit equipment, arms and ammunition was dried out and greased.

Normal routine was re-established and work on gunpost construction was recommended. It was decided to give this the highest possible priority.

The second pair of Browning M.G's was assembled. It was found that the difficulties previously found in the fitting of the short ammunition chutes did not recur.

Extensive firing tests on Browning M.G's assembled were carried out at stop butts. The feed assembly was found to function perfectly and., altogether, the tests were most satisfactory.
The first gunpit built by the Unit was completed.
Orders were received from Headquarters No.225 Group to renew liaison with Officer Commanding No.240 Squadron with a view to providing L.A.A. cover ar their new detachment base.

One pair of the twin Browning M.G's was mounted and manned on the airfield.

Officer Commanding Unit proceeded R.A.F. Redhills but was unable to see Officer Commanding NO.240 Squadron. Information was, however, furnished by the Squadron Adjutant that no aircraft would be at Narasapur before the end of the month at the earliest.

The 3rd assembly of M.G's was tested and found to be satisfactory.

Officer Commanding No.240 Squadron was visited by Officer Commanding Unit, and results of conference forwarded to Headquarters No.225 Group vide Unit's 4428/MS/3/Air dated 21/10/43.

The second pair of twin Browning M.G's was mounted and manned on the airfield.

Belting of Ammunition was temporarily halted on completion of 10,000 rounds. Routine with ammunition on Gunposts was established as follows:-

1st day – Lot A on post.

2nd day – Lost B on post. Lot A to Armoury for cleaning, examination and repacking.

3rd day – Lot A on post. Lot B to armoury.

Headquaretrs No.225 Group letter 225G/S.5510/6/Air dated 25/10/43 received, cancelling A.A. proposition regarding Narasapur.

Visit to Unit of Squadron Leader J.N. Briggs, Group Defence officer, No.225 Group, and Squadron Leader T. McKirdy, A.H.Q. (I). As a result of a conference with Officer Commanding Unit it was decided to continue with Gunpost construction at Priority I and to utilise old gunposts as an emergency measure. The question of bringing guns in to Flight Headquarters as night was discussed at length and, after experiment, it was decided that the bringing in of the whole assembly was quite impracticable, on the grounds of time involved, the virtual certainty of eventual damage to the extremely fragile aluminium ammunition chutes etc. It was finally decided to bring in at night all the recoiling portions, together with the lock frames and return spring of each gun. Satisfaction was expressed by both visiting Staff officers on the design and construction of the gun posts.

The third pair of twin Browning M.G's was mounted and manned on the airfield.

November
4428 A.A. Flight – Operational at St. Thomas Mount Airfield, Madras

In general the month of November was one of steady development of the plans made during the first eight weeks of the Unit's formation, with no exceptional events or modifications to interrupt routine. Unit morale remained high, and incidence of sickness remarkably low.

The fourth A.A. L.M.G. post to be constructed by the Unit was completed and manning commenced.

The fifth A.A. L.M.G. post to be constructed by the Unit was completed and manning commenced.

The sixth A.A. L.M.G. post was constructed by the Unit. This and all subsequent posts (while the current state of readiness is in existence) will only be manned during Air Raid Warning "red". Special cases to house and recoiling portions of the guns have been constructed and these, with ammunition, are held in the Unit armoury. An average of ten minutes is required to make this post operational. This compromise is, of course, rendered necessary by the low establishment of manpower in the Unit, the considerable amount of construction and routine work requiring labour, and the requirements of training.

Headquarters No.225 Group Signal AI.390 dated 25th November received at R.A.F. Station, St. Thomas Mount., calling for maximum alertness during December "Moon" period.

Conference held at R.A.F. Station, St. Thomas Mount incident upon instruction regarding "Moon" period alertness. Unit was detailed to institute 24 hours manning of A.A. L.M.G. Posts during this period (To commence 4/12/43).

4449 A.A. Flight – Entrained from R.A.F. Secunderabad, with orders to move to R.A.F. Cholavarum.

On the 3rd Nov. 1943 the Flight received orders to move to CHOLAVARUM. Entrainment took place at 09.00hrs 5th Nov. 1943 and the Unit duly arrived at CHOLAVARUM at 23.00hrs.

7th NOV. 1943. W/CDR CHATER D.F.C. Station Commander at CHOLAVARUM was contacted and gun-posts were sited to cover various dispersals etc. Work on same was commenced together with other necessary work, it being not possible to assemble gun mountings as Conversion Sets were not yet to hand.

Demand were raised for all deficiencies through No.12 Equipment Section. O/C Unit reported to S/LDR BRIGGS GROUP DEFENCE OFFICER No.225 Group on 15th November 1943. Various points were discussed and contacts made with other sections at No.225 GP including Welfare Section from whom a supply of amenities were drawn. On return to CHOLAVARUM O/C Unit ordered 1355684 CPL. MADAMS and 1 OR to proceed to SECUNDERABAD as it had been learnt that further equipment was now available.

December
4428 A.A. Flight – Operational at St. Thomas Mount Airfield, Madras

Bren L.M.G's to Unit Scale were received ex R.A.F. Regiment Depot, Secunderabad.
Unit commenced 24 hours manning of A.A. L.M.G. Posts (reference Entry dated 29/11/43 in November Section of this Unit's Operations Record Book).
Unit participation in Practice Stand To wide Airfield Defence Scheme. Army Garrison troops also took part.
A practice "strafe" of the Airfield was carried out by No. 135 Squadron. This was used by No.4428 A.A. Flight to test gun post dispositions, and as a result of this the siting of the 9th A.A. L.M.G. Post was altered.
"Moon" period alertness concluded and normal routine re-instituted in Unit. Unit received copy of Headquarters No.225 Group Operational Standing Orders for R.A.F. Regiment A.A. Flights. Unit's Standing Orders for A.A. L.M.G's Crews were amended following receipts of these Instructions.

4449 A.A. Flight – Moved and operational at Vizagapatam

CPL Madams returned with this equipment on 27th November 1943 and on 2nd December 1943 3 gun posts were fully operational and being manned 24hrs daily, a night patrol contacting during the hours of darkness. This was carried out in accordance with No.173 W. OP. ORDER No.36 dated 30th Nov. 1943, covering a period when EA was likely. At this a signal was received from H.Q. 225 GP ordering the Unit to move to YIZAGAPATAM. W/CDR CHATER was informed and he at once contacted H.Q. 225 GP. By telephone speaking firstly to S/LDR BRIGGS and then to G/CAPT BOWLES. As a result of these conversations W/CDR CHATER informed O/C Unit that the movement had been cancelled.
This however was not confirmed and verbal orders were received from S/LDR BRIGGS on 8th Dec. 1943 that the Unit was to proceed. This was done and the Flight arrived at VIZAGAPATAM at 23.00hrs. 11th DEC. 1943.

A report regarding the delay in movement was submitted to H.Q. 172 WING.

Gun Posts were sited and construction commenced, owing to nature of the ground it was decided that the Gun Posts could not be dug deeply, also that an oblong shape would lend itself more easily to camouflage.

General work and construction of Gun Posts continued.

No.1508224 L.A.C. WHITBY returned to Unit having completed Unit Armourers Course at Ambala.

On instructions received from S/LDR GODBER O/C VIZAGAPATAM the Flight was ready for action, as a signal had been received to the effect that an unidentified convoy was near the coast. This however was later confirmed to be friendly, and at 03.00hrs the Flight was given the order to "STAND DOWN".

At this time three Gun Posts were being manned permanently, it being decided to man this number only in order to have more men available for further construction work.

Work proceeding.

No.4428 A.A. Flight – Defence Orders

FROM: No.4428 A.A. FLIGHT. R.A.F. REGIMENT.

TO: HEADQUARTERS. No.225 GROUP. R.A.F.

(FOR ATTENTION OF GROUP DEFENCE OFFICER)

DATE: 2nd OCTOBER 1943.

REF: 4428/S/3/AIR.

<u>Defence: R.A.F. Concanada.</u>

Reference to verbal orders given to Officer Commanding No.4428 A.A. Flight, R.A.F.R., during his recent visit to Headquarters, No.225 Group, on the subject of temporary A.A. Defence, R.A.F. Concanada, contact has been made with Officer Commanding No.240 Squadron Detachment R.A.F. Cocanada, and the following facts established.

2. There are four Marine Craft at Cocanada, as follows:-
   i) <u>Refueller</u>: This is not suitable for, and, by reason of its special function, not available for the mounting of A.A. L.M.G's.

   ii) <u>Petrel</u>: This is apparently an old boat and the mounting on it and firing of A.A. L.M.G's from it, would, it is stated, render it dangerously unseaworthy.

   iii) <u>Bomb Scow</u>: Suitable for mounting A.A. L.M.G's subject to limitations outlined in para 3. Used for bombing and de-bombing aircraft, and ferrying of maintenance personnel to and from and between aircraft.

   iv) <u>Walton</u>: Suitable for mounting A.A. L.M.G's subject to limitations outlines in para. 3. Used for ferrying Aircrew and also as Flare Path Officer control boat.

3. It will be seen from the above that there are two marine craft on which A.A. L.M.G's could, as a practical consideration, be mounted. The Officer Commanding No.240 Squadron Detachment pointed out, however:

   i) That he had only just enough boats to cope with normal servicing and other requirement without leaving any boats out at the aircraft longer than was absolutely necessary. He could not even consider, if he was to carry on normal routine, leaving these two boats out at the aircraft in a role of semi-permanent gun "pits".

ii)   That the only type of mounting which they had been able to devise (an adaptation of the tripod type) would make it impossible for the boats to lie, as is apparently necessary, up against the aircraft, under the wings. If the guns were mounted on craft that were used for normal routine as well, they would have to be taken off the mountings when the boats were up alongside the aircraft. IF this system (i.e. dual purpose boats) was adopted, it would mean that for most of the only time that the boats were near the aircraft, the guns would have to be dismounted. It is not necessary, in addition, for this Unit to elaborate on the question of the mounting and dismounting of Twin Browning guns, with ammunition tanks, etc. on a small boat some two or three miles out at sea. Furthermore, for A.A. L.M.G's to be of any use, they would have to be some little distance away from the aircraft and this, could only be done at the expense of normal routine and other requirements. The additional weight and "space" of guns and crew would themselves interfere with these and, if installed would necessitate even more "runs" to and from the jetty and aircraft.

iii)   No.240 Squadron state that the guns of the aircraft themselves would appear to offer a far better form of protection than two sets of Brownings, even if there were the marine craft available to have these out in the neighbourhood of the aircraft on a semi-permanent basis. Then moored the guns in the aircraft can be elevated to approximately 80 degrees, an elevation equal to, if not greater than, A.A. L.M.G's mounted, as suggested on marine craft. There is apparently one man always in each aircraft as a guard/watchman as a matter of routine. The question whether R.A.F.R. Gunners could man guns in the aircraft was raised and declared quite out of the question. The manning of aircraft guns by No.240 Squadron personnel familiar with the mechanism of the aircraft turrets was not gone into by this Unit since, if it were ever adopted, it is obviously a matter that could best be settled directly between your Headquarters and the Squadron itself.

4. Having regards to the above, and the fact that it was obviously necessary for these facts to be brought to your notice, other considerations were not gone into in any great detail. Accommodation for the detachment could be provided by the Squadron (by tents) and while this would be very far from satisfactory, as a temporary expedient it would be adequate.

5. It is requested that your Headquarters will consider the information reported above and issue further or additional instructions to this Unit and/or to No.240 Squadron. It seems quite clear that with the position as it is at present this Unit can serve no useful purpose at all by proceeding with Detachment

to Cocanada. The core of the matter appears to be in the policy question of the use of the available marine craft at Cocanada: whether they are to be used as at present, or as floating gun "pits". This Unit is not qualified to express an opinion on the matter of combining the two functions, but the Officer Commanding No.240 Squadron Detachment, R.A.F. Cocanada, was very definite in his opinion that it was not a practical proposition.

Signed F/Lt.

OFFICER COMMANDING,

No.4428 A.A. FLIGHT,

R.A.F. REGIMENT.

No.4428 A.A. Flight – Sketch of Gun Post

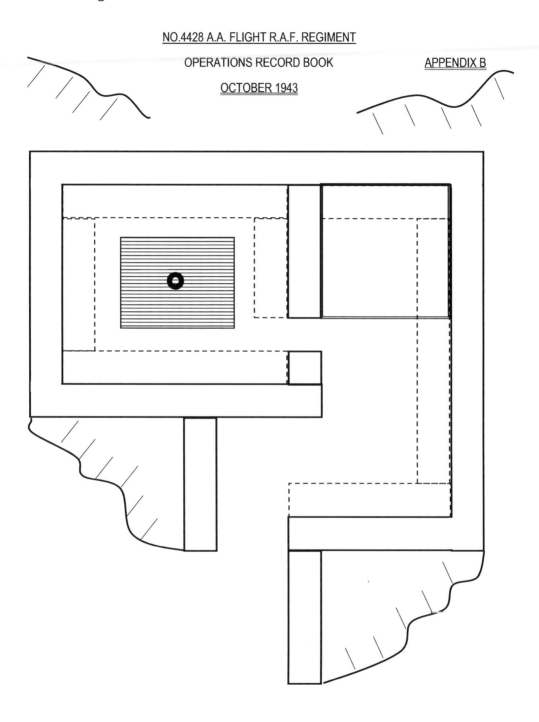

No.4428 A.A. Flight — Flying Boats Protection

MOST SECRET.

FROM: No.4428 A.A. FLIGHT. R.A.F. REGIMENT.

TO: HEADQUARTERS. No.225 GROUP.R.A.F.

(FOR THE ATTENTION OF GROUP DEFENCE OFFICER)

OFFICER COMMANDING, No.240 SQUADRON, R.A.F.

DATE: 21/10/43.

REF: 4428AA/MS/3/AIR.

A.A. Protection - Flying Boats.

1. With further reference to your Headquarters 225G/S.5510/6/AIR dated 12th October 1943, the question of the provision of A.A. M.G. protection for No.240 Squadron's Flying Boats Detachment, at Narasapur, has been discussed with Wing Commander Clayton, Officer Commanding, No.240 Squadron, R.A.F.

2. No.240 Squadron have not, as yet, moved into Narasaput, and do not anticipate having aircraft there before November 7th at the earliest. This is incident upon mooring having to be constructed, and living accommodation built and/or repaired etc., in accordance with medical instructions. An arrangement has been made whereby the Adjutant, No.240 Squadron, will notify this Unit when an Officer from that Squadron is next proceeding to Narasapur, and F/Lt. Yates of this Unit will accompany him and carry out a preliminary reconnaissance of the site.

3. During the general discussion between Wing Commander Clayton and F/Lt. Yates, it was decided that the various points brought out should be reported to your Headquarters by this Unit, having regard to paragraph 5 of your above quoted letter.

4. In the first instance Wing Commander Clayton would not understand why it was considered necessary to have a section of R.A.F. Regiment Gunners at Narasapur, when Red Hills was left entirely without R.A.F. Regiment A.A. protection. He felt that if the former was essential, then the latter was even more so, and that the ideal, from the Squadron's viewpoint, would be an R.A.F. Regiment A.A. Flight attached to No.240 Squadron with 2/3rds of its strength at Red Hills, and 1/3rd at Narasapur.

5. The current situation at St. Thomas Mount Airfield was next briefly discussed, and it was pointed out that since the question of A.A. protection for No.240 Squadron's Detachment was first raised, the situation in Madras had materially altered. St. Thomas Mount

Airfield is now being used as an assembly airfield for "Lightnings", in addition to its former function, and large numbers of these aircraft, awaiting assembly, are parked thickly on almost every available piece of ground. There has already been one armed reconnaissance enemy aircraft over the airfield, and it is considered more than likely that the enemy are aware of the location of these U.S. Army Fighters. It was felt that this fact should be brought to the notice of your Headquarters.

6. Returning to Narasapur, it would appear that it would be possible, prima facie, to place A.A. M.G's, land-based, reasonably close to moored aircraft. Details of siting etc., will have to be decided on the spot, and full particulars of this will be reported to you when a reconnaissance has been carried out. On the question of manning, Wing Commander Clayton suggested that Backers-Up could very well man the guns, provided that these were sited, orders formulated, etc., by an R.A.F. Regiment Officer. He was of the opinion that if, as is the case, Backers-Up are considered suitable to man the guns at Red Hills, then even more so can this be dome at the relatively less important base at Narasapur. No.240 Squadron has two R.A.F. Regiment D.T.I's attached, and these N.C.O's have been, of course, including Browning training in the Backers-Up course.

7. Having regard to paragraphs 5 above, F/Lt. Yates informed Wing Commander Clayton that he felt that he should suggest again to Headquarters No.225 Group that a special section be requested from R.A.F.R. Depot, Secunderabad, in order not to weaken the, at best, thin defences at St. Thomas Mount. Wing Commander Clayton did not agree, stating as his opinion that if a special R.A.F. Regiment Section were to be attached to No.240 Squadron at all, then Red Hills was the base first to be considered (vide paragraph 4 above), and not Narasapur.

8. The position at present can be summed up as follows:-

Both this Unit and No.240 Squadron would welcome your Headquarter's comments on the above information and suggestion but in the meantime, this Unit will carry on with the taking of the necessary steps to fulfil the instructions contained in your letter of 12th October.

Signed F/Lt.

OFFICER COMMANDING,

No.4428 A.A. FLIGHT,

R.A.F. REGIMENT.

No.4428 A.A. Flight – St Thomas Mount Airfield Defence Scheme

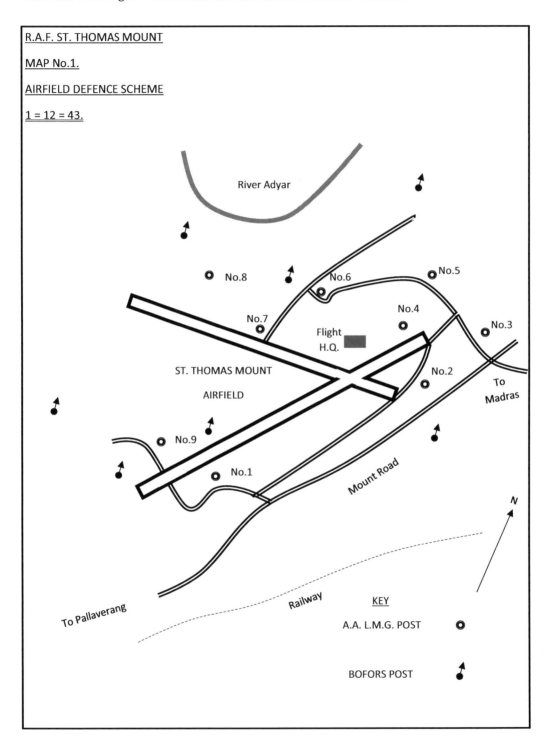

Group 231 – Heavy Bombers

Overview

The first new unit, No.4406 A.A. Flight arrived at Amarda Road Airfield, in early May, after an uneventful 3-day journey, their accommodation, south of the runway in No.3 Camp, was satisfactory. Settling in proceeded and in June the flight started to undertake it's routine training programme. A letter was received from A.H.Q., confirming the renumbering of flights, formerly changing its old No.4356 to No.4406. The flight commander instructed the station engineer to construct six Gun Posts around the aerodrome and although they estimated their completion in 6 days, it wouldn't be until the end of the month that the basic construction of the Gun Posts would be finished. As some men had not had any time off since arriving in India, the flight commander took the opportunity to get as many men as possible, off on 48-hour leave.

The months of July and August saw the heaviest rains of the Monsoon and the impact on the newly constructed Gun Posts was quite severe, with only half being able to be manned. The siting of the original Gun Posts and the porous nature of the ground, meant that four new posts had to be sited and constructed. With the assistance of the Photographic Section, a unique opportunity came about, between the flying squadrons and gun crews. With camera guns being fitted to the aircraft and guns, footage could be gained, through simulated runs, of what the pilots can see whilst attacking the aerodrome and what it looks like to be "shot up" by the Gun Crews.

September saw nine of the new A.A. Flights, including No.4436 and No.4437, in transit onboard S.S. "Varela", at Madras, for a 5-day journey to Chittagong. On arriving at Chittagong, the units in transit, found conditions very bad, with no lighting, or cooking equipment. For seven days, awaiting movement orders, the men were forced to cook their own meals using cleaned out, discarded petrol tins. Whilst work was still not being forthcoming on the completion of the Gun Pits, the new flight commander, No.4406 A.A. Flight, at the Amarda Road Airfield, spent a good part of the month re-organising his unit.

At the beginning of October, only 3 flights were waiting for their movement orders at the transit camp at Chittagong. Both No.4436 and No.4437 A.A. Flights embarked on a small cargo steamer H.T. "Bandra", for Calcutta. While No.4436 A.A. Flight waited in transit for another boat, to take them to R.A.F. Char Chapli and No.4437 A.A. Flight completed their movement, after a short rail journey, to R.A.F. Diamond Harbour. The flight was split into two sections, defending 544 A.M.E.S. at Diamond Harbour, initially taking over a Gun Post at the top of a 60ft tower and fifteen miles away, defending 258 A.M.E.S. at Mathrapur. During the month, the flight constructed a number of new posts and by the end of October manned a total of six Gun Posts. Due to accommodation shortages No.4436 A.A.

Flight split into two, one section, with 3 twin Brownings, stayed at 211 A.M.E.S., at Khulna and the remainder of the flight moved to R.A.F. Char Chapli. The Gun Posts were split to defend 375 A.M.E.S. and the beach area, providing A.A, as well as ground to ground cover, due to the high risk of probable Japanese raiding/sabotage parties.

The training programme continued for No.4406 A.A. Flight, at Amarda Road Airfield, with range firing of the Browning Guns, which resulted in a number of stoppages thought to be due to the "American" ammunition. All the Gun Posts, including the dummy sites were now complete in construction, with only sandbagging now to be done. The camera gun work with the flying squadrons took place mid-way through the month, with Vultee Vengeance and Hardvard aircraft, providing simulated dive bombing attacks. The Gunners were complimented on their "shots" and although more was needed, to help harmonise the equipment, much was learnt, on both sides.

The beach Gun Crews of No.4436 A.A. Flight, at Char Chapli, spent most of the first two weeks of November 'Standing To', due to numerous suspicious activities out at sea, all of which turned out to be local fishing boats. Still without the bolts for the Motley Stork mountings, the men experimented with wooden cross bases, which turned out to be quite satisfactory. The last two weeks of the month saw a high rise in men being admitted to hospital suffering with Malaria. By the end of the month a total of 12 men had been admitted to hospital. Soon operational at R.A.F. Diamond Harbour, No.4437 A.A Flight spent a large proportion of the month on the range and undertaking extensive advanced training on their Browning Guns. Around 90% of all Gunners met the standards set, those failing were put through elementary training again, before progressing to meet the advanced standard required.

Arriving at the airfield at Baigachi, No.4447 A.A. Flight soon settled in, and the Gunners from resident Defence detachments were attached to the flight, to increase discipline. Nine gunners were detached to No.176 Squadron, to attend a 3-day aircraft Refuelling and Rearming course.

The training programme of No.4406 A.A. Flight, at Amarda Road Airfield, focused on individual weapons training. In addition to this, the unit travelled to Chardipur A.M.E.S. and fired its Browning Guns at a range at between 250 – 1,000 yards, out to sea. The responsibility for the units M.T. vehicles was handed over to the flight, with each designated driver taking the full responsibility for their upkeep and servicing.

At the beginning of December, the bolts for the Motley Stork Gun mountings finally arrived for No.4436 A.A. Flight at Char Chapli, allowing the mounts to be erected. An air raid warning was sounded, when a large formation of enemy bombers was heard flying overhead. All A.A. posts were manned, but the aircraft were too high and no hostile act was committed. A second batch of enemy bombers were reported to be flying East to West later in the day. Ten men from the flight were still in hospital suffering with Malaria and confirmation was given from medical authorities, that the maximum length of tour on the station would be 6 months. On several occasions suspicious boats were sighted out at sea, again all ended up being fishing boats. Fresh rations were served for Xmas Day dinned, followed by a rifle range competition, football and cricket matches, ending in the evening with a concert. Near the end of the month, most of the men suffering from Malaria were now back on strength and the station personnel of 373 A.M.E.S., were also formed into three Rifle Defence Sections, who in an emergency, would man outer defence localities.

The same enemy aircraft formations were observed by No.4437 A.A. Flight at Diamond Harbour, the first formation believed to be six Zero's heading south west at approximately 25,000ft and the second batch was identified as eight Mitsubishi Army Bombers at 18,000ft heading south. No.4447 A.A. Flight at Baigachi received instructions to move to R.A.F. Alipore.

The training for No.4406 A.A. Flight, at Amarda Road Airfield, focused on Fieldcraft and Morse code, with range work and a full exercise in attack. Xmas and Boxing Day were fully celebrated, with the aid of the stations A.F.T.U., with a concert, comic football matches, athletics and a fancydress whist drive. Xmas dinner was served in the traditional, way with Officers and N.C.O.'s waiting on the men.

The table and maps below show all the new units locations as at the end of December 1943.

R.A.F. Regiment Units in 231 Group R.A.F. – December 1943

Area	A.A. Flight	Field Squadron
Amarda Road	4406	
Kharagpur	4412, 4446	
Cuttacj	4420	
Baigachi	4435, 4447	
Char Chapli	4436	
Dlamond Harbour	4437	
Establishment Numbers	8 A.A. Flights = 16 Officers and 296 Airmen	Nil

R.A.F. Regiment Units in 231 Group R.A.F. – December 1943

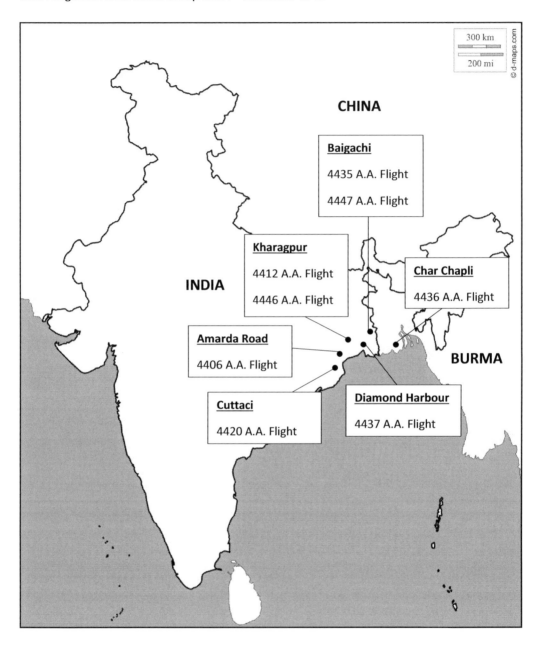

(Author Adapted - http://d-maps.com/carte.php?num_car=32142&lang=en)

Operational Diaries

May
4406 A.A. Flight – Settling in at Amarda Road Airfield

The flight arrived here after a 3 day journey from Secunderabad, via Nagpur, Raipur, Khargpur. The men are accommodated on No.3 Camp, SOUTH of the runway. No complaints have been received which cannot be rectified quickly, apart from scarcity of furniture such as tables for huts: & the men appear to be fairly happy considering the location of the station. 24 hours was given to them to settle down and have some rest after travelling.

Settlement has proceeded well & all accommodation difficulties have been overcome. During the month F/Lt. Chambers has been appointed Station P.W.D Officer. Owing to the wide dispersal employed here and the lack of transport for this unit the making of contact with Sections has been extremely difficult and much time has been wasted.

June
4406 A.A. Flight – Settling in at Amarda Road Airfield

The training of the Flight proceeds in the normal way. The work has been much more easily proceeded with and much work has been done as the Station M.T. Section has today lent F/Lt. Chambers a Motor cycle, pending the arrival of the Units own transport.

A letter has been received to the effect that A.H.Q. has renumbered the Flight with effect from to-day. It is now No.4406 AA Flight R.A.F. Regt.

Instructions have been given to the P.W.D. with plans for construction of six gunposts at various places on the actual aerodrome.

6 days delay has occurred in connection with the construction of the gunposts & no work has been done by the P.W.D., because, they say, they have had no letter of instructions. Letter handed to then within four hours of knowing this. They estimate completion in 6 days. It would appear that this policy of P.W.D.'s not carrying out work until the request has been given in writing, in spite of the fact that they are cognisant of what is wanted, is futile. In this case

they knew in detail because F/Lt. Chambers paid a personal visit to the Office & saw Mr. Laurie, the man in charge and yet for six days the work was not even started for want of a letter of confirmation. It is suggested that this matter be rectified. The Motor Cycle went U/S to day so we are back where we started.

A letter was received from 329 M.U. saying that four 15 cwt Trucks are awaiting collection.

1 Cpl & 3 airmen left to act as escort to the above which 329 M.U. have been requested to despatch. They will not be driven here. Two airmen also left today for 35 P.T.C. Calcutta for a course in Cookery under orders from Bengal Command. During all the time the Flight has been at this station & the normal working has been held up by the construction of gunposts every effort has been made to get men off on 48 hour passes. Some of them have had no leave, not even "48", since they have been in this country. Two vacancies occurred in a hill party and two men were sent who had been sick. They are not yet back.

Two vehicles of our establishment of four 15 cwt trucks have arrived. Two only became railway "flats" were not available & would not be for about a week. The four men of the escort were given driving tests at 329 M.U. and only two passed (1 Cpl. & 1 LAC) & they drove the two vehicles back.

12 Browning guns & six twin mountings are now ours having been taken over from the Station Armoury. We are still waiting for ammunition tanks, which have been demanded.

All gun posts are now constructed according to the specification given to P.W.D., but some modifications will be necessary when the mono pools for holding the mountings are fixed. This is a simple matter. As soon as the ammunition tanks arrive gun posts will be manned. 221 Group say the tanks are those for Nos. 5 & 6 Starboard & Port Guns for a Hurricane IIB. They cannot be borrowed here.

July
4406 A.A. Flight – Settling in at Amarda Road Airfield

In the course of this month training has proceed as much as possible. This unit is the only one on this camp (No.3) at this station. Information was given to us that a Squadron was coming to this camp as well as ourselves, & we were given orders, by S/L Admin, to clean it up, rearrange furniture in officer's quarters which was in officer & other billets, to make an inventory thereof, & so collect, make serviceable & redistribute all fire equipment on the camp. In addition to this all sanitary appliances were to be cleaned & put in order generally. This has all been done. It is now said that if the Squadron comes to this station at all, it will not come to this came!

In view if the time involved in waiting for the ammunition boxes for the Browning Gun mountings it was decided to make our own. Twelve boxes of the requisite size were made with wood and disused petrol tins. The effectiveness of these have not yet been tested by actual firing, but it is hoped to do it soon.

The gunposts are completed and three of the six have been manned. In spite of the P.W.D.'s assurance that the ground was sufficiently porous to allow any water to permeate into the earth there has been trouble caused by the monsoon causing further modifications to be necessary. There are partly completed. During the modifications gun post manning has still proceeded wen not hampered by waterlogged posts. Four further posts are being constructed.

The A.F.I.U. at this station is equipped with a film projector (16m.m.) & a letter has been written to Bengal Command asking if any films of an instructional nature are available which are suitable for the Regiment. No reply has yet been received. The same section has offered to lend us a camera gun to be fixed on a Browning Mounting so that films may be taken to test the Flight's ability the A.F.I.U. do practice "rhubarbs" in the courses. This is an extremely good idea & every effort is being made to carry it out. One mounting with two guns has been given to the Photographic Section for them to fix & harmonise the sights, camera and guns. The execution of this will give mutual assistance in that we shall see how we can "shoot", so will the pilot see his results (he is fitted with a camera gun too) & also what likelihood there us of his being "shot up" from the rear after his attack.

The 9 Motley Stalk Mountings cannot be used as there are not any proper brackets to fix the guns. Steps have been taken to rectify this.

August
4406 A.A. Flight – Settling in at Amarda Road Airfield

In the course of the month of August training and working of the Flight have proceeded normally. Gun Posts were manned for 6 nights over the full moon period. Still no reply has been received to the question to Bengal Command in conjunction with films for training purposes. The suggested plan of action with camera guns on our mountings against fighter aircraft with camera guns did not materialise owing to the fact that all our guns were wanted during the full moon period which coincided with the part of the programme of Fighter Flight. Every effort is being made to make arrangements for this to take place during the of September. Sickness has been on a heavier rate during the month of August than in any previous months, the most notable complaints being infected prickly heat & kinea. There have been three cases of dysentery. For the time being hill parties have ceased owing to dislocation of communication and hill stations are only open now for convalescence cases. This sickness has made the granting of leave somewhat difficult. It is estimated that all personnel who want it will have had leave or attachment to hill parties by the 15th October. This was the latest date quoted by the Bengal Command Defence Officer when he visited this unit in July.

The nine Motley Stalk Mountings are still incomplete, therefore they cannot be made use of. The four 15 cwt Chevrolets which were pooled with the station transport, by the Station Commander Orders, are all being used, two by us. The agreement(verbal)between the Station Commander & this Flights' Commander was that if any vehicles were wanted by us in excess of the two which this unit at present use, we were to have first claim on our own transport. This agreement has twice been broken by the use of this Section, and the vehicles when wanted, have not been called in from the Sections to which they are sent so that they could be at our disposal. In the first instance one of our own two vehicles was U/S. Application was made to the M.T. Section for another of our own giving one of our other vehicles which had been returned to M.T. for a regular inspection. It was imperative that we had it & so the inspection was lifted. In the second instance it was necessary to send two men to a police court to give evidence. Application was again made to M.T. giving them 24 hours notice, but we were given an unreliable 3 ton truck for the morning only, for our duty runs here and one of our own took two men to court.

September
4406 A.A. Flight – Operational at Amarda Road Airfield

Training programme as usual for the month.
National Day of Prayer held at No.1 Camp – football pitch – 16 men paraded from this unit. Colours were hoisted at 07.45 hrs. Service held by Padre S/Ldr. McIntrye at 08.00 Fourth Anniversary of Great War.
Medical Officer placed all native village out of bounds, with outbreak of Cholera in district.
Airmens' Messing Committee held. Complaints few, meals rather highly praised. Green vegetables lacking, this is due to time of year.
Supplies of hats; putties & Regiment flashes demanded as they are now available.
CO. visited P.W.D. in connection with four new gun posts, orders for the construction of them were given on 22nd July. Two of these are complete, one half complete and one not started. Letter had been handed with them concerning this on August 2nd, but nothing had been done. LAURIE has left and a new man arrived. He asked for time to settle down, and will be given it. Further action will be taken if nothing has been done about the pits by next month.
C.O.'s parade held at football pitch No.1 Camp. 18 personnel of this unit present.

A.H.Q. Orders No.89 contained new address of unit. This was communicated in new Unit daily detail as follows:-
No. Rank. Name. Initials,
4406 A/A Flight,
R.A.F. India.
1154814 Cpl. Coswell I.H. & 1404514 L.A.C. Richards G.A., returned from M.T. Maintenance Course at C.R.O., McKenzices Garage, Calcutta 208, Lower Cirenlai Road.

1404514 L.A.C. Richards G.A. admitted SSQ 15/9/43 and transferred to B.C.H. on 25.9.43, our first case of Malaria.

MR PARTI new P.W.D. man visited Gun Posts with C.O., will complete within a week.

990992 L.A.C. JENNSON A. admitted S.S.Q. & hence B.M.H to see specialist.

F/LT. H.W. FREEMAN the new O.C. Unit arrived, to take over command. Visit paid to all and sundry at S.H.Q. & Sections on camps.

F/LT. H.W. FREEMAN takes over command officially from this date.

Camp Sections reorganised.
1340862 L.A.C. McNab R. placed in charge of Equipment Section.
1545015 L.A.C. Chandler B.L. placed in charge of Fire Section.
990992 L.A.C. Jennson A. placed in charge of Camouflage Section.
A.P. 1918 procured and unit deficiencies of equipment etc. arms and ammunition checked & demands placed on appropriate M.U.'s and E.P.'s.

Independent Air Crew Candidates interviewed & J. 494 & F. 1739 completed & passed to Station Commander.

Letter answered ref. confidential report on N.C.O.'s. All considered satisfactory.

1467880 L.A.C. Grimshaw A. detailed as permanent Medical Orderly for the Unit. To report to S.S.Q. for instruction. M.O. agrees & is keen about the whole thing.

Advance party of 307 Sqn (Fighters Spitfire) arrived in camp. To be here for 3 weeks duration. Flight is with our organisation. All details arranged with S/Ldr. Tait. Squadron here for A.F.T.U. Course.

> Further members of 307 Sqdn arrive in all about 30. Sgts & Officers Messes being opened down here. Water supply station arranged.

4436 A.A. Flight – In transit at Chittagong

Arrived at Madras. Embarked on Troopship "Valera" at 10.00hrs. Left at 16.00hrs for Chittagong.
Called in at Vizag; left at 16.00hrs for Chittagong.
Officers' accommodation very good but men very crowded below deck.
Arrived Chittagong- unloaded and proceeded to 224 Group transit camp at Muslim School arrived at 19.00hrs.
Accommodation very bad, washing facilities bad, no lighting whatsoever, no cooking utensils in which to cook food. Remained here 7 days awaiting movement orders.

4437 A.A. Flight – In transit at Chittagong

We arrived in MADRAS at 09.00hrs. Immediately preparations were made to convey all our kit, ammunition and equipment aboard the S.S. VARELA of the B.I.S.N. Co., which is due to sail at 16.00hrs. Rations for Officers and Airmen are available aboard ship, consequently our supply of rations were returned to the R.I.A.S.C.
Here the S.S. VARELA dropped anchor for a few hours before proceeding to CHITTAGONG. Accommodation on board, for Airmen, was rather cramped but the food being good compensated for this inconvenience.
After a five day uneventful sea journey the nine A.A. Flights R.A.F. Regt finally arrived at the CHITTAGONG docks. Upon disembarkation, transport, awaiting our arrival, conveyed the nine Flights to the R.A.F. Transit Camp to wait further Movement Orders.
Accommodations are very poor. And due to our very limited supply of equipment Airmen were forced to cook their own meals in cleaned out discarded petrol tins. Cooking utensils were not provided by the Transit Camp. Our supply of rations left behind in MADRAS would have been useful on this occasion.

October
4406 A.A. Flight – Operational at Amarda Road Airfield

Training programme as usual for the month. Filing system and treatment of correspondence entirely reorganised on official "R.A.F. lines". Letter received from A.V.M. J. M. Williams, A.O.C. Bengal Command re poor saluting of officers & men in Calcutta. Digest of letter communicated to all ranks of Unit on Unit Detail, 1.10.43, letter reference HQB/1303/P.I. dated 23.9.43.

1562820 L.A.C. Riddell (J)(Gunner) arrived this Unit for attachment from R.A.F. Regt. Depot, Secunderabad, reason for attachment not known.

Flight fired MK.2 Browning Guns on 25 yards Range, stoppages rather frequent, due to faulty .303 "American Ammunition" in the main.

Communication received from A.H.Q. India - Amendment to establishment - Notes - 2 Gunners employed on Armament Maintenance duties may draw additional pay of 3d a day in accordance with AFI/131/43 - Authority:- G of I. No.3106/424/Org./A.F. dated 18/9/43.

No action taken by O.C. Unit, pending return of 2 Gunners at present attached, at No.2 S of T.T, Ambala. (For Armament Course) and a statement of results gained on course.

O.C. Unit had interview with R.A.F. Station Amarda Rd. O.C., Group Captain Champion de Crespigny, re "Backers Up" training of Station personnel. The Group Captain agreed that the present system of an hour a day be discontinued, & that the suggestion of a complete 5 day course every 3 weeks, i.e. in the "breaks" between A.F.T.U. courses be substituted.

A.M.O. N.675/43 which refers to the "thanks of the Houses of Parliament to his Majesty's Forces on the occasion of the victory in Nort Africa", was repeated in full on Flight Unit Orders dated today.

C.P.W.D. consulted re. Gun Posts and following arrangements agreed upon, coolies to prepare gun posts under supervision of a Cpl. & a party of B.O.R.'s.

Gun Posts started. 530314 Sgt. Kelly, 1143551 L.A.C. Ainscough detailed to collect stores from Calcutta, Stationery Store, Welfare

Goods at 221 Group, and spending of a portion of the stationary grant buying office requisites.

1562820 L.A.C. Riddell now definitely posted to this Unit – authority:- B.P.O. Draft Note BPO/13419 dated 7/10/43.

Firing of MK.II Browning Guns on 25 yards Range. Same fault noticed – stoppage due to faulty AMERICAN - .303 AMMUNITION.

All gun positions, dummy positions, now completed and inspected by O.C. Unit. Sandbagging now needed, and positions are fully prepared. Sandbags demanded through EQUIPMENT SECTION, RAF STATION, AMARDA ROAD.

530314 Sgt. Kelly and 1143551 LAC Ainscough returned from CALCUTTA with a large amount of stationery and a large assortment of Welfare articles, e.g. a cricket set, card games etc, a library of 50 books, and a gramophone and records.

1301774 L.A.C. HUNTBACH L.A., and 1562820 L.A.C. RIDDELL detailed to attend Aircraft Recognition course at 221 Group, CALCUTTA & proceeded same day.

101449 L.A.C. MABBOTT W.A. and 1554623 L.A.C. RALSSTON D. returned to unit from S of T.T. AMBALA (Armament Course) both passed course, detailed result awaited.

One N.C.O. & 4 Airmen proceeded to RAF 313 MU, Kankinara, to collect Browning Guns, Bicycles, & Stationery, escort guard armed.

M/Cycle Norton received from A.F.T.U. AMARDA road – No.c/4601622 (16.H) M.T. mow complete. Personnel of Flight were mustered and taken to Bomber Flight for a lecture on the Hurricane line camera gun, preparatory to ground to air firing at an attacking aeroplane, low flying attacks, hedge hopping on gun pits. S/Ldr. Sutton C.I.G.S. agreed & was pleased to cooperate, as it entailed good training for pilots. It is the intention of the O.C. Unit to cooperate with the A.F.T.U. gunnery courses on the station& to use the facilities, for training the Flight to a high level of accuracy in A.A.L.M.G. "ground to air" firing.

Attacks arranged & Flight assembled at No.3 Gun Post for firing. Vultee Vengeance dive bomber made the attacks, these "went off" successfully, but after third attack the plane had to land owing to engine trouble – oil pressure.

M.T. Section now completely reorganised and a driver is now made responsible for each vehicle, with a second driver to make a team. Each driver i/c a vehicle & the motor cycle keeps his own log book for M.T., which is inspected on M.T. parade weekly. Two of the Flight now service all M.T. vehicles at 500, 2,000 mile inspection. The M.T. MAINTENANCE personnel at R.A.F. Station, Amarda Rd, supervise and guide these Airmen. They are to be complimented on their first inspection, they were really well done. This makes the Unit almost self responsible for the servicing of its own M.T. & relieves congestion at M.T. Section Amarda Road, as they are very short staffed in M.T. maintenance personnel, and their number of M.T. is large.

The "camera gunning" of low flying aircraft was continued & completed this morning. A Harvard was the attacking aircraft. The shots were good and the pilot was thanked & complimented on the excellence of his attacks. This is an excellent form of training for our gunners.

W/CDR. J.E. Fowke, A.H.Q. Bengal (Command Defence Officer) arrived very unexpectedly at the Flight. Although he had sent a signal on before, it never reached the Unit in time. He inspected thoroughly the men, their quarters, & the camp. He asked me for a list of difficulties & shortness of equipment. His report which will include a detailed summary of his visit, is awaited. It will be published in the appendix to the next month's operational record sheet.

Alterations to Establishment - Communication received A.H.Q. DELHI - India 664/5 - A.A. Flight - R.A.F.R Flight H.Q. - add 1 F.M.T. authority - G of I No.3106/424/1/ORG A.F. dated 15/10/43.
W/Cdr. Fowke left the unit by air. In the afternoon the Flight paraded at the Photographic Section, R.A.F. Station, Amarda Road to see the films they took of the attack by the Vengeance & Harvard. Sqdn/Ldr. Sutton was present (C.I.G.S. A.F.T.U.) & said the "shots" were good, the but the camera needed harmonising, a reflector 100 mph sight is fitted to the gun & as this was new to the Flight, the results were gratifying. The Unit stayed on & saw the Air to Air "shots" film taken by 615 Sqdn & gained a great deal of information & experience in deflection, & range estimation of a fighter aircraft. He also listened with interest of the comments of the instructors,

& the Officer Commanding, Wing Commander F.R. Carey, D.F.C., D.F.M., of R.A.F. Station, Amarda Rd, he gave short hints which were of great interest& help to the Flight. Sgt. Malone & Cpl. Dalton arrived to replace temporarily the "B/UP" Cpls of this station who were granted 14 days leave w.e.f. 2-15/11/43. A precedent was established & has proved very successful, the N.C.O.'s were billeted and attached to the No.3 Camp.

This will always be the case in the future, as supervision of them is much easier, and the cooperation of the Officer Commanding Unit with "Backers - Up" training is more successful, if the Instructors are present in the camp.

The O.C. Unit was present as an officer under instruction at a Court Martial held at R.A.F. Station Amarda Road. The trial lasted until the morning of the 30/10/43.

GALE WARNING received:- "Deep depression" 17'N 87'E. moving N.W. will turn in later during next 24 hours over coastal region of Grissa and Bengal W of 90'E wind becoming E to NE.at 25 to 35 mph with gusts of 40 to 50 M.P.H. with local gusts at 30 to 35 m.p.h..

All Unit personnel warned to secure all unit stores & huts, gale warning published in Unit Orders dated 31/10/43. The gale did not materialise, the weather was merely, overcast sky & slight drizzle of rain.

The Command Education Officer (S/Ldr. Duckett) visited the Flight & talked to men with the result he had many enquiries re: Air Crew Maths, & Correspondence Courses, he promised to relay his answers direct to me. Enquiries also made re: a Welfare Grant, for the setting up of a Model Handicraft Club. An answer to all these enquiries is awaited.

4436 A.A. Flight - En-route to R.A.F. Khulna and R.A.F. Char Chapli

Flight awaiting movement order. 6 other flights moved off 4435, 4436, 4437 awaiting boat for Calcutta, moved kit and equipment to quayside at 16.00hrs.

Given movement orders to be on quayside by 10.00 hrs. embarked on boat at 11.00Hrs, left Chittagong at 12.30Hrs. Took own rations on board, again difficulty in preparing meals owing to shortage of cooking utensils. Spirit of men still high and no sickness.

Arrived Calcutta, men and equipment transported to 35 P.T.C. arrived at 16.00Hrs. This move was handled most efficiently by the embarkation unit concerned.

Reported personally to 221 Group Defence Officer, re the badly equipped flight, great assistance was given in a very short while fire-safe units were obtained, mountings, cooking utensils, and training pamphlets, also games-sports from Welfare Officer. Forms-stationery urgently required.

Arrived at Khulna, met by O/C 211 A.M.E.S. who had arranged transport and a meal for the flight and much appreciation is felt by all concerned for the considerations and comfort afforded by 211 A.M.E.S.

4436 Flight originally posted to Khulna is now to proceed to Char Chapli, the original order for half the flight to remain at Khulna and half at Char Chapli has been amended and the whole flight will now be stationed at Char Chapli, this having been decided by 221 Group Defence Officer in consultation with W/C Smith of 180 Wing. Equipment checked, and a signal sent to Char Chapli asking for maximum accommodation.

Signal received from Char Chapli "Maximum accommodation 16 men, bring own charpoys".

Move to Char Chapli by first available boat which leaves Khulna at 01.30Hrs, 10/10/43. Telephoned 175 Wing Jessore and arranged for escort party to take 30,000 rounds of .303 to 175 Wing which was belted for use with the Browning Guns, (This should have been sent from the Depot ready for use).

Two N.C.O's reported sick Cpl. Maxwell and Cpl. Casey to proceed to hospital at Calcutta.

1 Officer, 1 Sgt, 1Cpl. and 17 A.C's and all equipment and ammunition to form first party for Char Chapli, 1 Cpl., 14 A.C's to remain at Khulna and will be signalled for when accommodation is available. Party boarded steamer at 23.59Hrs.

Sailed from Khulna at 04.30 Hrs. Road and rail rations taken and cooked on board, arrived at Barisal at 23.00Hrs. transhipped all equipment on to another boat.

Left Barisal arrived at Pataukhali at 08.50Hrs. transferred all equipment again to another steamer at 10.00Hrs, left guard on board, all embarked at 20.00Hrs.

Steamer sailed at 06.00 Hrs. arrived Khepupara at 13.30Hrs. The party had to split, 10 men and half the equipment boarded the small launch and 1 N.C.O. and 9 men left at Khepupara with half the equipment until the following day.
First party arrived and moved billets at 375 A.M.E.S.

Second party arrived, all equipment checked and found correct. Accommodation very short, a new basha or tents must be erected before the party at Khulna can proceed. No armoury available and storage of equipment a difficult problem. O/C 373 A.M.E.S. has given every assistance in a somewhat situation.

Two LACs. Proceeded to 221 Group for Aircraft Recognition course. Unable to use Motley Stork mountings until bolts for base plates are obtained. Three sets of twin Brownings assembled and ready in case of air attack. Three new A.A. posts to be sited and construction two others on beach for ground to air and ground to ground. Beach patrols to be commenced, also patrols on technical site and domestic site.
Reports of a submarine or boat seen at sea to be investigated, look outs to be detailed, a great deal of drift-wood trees etc. have been observed but every precaution will be taken. Owing to the isolated position of the station it is a very tempting and east target for a Japanese raiding party, not necessarily to sabotage, but to obtain much valuable equipment and plans, therefore the defence of the station from the ground is considered as important, even more so than attack from the air. A defence scheme will be drawn up immediately to offset any such attempt by air or ground forces.

Twin guns tested, very satisfactory. Gun posts sited and construction commenced. S/Ldr. Last arrived from 221 Group and matters regarding deficiencies taken up. It has been decided to leave 1 N.C.O. and 9 men at 211 A.M.E.S. Khulna with a third of the equipment. Signal sent to Khulna instructing 2 Cpls. and 5 men to report to Char Chapli.

LAC. Pugh taken to hospital Calcutta by plane. Malaria.

Two gun posts completed near beach, giving ground to ground and ground to air defence, beach patrol commenced. Three other A.A. posts sited, all guns mounted ready for action.

Escort party of three left for 211 A.M.E.S. Khulna with six Browning guns, three Motley Stork mountings, ammunition and equipment for A.A. Defence of Khulna. Airmen of 4436 A.A. Flight have settled in well, general fitness good.
2 Cpls. and 5 A/Cs. arrived at Char Chapli from Khulna. The flight is now split up as follows 1 Cpl. 9 A/Cs stationed at Khulna, 1 Sgt. 3 Cpls. 22 A/Cs stationed at Char Chapli.

Two beach gun posts now fully manned and beach patrol at night commenced, special look out being kept out to sea. Orders for patrols, sentries and gun posts made out.

Training syllabus for whole squadron made out to commence 25-10-43 for 6 weeks' duration. All personnel to be trained in all weapons and field craft and to take up their positions in the defence of the station.

At least 4 180lb. tents should form part of each flight's equipment, very necessary for guard tents. Bolts for Motley Stork mountings not yet to hand, cannot install in gun posts till received.

Training of "backers up" all stationed personnel commenced to-day, course of 6 week duration in which all personnel will be trained in the following:- Rifle, Sten, Browning gun, hand grenades, unarmed combat, gas (personal decontamination), aircraft recognition, and field tactics in defence of the station, Bayonet fighting.

Rough draft of Defence Scheme of Char Chapli completed. Two airmen detailed to attend No.1 School of M.T. Ambala (M.T. Course) left to-day.

Detachment of gunners absorbed into Flight, duties and training.

Escort party of 3 arrived back from Khulna, difficulties experience in getting messages down to the guard tent and A.A. posts by runner, also urgent messages up from beach at night by runner 7 minutes in getting message down. Request for two field telephones made on Monthly Defence Report to 211 Group.

Two 180lb. tents and camouflage nets arrived to-day in reply to signal. F/Lt. W.G. Chaffin proceeded to Calcutta on temporary duty. 1 - To collect as much outstanding equipment as possible. 2 - To report to E.N.T. Specialist reporting ear trouble. 3 - En route to Khulna on inspection of detachment of R.A.F. Regiment stationed there. One more gun post completed, now 3 in number.

4437 A.A. Flight – Settling in defending A.M.E.S. at Diamond Harbour and Mathrapur

The three remaining Flights at the R.A.F. Transit Camp have received orders through No.224 Group Defence Officer to prepare for the next stage of their journey i.e. CHITTAGONG to CALCUTTA by sea.

No.79 Embarkation Unit have issued the Movement Orders to proceed by sea to CALCUTTA on the 3rd October 1943. All arrangements for the transport of kit and equipment have been made.

By 11.00hrs all personnel of the three A.A. Flights were aboard the H.T. "BANDRA" of the B.I.N.S. Co., and all equipment stowed in the hold. We set sail at 13.00hrs.

The H.T. "BANDRA" is but a small cargo steamer not equipped to convey Troops. Troop decks were not installed. Airmen had to cook their own meals and were forced to sleep on the top decks on the forward part of the ship.

Mechanical Transport awaited our disembarkation, to convey the three A.A. Flights to the R.A.F. Transit Camp in CALCUTTA.

The final stage of 4437 A.A. Flights' movement was completed by rail. We departed from CALCUTTA at 14.40hrs and arrived at DIAMOND HARBOUR, R.A.F. Station at 18.00hrs. Airmen are accommodated under canvas until two busty huts can be erected.

The Unit will be divided into two parts:-

1. It will provide Light A.A. Defences for 544 A.M.E.S. at Diamond Harbour

2. It will provide Light A.A. Defences for 258 A.M.E.S. at MATHRAPUR.
3. Consequently the Senior N.C.O. plus 17 B.O.R's will proceed immediately to MATHRAPUR. Approx. 15 miles distant.

The Officer Commanding 544 A.M.E.S., Diamond Harbour has been most generous in helping to establish my Headquarters and Orderly Room. It is most considerate of him to oblige in the use of his stationery, typewriter, forms and information to attain perfect functioning of this Unit.

A Motorcycle collected from 329 M.U. is one of our first acquisitions of Mechanical Transport.

A.M.E.S. personnel manning a 60ft high tower Gun Post, used for identification of aircraft as well, of vital importance of an A.M.E.S., were relieved of their post by this Unit. This Gun site is linked by field telephone with the Technical building. All aircraft within visual distance must be identified and reported.

The guarding of the Technical building by night has also been taken over by this Unit.

The first P.O.R's made by this Unit were signed and despatched.

Our first set of D.R.O.'s were written and posted on the notice board at MATHRAPUR and DIAMOND HARBOUR.

Two new Ford 15cwt trucks were acquired from 329 M.U. with the necessary tools and spare wheel.

Two derelict Gun Sites are being renovated by our personnel. One of which is being manned today. Termed No.2 Gun Post.

Our No.3 Gun Post has been reconstructed and is being manned. Twin .303 Brownings have been installed to replace the Twin .303 Lewis Gun.

A conference with all N.C.O.'s present was held for the first time. Its object is threefold:- (1) To bring to light ideas and plans worth consideration to improve the general routine of the Unit. (2) Discuss plans relating to Airmen's Welfare. (3) Detail duties for forthcoming week.

These conferences will be held on the Saturday of every week.

The five N.C.O.'s were allotted a specific task each besides their daily routine orders i.e. Sgt FENWICK i/c ARMOURY; Cpl MERCER i/c M.T.; Cpl BULL i/c Equipment and Stores; Cpl CRUST i/c Works, Buildings, Gas and Camouflage; Cpl REED i/c Rations, Canteen Supplies and Welfare.

Two ancient Gun Posts are being reconstructed. Materials for a cement foundation have been obtained from 180 WING Equipment Stores. Within five days the posts should be completed. All work appertaining to Gun Sites will be carried out by our personnel.

A few armoury tools, Gun oil and 4 X 2 flannelette was acquired from 75 E.P. CALCUTTA. A very small percentage compared with our entitlement.

A new Gun Site has to be erected to complete a triangular position of three posts. Construction of such will start within a few days and should be ready for manning in seven days time.

The two outstanding Ford 15cwt trucks were collected from 329 M.U. bringing our M.T. up to establishment i.e. Four – 15cwt Trucks and One – Motor Cycle.

The three Gun Sites under construction are nearing completion. Two of these will be manned on the morrow. Twin .303 Browning Guns will be used. The third Gun Post should be ready by the 31st of this month.

A further issue of Armourers tools and equipment was collected from 180 WING CALCUTTA, i.e. Armourers Tool Chest, Barbed Wire, Picks and Shovels, Camouflage Nets were obtained from 75 E.P.

The construction of the new Gun Site has been completed. Bringing the total amount of Gun Posts, fully manned, to six, located as follow:-

MATHRAPUR (3) – Two Gun Posts with twin .303 Browning Guns on cradle mountings. One Gun Post with twin .303 Browning fitted on a Motley Stork mounting.

DIAMOND HARBOUR (3) – Two Gun Posts with twin .303 Browning Guns fitted on cradle mountings. One Gun Post with twin .303 Lewis Guns (to be replaced by Brownings on Motley Stork mountings).

November
4406 A.A. Flight – Operational at Amarda Road Airfield

General training programme was commenced, with the emphasis on individual weapon training.
W/Cdr. Carey D.F.C., D.F.M. officer commanding, A.F.T.U. visited the Unit, with M.T. this morning at 09.00 hrs. He complimented the Flight on their appearance and the good appearance & serviceability of the M.T.
The complete Flight visited S.H.Q., Photographic Section to view an instructional film on the "Flight Fighter sweeps & Train Busting". It was instructive.
Airmens' Messing Committee formed – to meet at regular interval as & when complaints are received. Consulting of O.C.4406 AA Ft. & 2 members, plus 2 members of 1573 Gunners Flight & a squadron representative of the visiting squadron in its care No.136 Sqdn. 1562820 L.A.C. Riddell Gunr (V) proceeded to Palam, on a court martial case, as a witness.
Flight had range practice with Browning MK II Six Guns on 25 yard range.
This unit took over from M.T. Section, Amarda Road, all its own transport & became responsible w.e.f. this date for its own M.T. vehicle servicing & general running etc. Its own F.M.T. is still unposted. Each diver became responsible for the maintenance of his own vehicle.
1600035 L.A.C. Foster C. & 1134824 L.A.C. Duffield L. detached from this Flight to 221 Group for A/Recog. Course – authority 221G 221G/S/810/7/DC/dd 9.11.43. Section training began wef. 0900 hrs14/11/43.
OC Unit paraded the Flight informally & 1573 Gunners Flight at 1400 hrs read an airstrip Order of the Day from the new O.C. Lord Louis Mountbatten. This unit is now part of the SE Asia Command, although it is still under the orders of AHQ Bengal, which is in turn controlled by Orders from A.H.Q. India, New Delhi. Signal rec'd from S.E.A.A.C. – AOB 622 dd 16/11/43 to this effect.
Information received from A.H.Q. Bengal that this Flight is now in reserve for combined other actions, establishment of Gun Mtgs now

changed from M/S Mtgs to Flight Mtgs. Plus 3 Bren Guns & 3 V.G.O mounts have to be collected from 221 Grp under armed escort on or about 20.11.43. Authority for these changes Letter HDB/S/151/8A/Air dd 4/11/43.

Unit proceeded to Chardipur A.M.E.S. Station, for training. Browning Guns fired over range at sea from 250 - 1000 yds, Ground dial for combined operations, (of which whilst a reserve flight) preliminary training Browning firing fairly goo in the whole.

118734 FL/LT FREEMAN proceeded by AIR to Calcutta to 221 GP for conference re collection of Browning Mounts and V.G.O. Mounts & also to collect more Welfare Equipment from Welfare Officer. Officer also made enquiries re Christmas Catering at C.B.I.D. Officer returned by Air on 23.11.43 all duties successfully accomplished.

990992 L.A.C. Jennson A. posted ineffective sick to B.H.Q. Calcutta. Flight training commenced.

Sgt Kelly 538314 & 3 personnel detached to 221 GP Calcutta, 313 M.U. & Welfare Officer 221 FP to collect armament as listed on 19/11/43. Part of Flight proceeded to Chandipur for range firing up to 1000 yds of Brg NK II & throwing of grenades. All successfully accomplished.

1435790 L.A.C. Maloney posted this unit from B.H.Q. Calcutta to replace 990992 L.A.C. Jennson posted non-effective sick.

Sgt. Kelly returned shortly returned from Calcutta, with equipment & Welfare material.

FT/LT H.W. FREEMAN left on duty to 2 R & SS to enquire re Armamment matter, he returned on 29.11.43.

Flight training commenced.

4436 A.A. Flight – Operational at R.A.F. Khulna and R.A.F. Char Chapli

F/Lt. Chaffin visited 221 Group and 180 Wing, and secured a further quantity of unit stores, also reported to M.O. 180 Wing.

Second case of Malaria, gunner flown to hospital.

Further A.A. Gun post completed, now 4 in number.

Guard tent erected and camouflaged.

F/Lt. Chaffin visited detachment of 4436 A.A. Flight stationed at Khulna. Three A.A. Gun posts completed with Motley Storks Mountings. Duties of detachment to man 3 posts dawn till dusk, and to patrol Technical Site during the hours of darkness. All necessary orders for run posts, patrols and N.C.O's drawn up. Bolts for mountings were made locally, as the delay through Services sources now 5 weeks. Guns and mountings very satisfactory.

Held practice alert 11.05 hours, very satisfactory, posts ready for opening fire minimum time 25 seconds, maximum 75 seconds.

At approximately 21.20 it was reported that lights were being flashed from a boat ½ mile out to sea, also possibility that this might be an enemy submarine. All R.A.F. Regt. And station personnel were immediately put under arms, and beach gun posts manned with two sets of twin Brownings. Sections were deployed along the beach and around the Technical Site. Signal was made out to 180 Wing asking for plane to make a recce. Signal was not despatched as a no reply could be obtained through Filter Room. Constant watch was kept all night. At 06.00 hours the boat proceeded in a westerly direction, and at dawn was confirmed a being a fishing boat about 55ft. long. A smaller boat in tow about 35ft. long headed for the beach, this being met and occupants interrogated and escorted to the Guard Room. The larger vessel was inspected and certified as a fishing boat off course, occupants were duly warned.

Another fishing boat was sited and occupants made to come ashore, a smaller boat than the previous occasion.

At 08.30 hours a further two fishing boats with sail were seen 1 mile S.W. of station about ½ mile out to sea. Beach guns posts were manned, attempts were made to bring them in and two shots were fired from a rifle, the boats continued on their way, and three bursts were fires from one gun post overhead, but this too failed to bring them in.

In the evening at 17.00 hours two further boats were observed 3 miles S.E. of station and ¼ mile out to sea. A small rowing boat and occupants (5 in number) were seen on the shore. Before contact could be made, the small boat was rowed out to sea and could not be induced to come in. Thought to be a fishing boats.

On the night of the 16th lights were seen at sea and thought to be fishing boats.

Third and fourth case of Malaria taken to hospital.

Rifle range on beach completed. F/Lt. Chaffin returned to unit after inspection of Khulna A.A. Defences.

Fifth Malaria case taken to hospital.

Sixth case of Malaria amongst gunners taken to hospital by air.

Seventh case of Malaria amongst gunners taken to hospital by air. 1 N.C.O. and 6 gunners now down with Malaria.

Letter sent to 221 Group and 180 Wing regarding high sickness rate. 4436 A.A. Flight are not on suppressive treatment (Mepacrin tablets) and it is thought that stoppage of treatment was rather premature. Have asked that the Flight be put on immediate treatment to prevent further sickness. 27% of detachment here, now in hospital with Malaria.

Confirmation by S.M.O. 180 Wing that all gunners be put on suppressive treatment immediately. Mosquito menace considerable.

Owing to stoppage of plane on 11-11-43 by comm. Flight, mail seriously delayed. Three postagrams arrived to-day dated 1-11-43, 8-11-43, and 9-11-43, one requesting gunners to attend a course at H.Q. 221 Group on 14-11-43 too late to comply. All personnel now on hard rations, no fresh rations available, these previously brought in by plane. Staple diet now:- tinned sausage, bully beef, dehydrated potatoes and biscuits. All personnel of 4436 A.A. Flight commenced Mepacrin tablet suppressive treatment for Malaria to-day.

All equipment deficient has been demanded on vouchers 674s.

Bolts for Motley Stork Mountings not arrived yet, to be made at Khulna to save further delay. Only two posts can be manned until these are received. One further case of Malaria, the eight case, gunner flown to hospital, one other appears likely.

Motley Stork Mountings being erected in 3 A.A. Posts. Two beach gun posts to have monopod mountings to enable quick manning of guns on alarm.

F/Lt. Lacey C.O. 375 A.M.E.S. proceeded to Barisal, to be away about 10 days, meanwhile F/Lt. Chaffin to act as C.O. Station until his

return. Ninth hospital case, gunner flown to hospital, Cholera suspect.
Experiment with cross base of wood for Motley Stork Mountings satisfactory, will be used on all posts. Report sent to G.D.O. 221 Group. Main advantage, makes mountings mobile and very quickly erected. Percentage of R.A.F. Regt. Gunners now non-effective due to Malaria and other sickness now 48%, attached gunners 373 A.M.E.S. One in hospital with Malaria, two in S.S.Q. with Dengi fever. Percentage non-effective 37%. First Motley Stork Mounting erected. Three A.A. posts now manned. Two beach gun posts to be manned in an emergency.
Tenth case of Malaria. One other gunner on course in Calcutta reported in hospital with Malaria.
Total in hospital for month with Malaria 11 gunners, 2 S.S.Q. Dengi fever. One gunner returned from M.T. course.
Eleventh gunner of 4436 A.A. Flight frown to hospital with Malaria. One attached gunner of 373 A.M.E.S. in hospital, total gunners for month in hospital with Malaria 12.

4437 A.A. Flight – Operational defending A.M.E.S. at Diamond Harbour and Mathrapur

Amendments to Form 540 (September and October) for Mathrapur read Mathurapur and for 548 A.M.E.S. read 848 A.M.E.S.
One Ford 15cwt. Truck which has been unserviceable since it's issue by 329 M.U. was towed to C.R.O., M.T. Calcutta for repairs.
A Church Service (C of E) was held today. Given by S/Ldr. Padre M. Corner visiting the station form H.Q. 211 Group
A copy of Operational Standing orders were received from No.221 Group Defence Officer. Extracts will be incorporated in our Unit Standing Orders now being published.
Two hundred rounds of belted .303 ammunition were expended in testing the Twin Browning guns.
One hundred rounds of .300 ball ammunition were expended on the rifle range for training purposes.
Five hundred rounds of belted .303 ammunition was fired in testing the Twin Brownings of this station

Three hundred and fifty rounds of belted .303 ammunition was expended for training purposes on the Twin Browning.
One hundred and twenty rounds of 9mm ammunition was expended in practice firing the Sten machine gun. 933083 LAC DAYNES has been posted non-effective sick to base Headquarters Calcutta, w.e.f. 23/10/43. Having spent 28 days in No.47 B.G.H. Calcutta.
One hundred rounds of 9m.m. ammunition was expended in practice firing the Sten machine carbine.
One hundred and eighty rounds of belted .303 ammunition was expended in practice firing the Twin Browning guns.
Amendments to Operational Standing Orders were received from the Group Defence Officer of H.Q. No.221 Group.
S/Ldr. Padre Maxwell (CofE Chaplain) from 293 Wing is holding an evening service at 20-00 hrs. Tomorrow morning Padre Maxwell intends to give early morning communion before proceeding on his visiting tour.
Fifty rounds .303 belted ammunition was expended in testing a reserve set of Twin Brownings for No.3 Gun post.
One hundred and sixty rounds of 9m.m. ammunition was expended in practice firing the Sten machine carbine. 1181606 A.C.1 Alldixs F.M.T. attached to this unit, pending posting by B.P.O. Bombay, arrived today from his parent unit No.42 Squadron.
One hundred and fifty rounds of .303 Ball ammunition was fired on the rifle range for training purposes.
A copy of the training programme for the coming week is hereby appendiced. Unit Standing Orders published under para.61 of Kings Regulations has been completed.
1061634 LAC Royds L. has been posted non-effective sick to base Headquarters, Calcutta w.e.f. 2/11/43, having spent 28 days in No.47 B.G.H. Calcutta.
During the past month extensive advanced training in Twin Browning M.G's, Rifle and Sten machine carbine was enforced for all personnel of this unit. A practical test was put forward which all airmen had to undergo. Gunners failing to comply to the necessary standards

required are being put through an elementary course proceeding to advanced handling. Only 10% of the total strength of this unit, failed. The remainder being thoroughly conversant with all weapons held on our charge.

During the recent period of training up to the end of this month, 1310 rounds belted ammunition was expended on the Twin Brownings, 275 rounds .303 ball ammunition fired by rifle and 380 rounds of 9m.m. ammunition was expended during Sten Machine Carbine practice.

4447 A.A. Flight – Settling in at R.A.F. Baigachi

Flight arrived ALIPORE.
Flight left ALIPORE for BAIGACHI.
Flight arrived BAIGACHI.
S/L LAST (221 Gp GDO) with Station Comdr. W/C GODDARD inspected & approved camp accompanied by Flight. In absence of Flight Vehicles (not yet allocated) a 3 Ton Truck was lent to the Flight by 136 SQDN. Gunners of 293 WING & 261 SQDN. Attached to 4447 A/A Flt. for discipline. 1303578 LAC SHEPHERD, J & 1451654 LAC WEBB, L attached to S. of A.F.T.T. AMBALA for Armourers Course.
993373 LAC HISH H & 934291 LAC SMITH D attached to No.221 Group for Aircraft Recognition. Course. The following Airmen were detached to 176 SQDN. For 3 day Refuelling & Rearming Course:- 1451516 LAC WEBB, W; 1453232 LAC ALDERMAN, C; 1165248 LAC JONES, A - 17/20 Nov 1943. 1357829 LAC GERDINER, C; 956953 LAC STEGGLES, E; 1228749 LAC FORD, R - 22/24 Nov 1943. 1546871 LAC HAWKER, A; 1356979 LAC McMANUS, J; 1465543 LAC TREGOING, A - 25/27 Nov 1943.
1478855 LAC LOADER, D admitted to 47 B.G.H.
1356979 LAC McMANUS, J & 1541336 LAC GRUNDY, A attached 221 Group for Aircraft Recogn Course. 934291 LAC SMITH, D admitted 47 B.G.H. 1230205 LAC SAINT, R (CLB III) att. Flight pending posting from 176 SQDN.

December
4406 A.A. Flight – Operational at Amarda Road Airfield

Flight training continued for the month, with emphasis on Fieldcraft, practical exercises. Morse will also be taught to all personnel with the aid of the Aldis Lamp.
3126 Chevrolet Truck came in 10,000 mile inspection at A.F.T.U. Maintenance Section caught fire, & the light harness, light switches / dynamo, etc. were damaged. Full report made to A.H.Q. Bengal & their instructions awaited. Actual cause of fire unknown & interview of A.F.T.U. Engineering Officer, will be almost impossible to actually pin down.
1034683 A.C.1 CURRY J. attached to this Unit from B.H.Q. Calcutta pending posting to take place of 1404514 L.A.C. Richards G.A. (non-effective sick).
1642172 A.C.1 MORRISON-JACK J.A. (F.M.T.) arrived this Flight ex. U.K. agreed to lend him to A.F.T.U. M.T. Section should he be needed there, provided that the vehicles of this unit were not in actual need of his services at that particular time.
1218841 L.A.C. LEWIS (Gnr) & 626344 L.A.C. Parker C.F.(GNR) returned from A/Recog. Course H.Q., both men obtained "A" passes.
Full exercise & attack at Chandipur carried out- Results fair - Remainder of day spent in firing rifle from the hip, advance in extended line, & advance in 3 extended lines each line passing thru firing, results good. A valuable exercise to get men used to firing in battle, & giving them confidence in their weapons.
1305616 Cpl. DALTON in charge of escort proceeded to Calcutta to collect 9 sets conversion for Browning Guns & bolts or Motley Stork mountings, from 75 E.P. Calcutta.
Flight takes full share in Xmas Festivities being organised by A.F.T.U., being actively engaged in Committee for following programme:-   Concert "ARMADILLAS" - shows on 23 & 30/12/43.   Comic Football matches etc. - 25/12/43.   Athletic Meeting - 26/12/43.   Whist Drive & Carnival (Fancy Dress) 27 & 28/12/43.   Smoking Concert, etc. 31.12.43.

Athletic Meeting (organised for A.F.T.U. by O/C 4406 A/A Flight) & being run almost entirely by 4406 A/A Flight.
Training & Gun Post duties continue. Training relaxed from afternoon 24.12.43 to morning of 27.12.43 in line with A.F.T.U.
Commanding Officer A.F.T.U. W/Cdr. F.R. Carey, D.F.C., D.F.M. present at Xmas Dinner. Officer & N.C.O.'s of Flight give service at Dinner in traditional service manner
Flight are second at Boxing Day Athletic meeting. Trophy won by S.H.Q. A.F.T.U. Prizes presented by W/Cdr. F.R. CARY, D.F.C., D.F.M. O/C A.F.T.U., Amarda Road in organisation & general conduct of sports. 19.30 hours Flight Dinner - a most successful affair, attended by whole Flight, plus selected personnel of A.F.T.U. from sections, with whom the Flight personnel are in contact.
Flight training continues.
Training & Gun post duties as usual. Letter received from A.H.Q. Bengal to the effect that a formal investigation will be held on accident in Flight vehicle - Chevrolet 15 cwt, No. T.I.Y. - 3126.

4436 A.A. Flight - Operational at R.A.F. Khulna and R.A.F. Char Chapli

LAC. Ryall posted to R.A.F. Regiment Depot, Secunderabad to be replaced by 221 Group. Aircraft log books issues out to gun posts for recording all aircraft. Serious delays in cables for personnel experienced, one cable taking 31 days and another 20 days from R.A.F. Post Bombay, subject taken up with R.A.F. Post Bombay. All monthly returns despatched for November.
F/Lt. Lacey O/C 373 A.M.E.S. returned to unit and took over duties. Bolts for Motley Stork Mountings arrived, manufactured in Khulna. Motley Storks can now be erected. Replacement arrived for LAC. Ryall.
N.C.O. i/c and 5 gunners of 211 A.M.E.S. posted to Kharagpur. Strength at 211 A.M.E.S. now 1 Cpl. And 9 ACs. All 4436 A.A. Flight duties, manning 3 A.A. Posts and night patrol of Technical Site.

Air raid warning alarm, large formation of enemy bombers could be heard flying overhead, no hostile act committed, all 5 A.A. posts manned.

Friendly fighter aircraft flew over camp (Spitfire)

Enemy plane reported to have crashed into sea south of station over the horizon, also report that two parachutists were seen to have bailed out S.S.E. of station.

R.A.F. Service launch put out to sea to investigate with armed party, returned 16.00 ours, nothing was seen. Two large boats lying out as sea, were investigated but proved to be fishing boats.

Second batch of enemy bombers reported flying East to West.

Two aircraft seen flying very high N.W. to S.E.

Hostile aircraft reported 4 mile N.E. of station.

All clear given

---

1 N.C.O. and 9 ACs. Of 4436 A.A. Flight still in hospital with Malaria.

Two gunners sent to 293 Wing for Aircraft Recognition Course No.5. On completion of course to report to 211 A.M.E.S. on 27-12-43 and relive two other who will report to 295 Wing on 27-12-43 for two weeks' course.

Fitter M.T. posted to this unit, arrived 211 A.M.E.S. Signal sent to instruct him to report to 375 A.M.E.S.

Confirmed by medical authorities that maximum tour of duty on this station is 6 months if personnel volunteer for this period. All unit personnel consulted and all volunteered for the 6 months period.

Intensive training commenced of all R.A.F. Regt. personnel, 8 forty five minute periods each day for 6 days a week. Weapon training, aircraft recognition, unarmed combat, field tactics and exercises, construction of rafts and ferrying equipment to overcome water obstacles, bayonet fighting etc. included in syllabus.

Series of red flashed or very lights reported on several occasions during the night, reported by signal to 180 Wing, friendly aircraft heard and seen overhead on each occasion, reason for lights unexplained.

All gunners of 373 A.M.E.S. (8 ACs.) posted from station to Kharagour wef. 4-12-43, instructions to report to 180 Wing S.S.Q. before proceeding to undergo blanket treatment, after suppressive treatment.

Three gunners of 4436 A.A. Flight returned to unit from hospital and sick leave. Fitter M.T. arrived from 211 A.M.E.S.

Twin Browning guns tested at 211 A.M.E.S. found satisfactory, each man fire 20 rounds.

Sixth set of twin A.A. guns completed ready for manning in an emergency. 1 N.C.O. and 3 ACs. Reported back to unit from hospital and sick leave, position now much relieved.

Cpl. Morley arrived 211 A.M.E.S. instructed by signal to report here, no information to hand re this posting.

Five suspicious boats sighted 4 miles W.S.W. of station, 1 paddle steamer, and two large boats with masts, about 35 ft long, and two others 20 feet long observed near beach, patrol sent to investigate, proved to be fishing boats.

Further Cpl. Posted to this unit, as yet no information to hand for reason of posting, posted strength now;- 1 Sgt. 6 Cpls. 31 ACs. And 1 F.M.T.

Christmas day, Fresh rations arrived and an excellent menu put on. Entertainments provided, rifle range competition, football match and cricket match, concert given in the evening.

All personnel ex hospital with Malaria with the exception of two gunners.

Two gunners attached to 211 A.M.E.S. proceeded to No.6 Aircraft recognition course, Calcutta.

All 373 A.M.E.S. station personnel have completed a 6 weeks' Defence Training Syllabus. All personnel today fired a range course, consisting of rifle, grouping, application, and rapid and also Sten gun.

All personnel of 4436 A.A. Flight completed a range firing practice, consisting of Rifle: grouping, application and rapid and also Sten gun.

Station personnel 373 A.M.E.S. approximate strength 45, have been formed into 3 Rifle Defence Sections and will man 3 Outer Defence localities in an emergency. Owing to limited numbers of personnel available, only 3 small defence sections can be formed. Of the 45 personnel, 18 will be required for carrying on with normal duty. Of the balance of 27 men, three sections of 8 men, with a Cpl. Gunners R.A.F. Regt. i/c will be available for the defence of the station. One further section of R.A.F. Regt. personnel who will not be manning A.A. posts will act as mobile reserve.

4437 A.A. Flight - Operational defending A.M.E.S. at Diamond Harbour and Mathrapur

The alarm siren sounded at 11-45 hours predicting two large formations of hostile aircraft approaching from a Northerly direction i.e. Calcutta. At 12-05 hours the first scattered formation of 6 hostile fighter aircraft (believed to be Zero's) were spotted at an approximate height of 25,000ft, travelling south west. At 12-20 hours a second group of eight aircraft approached, identified at a height of 18,000 ft to be Mitsubishi T97 Army Bombers and one hostile fighter heading south.

No bombs were dropped in this area. Stand down was sounded at 13-05 hours.

1372769 AC2 Reynolds posted to this unit, ex U.K., as a fitter M.T. arrived.

1181606 AC Alldis, F.M.T. attached to this unit pending posting, was posted to No.186 Maintenance Wing, Auth: B.P.O. Draft Note BPO/13949 dated 2/12/43.

The 15cwt Ford Truck having been at C.R.O. M.T. Calcutta for a month nearly returned to its base. The truck was collected from C.R.O. but barley reached the outskirts of Calcutta when the same trouble (petrol feed) for which it had been taken in for repairs reoccurred. The vehicle was towed to base and is now in the hands of our F.M.T.

Cpl. Reed has been detailed to attend an N.C.O's course on Aircraft Recognition ay RANCHI. The course commences on December 16th. Duration 3 weeks.

A Church Service (C of E) was held by S/Ldr. Padre M. Corner visiting this station before proceeding to Matharapur.

Sgt. Fenwick, second in command of this unit was posted to B.R.D. Worli ex-India for training as Air Gunner.

Col. Bull has been appointed Acting Sergeant unpaid whilst filling Sergeant vacancy with the posting of Sgt. Fenwick.

The alarm siren sounded at 12-15 hrs predicting hostile aircraft approaching from a northerly direction. The only aircraft seen were two friendly Spitfires patrolling this area at the approximate height of 20,000 ft. No enemy aircraft appeared. Stand down 12-45 hrs.

LAC. Daynes non-effective sick w.e.f. 23-10-43 has returned to duty. No replacements were sent to cover this vacancy, or no notifications of posting. Consequently this airman will remain with this unit until further notice.

S/Ldr. Padre Maxwell (C of E) from 293 Wing paid a visit to this station and gave early morning communion. His unit extended to Mathurapur where a similar service was held

4447 A.A. Flight – Flight en-route to R.A.F. Alipore

Flight moved to No.1 Camp.

1419828 LAC LANAGAN J (FMT-I) posted to Flight ex U.K. 142227 LAC O'LEARY, J admitted 47 B.G.H.

Flight moved from BAIGRACHI to ALIPORE (Arrived same day).

1232103 LAC COATES, D & 1531177 LAC REDMAYNE, R attended Aircr. Recogn. Course at ALIPORE.

1092507 LAC EDMONDS, I admitted 47 B.G.H.

1347679 LAC, J admitted 47 B.G.H.

LAC EDMONDS, discharged 47 B.G.H.

LAC SHEPERD & LAC WEBB, L C.T.B.A 1 S. of A.F.T.T. AMBALA on completing Armourers Course. LAC LOADER posted N/Effective Sick & A/CP1. GREENFIELD appointed to paid rank WEF 18/10/43.

LAC SMITH posted N/Effective Sick.

LAC O'LEARY discharged 47. B.G.H.

No.4437 A.A. Flight – Movement Order

Appendix "AC"

to

FORM 540

No.4437 A.A. Flight R.A.F.R.

September 1943.

SECRET   COPY NO.   2

DATE. 16.9.43.

MOVEMENT ORDER

INFORMATION :- Formation Order No.94952/iv/Con. Code Address.

INTENTION :- To carry out the move on 19.9.43 in accordance with orders detailed below.

ADMIN :-

1. Nominal Roll   APPENDIX "A"

(Full numbers to be verified and initials and spelling of names checked in alphabetical 1 order).

2. Arms and Ammunition   APPENDIX "B"

Details of times of drawing from armoury, signatures, guards and care en route.

3. Rations   APPENDIX "C"

Include the daily allocation of rations en route, labelling of boxes, duty sections, water arrangements.

4. Dress   APPENDIX "D"

Parade Order. Contents of small pack. Contents of large pack.

5. Baggage   APPENDIX "E"

All lit and baggage is marked. Baggage will be placed outside huts for inspection as per Appendix "E". Loading arrangements and baggage party detail as per Appendix "F".

6. Timetable   APPENDIX "F"
7. Halts – Discipline

No one will leave the train unless with the permission of the Flight Commander. Minerals and Ice-cream are prohibited. No-one will alight at any station unless properly dressed. During the hot hours of the day, sun blinds should be drawn.

Appendix "A"

to

MOVEMENT ORDER

Nominal Roll in alphabetical order

NUMBER	RANK	NAME AND INITIALS
610478	T/Sgt	Fenwick G.H.
1351995	T/Cpl	Bull E.H.
628918	"	Crust H.J.
972001	"	Mercer B.
624171	"	Reed J.H.
1418664	Lac	Anderson W.
1359141	"	Belcher R.F.
1305852	"	Bateman G.E.
1543822	"	Beattie A.
1355856	"	Chapman J.
1458622	"	Connor J.W.
1110874	"	Cole J.H.
1306880	"	Colley C.G.
933083	"	Daynes F.A.
1515631	"	Davies B.J.
1255657	"	Edkins S.A.
1406986	"	Edgar W.
1355865	"	Hart L.J.
1467878	"	Histed A.E.W.
1469350	"	Horne L.H.
1305866	"	Ingleson W.E.
1446274	"	Lovell E.P.
1347574	"	Murray J.
1347616	"	Moor R.
1053822	"	MacCartan T.
1487925	"	Phillips J.

1061634	"	Royds L.
1301668	"	Rosewarne E.R.
1416763	"	Russell R.
1482011	"	Russell J.W.
1512229	"	Spencer F.
1472472	"	Stringer S.H.
1445992	"	Turner L.G.
1352969	"	Taylor J.
1354611	"	Talbot D.J.
1474048	"	Wood F.R.

Appendix "B"

to

MOVEMENT ORDER

1. Type and Number.

....

L.M.G.	Number	Mountings	Rifles	Discharges	Sten Grenades
	Guns Mags		Bayonets		Number
					Guns Mags

....

L.M.G.	Number		Mountings	Rifles	Discharges	Sten		Grenades
Brownings	19		9 Complete	17	–	20	40	72
			9 Bases extra					

....

2. Ammunition. – Number of rounds

....

Ball	A.P.	TRACER	INCEDIARY

....

Ball	A.P.	TRACER	INCEDIARY
30,600	1,800	3,600	NIL.

....

3. Ammo. will be drawn by duty section and loaded as detailed below.
        11.00hrs 16.9.43.
        Will be loaded first in lorry 17.9.43
        ....

4. Duty section as detailed below will provide guards.

                Cpl Bull

                Lac Colley

                ....

5. Collected by NIL R/T Sets and stored as follows.

Appendix "C"

to

MOVEMENT ORDER

Rations to scale for   days.

1. Rations to be sorted out and divided into number of days rations. Boxes labelled 1st day, 2nd day etc.

2. Duty Sections as detailed.

3. Water arrangement as circumstances dictate.

4. Advice to S.H.Q. Rations stores stating:-

....

Number of troops	Number of days rations	To be ready for Collection from Ration Stores
36	14	at ....08.00hrs 17.9.43.

....

5. Details of duty flights.

6. Arrangements for M.T. 658's to be submitted at least 24 hours ahead.

Appendix "D"

to

MOVEMENT ORDER

Large pack to contain one complete change.

        (a)   Slacks.

        (b)   Shorts.

  (c) Shirt.
  (d) Towel
  (e) Underpants.
  (f) Vest.
  (g) Hose tops and socks, 3 pairs advisable.
  (h) Gym shoes on top.
  (i) One blanket folded neatly on top with ground sheet
     overlapping last item.

Haversack to contain.

  (a) Small kit.
  (b) Mug, knife, fork and spoon.
  (c) Mess tin or plate.
  (d) One towel.
  (e) Shaving kit, soap, tooth brush, and tooth paste.

Mosquito Net in Bedding Roll.

. . . .

Appendix "E"

to

MOVEMENT ORDER

BAGGAGE

(a) All kit and boxes to be marked clearly.

(b) Place neatly outside huts by 07.45 hours. Date
    17.9.43.

(c) Duty Section to load on to truck at 09.00 hours and
    proceed to OLD MILITARY siding Secunderabad by
    .....hours. Date...........

(d) Guard on truck will be as under:-

     Names:- N.C.O.   Cpl Bull
               Lac Colley

(e) Section Bedding Roll, (labelled).

(f) Arrangements for weighing are as follows:-

(g) Duty Section Detail.

Appendix "F"

to

MOVEMENT ORDER

Time Table (tick off each item as attended to).

....

| DATE | TIME | DETAIL |

....

DATE	TIME	DETAIL
18.9.43	08.00 hrs	Roll Call and Inspection
"	10.30 "	FFI.
"	09.15 "	Check Pay Books. AB 64 up to date Identity Cards and Discs.
"	14.15 "	Pay Parade.
19.9.43	05.30 "	Breakfast or Tea or Tiffin In Depot.
17.9.43	10.00 "	Times of drawing Ammunition.
18.9.43	08.00 "	Draw Rations.
"	08.00 "	Baggage to be ready stacked outside hut.
"	"	Baggage party and parades at 08.30.
19.9.43	06.30 "	Final Parade and Roll Call.
		R.T.O. arrangements.
		Clearance Chits & Inspection of quarters vacated.

TRAIN TIMES

Depart Secunderabad After 09.00 hours

No.4437 A.A. Flight – Part 2 Standing Orders - Defence (614)

UNIT STANDING ORDERS.

PART 2.

DEFENCE.

Orders for Gun posts.

The following orders will be carried out by personnel mounting No.1. gun site and O.P.

1. Airmen will be detailed in D.R.O's to man No.1 gun post from half an hour before dawn until half an hour after duck. Times will be laid down in D.R.O.'s.

2. Between the hours of 19.00 and 08.00, the Technical Building will be guarded by these same airmen. Airmen will make themselves acquainted with guard orders for Technical Building.

3. Airmen off sentry duty are to rest in the tower and on no occasion are they to leave No.1gun site without permission from the Duty N.C.O.

4. Posts will be manned by one man who will act as Air Sentry. Air sentries will be relieved every two hours.

5. (Alarm Signal)
   When hostile aircraft reach a range of 25 miles from this station the alarm siren will be sounded. All gun posts will Stand to. The alarm signal will also come through the field telephone which is linked with the Technical Building.

6. Stand To.
   a) Gun positions will be fully manned form one half hour before to one half hour after dawn and from one half hour before to one half hour after dusk.
   b) Gun positions will be fully manned on sounding of the alarm signal, verbal instructions, or field telephone.
   c) Personnel will wear steel helmets with camouflage nets.

7. Engagement of Hostile Aircraft.
   a) After receipt of a warning, any aircraft positively identified as hostile or committing a hostile act by opening fire or dropping bombs will be fire upon.

b) When no warning has been received, <u>all</u> aircraft will be followed by the guns on all posts within range, but will <u>NOT</u> be fire upon unless positively identified as hostile or committing a hostile act.

c) Aircraft will normally be engaged at a range not greater than 800 yards.

d) Dive bombers will be engaged from the point of straight dive, provided they are within range.

e) Single reconnaissance aircraft are unlikely to be within range of small arms fire and will only be engaged upon instructions form the Flight Commander.

f) All guns will <u>cease fire</u> when friendly fighters are seen to be about to engage the target.

8. <u>Stand down</u>
The Air Sentry will remain guarding the gun post.
Signal:- Word of mouth.

9. <u>Night Ops.</u>
a) During the period of 6 days before and 6 days after full moon all gun posts will be manned and during all periods of night flying.

b) In the event of an alarm signal preceding the above mentioned period, two gunners will take up Action Stations and comply with instructions as per <u>Stand to</u> and <u>Engagement of Hostile Aircraft</u>. Whilst remainder of No.1 gun posts carry on guarding the Technical Building.

c) During periods when there is no night manning, personnel will patrol gun posts localities between the hours of dusk and dawn Stand to (as per patrol orders).

10.   <u>Visual Identification.</u>
Air sentries will give the following information on <u>all aircraft</u> within visual distance:-
a) Number of aircraft.
b) Type of aircraft, whether single or twin engine.
c) Identification.
d) Direction aircraft is travelling i.e. heading east or west.
e) Height.
f) Distance from station.

Each Air Sentry will keep an Aircraft log laid out as follows:-

Date Time	Type & Make of A/C	No.	Approx. Height.	Direction	Distance
21/3 09.45	Fighter, Hurricane.	3	1500	East	25 miles
10.05	Bomber, Liberator.	1	5000	N.N.E.	17 miles

11.   Airmen will have their personal weapon, steel helmets, F.A. field dressing and filled water bottles with them in gun positions.

12.   Guns will be checked by Air sentries taking post i.e. feed mechanism, ammunition, etc. All defects will be reported immediately to the Duty N.C.O.

13.   Smoking in gun positions or in the vicinity of the gun posts, whilst on duty is prohibited.

14.   Gun posts will be kept clean and tidy at all times.

Orders for Gun Posts.

The following orders will be carried out by all personnel mounting all other gun positions:-

1) Airmen will be detailed in D.R.O.'s to mount each gun site from half an hour before dawn until half an hour after dusk. Times will be laid down in D.R.O.'s.

2) Posts will be manned by one man who will act as Air Sentry. Air Sentries will be relieved every two hours.

3) Alarm Signal.
     When hostile aircraft reach a range of 25 miles from this station the alarm siren will be sounded. All gun posts will Stand to.

4) Stand to.
   a) Gun positions will be fully manned from one half hour before to one hour after dawn and from one half hour before to one half hour after dusk.
   b) Gun positions will be fully manned on sounding of the alarm signal or verbal instructions.
   c) Personnel will wear steel helmets with camouflage nets.

5) Engagement of Hostile Aircraft.
     As laid down in para.1. (Orders for Gun Posts) Section 7.

6) Stand down.
     As laid down in para.1. (Orders for Gun Posts) Section 8.

7) Night Ops.
   a) During the period of 6 days before and 6 day after full moon all gun posts will be manned and during all periods of night flying.
   b) In the event of an alarm signal preceding the above mentioned periods, personnel will man the same gun sites which they

mounted during the day. Gunners will take up Action Stations and comply with instructions as per Stand to and Engagement of Hostile Aircraft.

c) During periods when there is no night manning, personnel will patrol gun post localities between the hors f dusk and dawn. Stand to (as per patrol orders).

Guard Orders for Technical Building.

Between the hours of 19.00 and 08.00 the Tx door will be kept locked and the guard mounted in front of Rx door. ALL personnel are to be conversant with the following guard orders.

The guard at the Technical Building will:-

i) Keep on the alert continually.

ii) Ensure that NO PERSON approaches the building unchallenged.

iii) Patrol around the Technical block once every five minutes.

iv) All persons approaching will be challenged and halted as such a distance that the person challenged cannot be sudden or surprise action:-

    (a) Harm any R.A.F. equipment.

    (b) Harm the sentry challenging.

v) All persons approaching will be challenged as follows:-

1st TIME.
"Halt, who goes there?."- If the reply is friend the sentry will order "Advance one". If more than one person is challenged, the sentry will order each member of the party to advance and be recognised singly.

2nd TIME.
If the person or persons are challenged as above and no reply is received in answer to the sentry's challenge, the sentry will order "Halt or I fire".

3rd TIME.
If no reply is given to the challenge the sentry will again order "Halt of I fire".

ACTION.
If no reply is given the sentry will load and fire. Aiming if possible to disable rather than kill.

vi) Rifles will have five rounds in the magazine, but no rounds in the chamber except as permitted above.

vii) The sentry's tour of duty will normally be two hours but in no circumstances will he leave his post until relieved.

viii) During hours of daylight, sentries will not challenge R.A.F. personnel known to them and on the strength of the station. All other personnel will be challenged and checked for A.M.E.S. permits to enter the Technical Building.

ix)   During the hours of darkness all persons will be checked for A.M.E.S. permits to entre Technical buildings and on no account will any person be allowed to entre unless in possession of the aforesaid permit.

x) Guards are responsible for the general security of the Technical Building and personnel employed therein.

xi)   The guard is to check for gas during each patrol around the Technical Building. Should gas or spray be detected he will immediately sound the gas rattle and take personal anti-gas measures.

*NOT APPLICABLE UNTIL FURTHER NOTICE.

Orders for A.A. Vehicles.
The following orders will be carried out by personnel mounting A.A. vehicles.

1) A.A. Trucks will be manned by the undermentioned Airmen:-
   A - Truck:- N.C.O. i/c M.T. (Section Commander).
                 Driver.
                 Armourer.
                 Signaller.

   B - Truck:- Driver.
                 Armourer.
                 Carpenter.

   C - Truck:- Driver.
                 Spare Driver.
                 Armourer.

2) On sounding of the alarm siren or verbal instructions all A.A. vehicles will be fully manned. Personnel detailed to man vehicles will collect guns and ammunition from the armoury and install such on their allocated trucks. Drivers will, after completion of the aforeseen task, drive immediately to their prearranged site and Stand to.

3) Engagement of Hostile Aircraft.
   As laid down in para.1 (Orders for Gun Posts) Section 7.

4) Stand down.

Vehicles will return to base upon written instructions from the O.C. by D.R. or Runner.

5) Airmen will have their personal weapon, steel helmets, First Aid field dressing and filled water bottles with them on A.A. vehicles.

About the Author

After serving 10 years with the R.A.F. Regiment (the Regiment), and leaving in the early 1990s, I settled in Oxfordshire, and for more than 25 years have worked in Local Government. My passion for the Regiment, and in particular, the people who have served, has always been strong. After recently finishing my Master's, my thirst for knowledge remained and having read the main published books on the Regiment, I decided to delve deeper into understanding its early evolution and the men who had served.

It was while I was writing a book on the Squadrons, Men and Equipment of the R.A.F. Regiment 1942 – 45, that I realised I had significant gaps in my understanding of early unit structures and their evolution. So, I decided to spend a day at The National Archives to find out more.

That day at The National Archives, looking through the Operational Record Books (the records) of several units, introduced to a wealth of information and 'gems' that brought to life, what really happened in those informative years.

This book is the result of many more days at the National Archives and the bringing together of several different strands of information. I hope you enjoy this slice of history.

Other books by the Author

Operation 'Torch' and the North African Campaign 1942- 43 – Paperback August 2017

Operation 'Husky' and the Sicilian Campaign 1943 – Paperback/ eBook November 2017

Planned books for this operation and campaign series

Operation 'Diver' the Campaign against the German V- Rockets 1944

The Mediterranean Campaign

Operation 'Overlord' and the North West European Campaign

Bibliography

Batt. Keith (Gp Capt), *'The RAF Regiment - A Short History'*, 40th Anniversary Edition, 1982

Oliver. M. Kingsley (Gp Capt), *'The RAF Regiment at War 1942 - 1946'*, 2002

Oliver. M. Kingsley (Gp Capt), *'Through Adversity – The History of the Royal Air Force Regiment 1942 - 1992'*, 1997

Warwick. W.M. Nigel, *'Constant Vigilance – The RAF Regiment in the Burma Campaign'*, 2007

'Third Supplement to The London Gazette', 13th March 1951

Operational Record Books (The National Archives)

AIR 29/134 - **2941 -2943 Field Squadrons**

AIR 29/136 - **2945 Field Squadron**

AIR 29/138 - **2941 -2945 Field Squadron Appendices only**

AIR 29/884 – **4401 – 4408 Anti -Aircraft Flights**

AIR 29/885 – **4410 – 4436 Anti -Aircraft Flights**

AIR 29/886 – **4437 – 4450 Anti -Aircraft Flights**

Printed in Great Britain
by Amazon